INTERCOLLEGIATE ATHLETICS, INC.

Intercollegiate Athletics, Inc. examines the corrupting influence and damaging financial effects of big-time intercollegiate athletics, especially football and to a lesser extent basketball, on American higher education.

Including historical and contemporary perspectives, the book traces the growth of intercollegiate sports from largely student-run activities supervised by faculty to the gargantuan, taxpayer-supported spectacles that now dominate many public universities. It investigates the regressive student fees that have helped subsidize big-time sports at public universities and prop up chronically unprofitable athletic departments, as well as the corrosive effects of athletics on the university's academic enterprise. A review of the alleged salutary effects of massive sports programs, such as spurring alumni donations and student applications, reveals that such benefits are largely illusory, more myth than real. The book also pays special attention to the often prescient, if largely unsuccessful, opponents of these developments, and considers the alternatives to big-time athletics, from abolition to professionalization to club sports.

Students, scholars, sports fans, and those interested in learning how big-time football and basketball have cast such an enormous—and often baleful—shadow upon American colleges and universities will profit from this provocative and engagingly written book.

James T. Bennett is Professor of Political Economy and Public Policy at George Mason University, USA, and a prolific author. His research interests focus on public policy, political economy, and labor economics.

INTERCOLLEGIATE ATHLETICS, INC.

How Big-Time College Sports Cheat Students, Taxpayers, and Academics

James T. Bennett

Routledge
Taylor & Francis Group

LONDON AND NEW YORK

First published 2020
by Routledge
2 Park Square, Milton Park, Abingdon, Oxon OX14 4RN

and by Routledge
52 Vanderbilt Avenue, New York, NY 10017

Routledge is an imprint of the Taylor & Francis Group, an informa business

British Library Cataloguing in Publication Data
A catalogue record for this book is available from the British Library

Library of Congress Cataloging-in-Publication Data
A catalog record has been requested for this book

ISBN: 978-0-367-35387-2 (hbk)
ISBN: 978-0-367-35388-9 (pbk)
ISBN: 978-0-429-33113-8 (ebk)

Typeset in Bembo
by Taylor & Francis Books

CONTENTS

1

INTRODUCTION

"American exceptionalism"—its meaning and even its very existence— has been the subject of considerable debate among historians and foreign policy analysts in these first years of the twenty-first century. But in one realm not even the most dedicated contrarian can dispute the existence of American exceptionalism, and that is big-time college sports. The essence of this exceptionalism in the context of athletics vis-à-vis academics is emphasized by the observation of legendary football coach Paul "Bear" Bryant at the University of Alabama that "Fifty thousand people don't come to watch an English class."[1] And, as Janice M. Beyer and David R. Hannah of the University of Texas at Austin—epicenter of the college athletics boom—write, "In no other country is college sports taken so seriously, given such large budgets, or so embedded within the structure of universities."[2] Moreover, no other nation in the world has a university system that functions as a minor league for professional sports—or as, in a sense, a professional league itself.

We live in a sports-mad country. A whopping 85 percent of American males go first to the sports pages when opening a newspaper.[3] (Of course, this statistic was discovered back in that antediluvian era before the newspaper was so thoroughly routed by online news.) That college athletics have become big business is a truism. In 2012, ESPN agreed to pay $7.3 billion for the rights to broadcast the next 12 years of the football Bowl Championship Series.[4] In 2016, CBS and the Turner networks extended their deal to broadcast the NCAA men's basketball tournament—"March Madness"—through the year 2032 at a rate of about $1.1 billion per year.[5] For each game a team plays in the men's tournament, its conference receives about $1.7 million, which is then divided among member schools. In defense of this state of affairs, Syracuse University's then-chancellor Kenneth A. "Buzz" Shaw told the *Chronicle of Higher Education* in 2003:

I have yet to see the networks pick up on the national competition for drama programs. It isn't that we're overemphasizing sports. It's that people like it, they watch it, and the NCAA and the networks give them what they want.[6]

March Madness has come a long way—or has it gone in the wrong direction?—from humble beginnings. The first NCAA basketball tournament in 1939 featured eight teams. The Oregon Webfoots (later Ducks) beat Ohio State in Evanston, Illinois, on the campus of Northwestern, for the title, though the National Invitational Tournament (NIT), founded in 1938 and centered around Madison Square Garden in Manhattan (New York, that is, not Kansas), was a bigger deal. The NCAA tournament eclipsed the NIT by the mid to late 1950s, and in 2005 the NCAA actually purchased the NIT, which has settled into its middling condition as a not terribly attractive consolation prize for teams not invited to the 68-team NCAA tournament. (It's really no fun shouting "We're Number 69!" when your team brings home the NIT title.)

Before we trip over these letter-clots, a word on acronyms and the groups they denote is in order: The largest association of schools fielding intercollegiate athletic teams is the National Collegiate Athletic Association, or NCAA, which in 2017 had 1,123 members separated into three divisions. (College athletic officials are as hierarchy-obsessed as any ambitious arriviste.) In 1922, Fielding Yost, then athletic director at the University of Michigan, urged the NCAA convention to divide its membership according to each school's "attitude toward athletics."[7] But not until 1956–7, when the NCAA created College and University Divisions for the purpose of holding tournaments, was there a fissioning based on attitude toward athletics. In 1968–9, 223 schools chose to compete in the upper-level University Division, while 386 were lodged in the College Division.[8] In 1973 the bipartite arrangement became tripartite, with schools choosing to compete in Divisions I, II, or III. This trisection was based less on size than on athletic philosophy, particularly with respect to athletic scholarships. Five years later, spurred by the threat of an alliance of big-time football programs calling itself the College Football Association (CFA), the NCAA separated the Division I wheat from chaff, or powerhouses from pretenders, by creating a Division I-A and Division I-AA. In 2007, to spread nomenclatorial murk if nothing else, Division I-A became the Football Bowl Subdivision (FBS) and Division I-AA was renamed the Football Championship Subdivision (FCS).

Today, Division I, which offers full scholarships or grants-in aid, has about 350 members; Division II, which offers partial scholarships, has about 300 members; and Division III, with about 450 member schools, does not offer athletic scholarships and is often, though not unanimously, held up as the repository of old-fashioned "play for the love of the game" purity.

Within NCAA Division I, 130 schools are members of the Football Bowl Subdivision (FBS), whose season culminates in the Bowl Championship Series—the famed national championship fought over by the Alabama and Ohio States, the Michigans and Clemsons. (The FBS schools include about 25 percent of the nation's college students.)[9] The FBS has minimum attendance levels, among other requirements. Schools competing in the Football Bowl Subdivision must sponsor a minimum of 16 teams (with a minimum of eight being all-female squads), have an average home attendance of at least 15,000 over a rolling two-year period (the methods of counting are, ah, flexible), provide a minimum of 90 percent of the available football scholarships over a two-year rolling period, and schedule at least five home games a year against FBS opponents.[10] Another 125 schools compete in the second-tier Football Championship Series. The remaining Division I schools do not field football teams. These are, disproportionately, Catholic basketball powers and quondam powers: Gonzaga, Providence, St. Bonaventure, and the like.

Much less prominent than the NCAA is the National Association of Inter-collegiate Athletics, or NAIA. The NAIA grew out of a 1937 basketball tourna-ment for smaller schools under the grandfatherly eye of Dr. James Naismith, inventor of the game. Midwestern in flavor, it was formalized in 1940 as the National Association of Intercollegiate Basketball before adopting its current name in 1952. It consists today of about 250 small colleges and universities whose 65,000 athletes compete in baseball, basketball, bowling, cheerleading and dance, cross country, football, golf, lacrosse, soccer, softball, swimming and diving, tennis, track and field, volleyball, and wrestling.[11] Membership took a hit when in 1973 the NCAA carved itself into three segments; many of the then-561 NAIA schools defected to the larger and wealthier organization.[12] It has contracted in recent decades, but it endures. The National Junior College Athletic Association (NJCAA), founded in 1938, has 525 members in three divisions. The NAIA and NJCAA are peripheral to the concerns of this book, though the pernicious effect of athletics on academics is visible in those schools, too.

American colleges and universities award about $2.9 billion annually in full and partial scholarships to over 150,000 athletes at the Division I and II levels. These are not handed out promiscuously, or to every rag-armed pitcher or brick-laying forward: only about 2 percent of high school athletes receive such aid.[13]

In the case of football and basketball, and to a lesser extent hockey, big-time college athletic programs act as farm systems for professional leagues. Promising, if callow, players are given first-tier training, deluxe (compared with their fellow "students") accommodations, and compete before large crowds, winning laurels of various stripes. They are also offered—as long as it doesn't interfere too much with their athletic obligations—a four-year education and a bachelor's degree. The best—1.1 percent of Division I men's basketball players, 1.6 percent of NCAA football players—will appear, at least briefly, in the National Basketball Association or the National Football League.[14]

Division I coaches are typically the highest paid people at the university, and at public universities, they may be the highest paid government employees in the state. Remarkably, the highest-paid public employee in 39 of the 50 states is a college football or men's basketball coach. The eleven exceptions are Alaska (whose best-compensated public employee is president of the state's Gasline Development Corporation), Delaware (public school superintendent), Hawaii (neurosurgeon), Maine (University of Maine chancellor), Montana (commissioner of higher education), Nevada (aptly, a plastic surgeon at the University of Nevada—alas, he died as this was being written), New Hampshire (president of the University of New Hampshire), New York (CEO of SUNY Stony Brook Hospital), North Dakota (dean of the University of North Dakota School of Medicine & Health Sciences), South Dakota (dean of the University of South Dakota School of Medicine), and Vermont (dean of the University of Vermont's College of Medicine). The salaries of these eleven never top $1 million, in contrast to the salaries of the coaches, which in a majority of cases are well over the $1 million mark.[15]

Despite appearances, American universities do spend more on books than on balls. Or, more pertinently in this day and age, smart boards and new technology buildings. Athletic operating expenditures as a percentage of total institutional expenditure is about 5.6 percent for FBS schools, 7.0 for FCS schools, and 6.0 for schools with Division I basketball but no football.[16]

Yet despite all this money being thrown around as so much legal tender confetti, only a handful—between five and 25, depending on the year and the source—of the approximately 350 Division I athletic programs have revenues that exceed expenses. These schools are, inevitably, drawn from the "Power Five" conferences whose teams occupy a privileged position in the football Bowl Championship Series. In the most recent accounting, only 23 Division I public universities of the 230 Division I public university athletic departments finished in the black, by NCAA accounting standards.[17] (This book focuses primarily on public, taxpayer-supported schools.)

As discussed in Chapter 4, most athletic departments rely on student fees extracted from a student body that is somewhere between unaware and resentful of this regressive transfer of wealth from often hard-pressed undergraduates to gold-plated football programs. The scholarly consensus, based on empirical evidence, was stated plainly in a 2013 report by the Delta Cost Project of the American Institute for Research:

> The belief that college sports are a financial boon to colleges and universities is generally misguided. Although some big-time college sports athletic departments are self-supporting—and some sports may be profitable enough to help support other campus sports programs—more often than not, the colleges and universities are subsidizing athletics, not the other way around.[18]

Nevertheless, the myth endures: a Knight Commission on Intercollegiate Athletics poll found that 78 percent of Americans believe that college sports turn a profit for their schools.[19]

For every University of Texas at Austin, flush with television and ticket and donor revenue, there are five University of Texas at El Pasos or San Antonios or Texas States, which survive in part by beggaring students through mandatory fees—sometimes in the thousands of dollars per student annually. And even the UTs of the world have to answer, or sedulously avoid, the question of whether their pursuit of athletic riches and glory is consistent with the putative academic mission of the university.

The athletes—the term *student-athlete* is, at the Division I level, a faintly ridiculous euphemism, a "legalistic confectio[n] propagated by the universities so they can exploit the skills and fame of young athletes," in the words of historian Taylor Branch—whose performances draw the viewers and sell the tickets make nothing from these spectacles.[20] The cartel that is the National Collegiate Athletic Association forbids their payment, as well as payments for a long and excruciatingly detailed list of perks and small gratuities to which one might think the generators of multimillion dollar enterprises might be entitled. What the athletes *do* receive are tuition, room, board, adulation, and sometimes fame and sexual access that their coevals can (and do) only dream of, i.e., non-negligible benefits, though of wildly varying usefulness depending on the athlete.

Still, the ordinary student, burdened by loan debt, struggling to pay her bill at the bookstore, subsisting on ramen noodles and energy drinks, might cast an envious, even bitter eye toward the jocks. One recent study found that Division I schools spend, on average, from "three to six times as much on athletics per athlete as on academics per student." In the Southeastern Conference, ground zero of college football mania, the gap is an astounding twelvefold.[21] All this at a time when public colleges and universities are being squeezed, in most states, by a serious budget pinch. At my own school, George Mason University, several academic departments have removed the faculty phones because of tight budgets—but, you may rest assured, the university phones remain in the athletic department. Nonetheless, something's gotta give: a situation in which legislatures cut funding to state schools while athletic budgets swell, and the ordinary Joe or Jill College is left paying the bill, is untenable.

Sitting on the porch

Proponents of the athletic ideal hold up sport as a great molder of character and physique and a uniter of disparate people in a common cause. For the athletes themselves, the benefits are, or can be, undeniable. In 1945, Pope Pius XII even gave it a papal imprimatur: "Sport, properly directed, develops character, makes a man courageous, a generous loser, and a gracious victor. It refines the senses, gives intellectual penetration and steels the will to endurance."[22] Generations of Notre Dame football fans will not disagree. Even those who sit and watch, or read about the game the next day, are said to derive benefit. Michigan coach Fielding Yost went so far as to claim that the mere act of watching a game had a civilizing influence on spectators. The discipline exhibited by players on the gridiron created a "spirit which reaches out from the athletic field through the campus and into the very recitation room."[23] Inspired by the quarterback on Saturday, the philosophy major leaves it all on the lecture-room floor when discoursing on Kant on Monday morning.

Columbia historian John Krout wrote in 1928 of the role of sport in American life: "During depressions, with thousands out of work, sports helps refocus our attention on the great American values and ideals and also helps us to remember that life does not begin and end with the dollar."[24] They can foster school or community spirit, bring together disparate people in a common (and, happily, nonpartisan) cause, and encourage an appreciation of achievement, personal excellence, and teamwork. For the players, they provide lessons in discipline, cooperation, physical training, and diligence. Sport can be a challenging environment in which to set and achieve goals. It often encourages teamwork and even a sense of brotherhood or sisterhood among people from very different backgrounds. But does it belong at the center of university life?

One of the more excessive extollers of the role of football in college life was the University of the Pacific president who in 1953 engaged in this rhetorical flight:

> The curriculum has become diversified; there are numerous electives. Few study the same courses or sit under the same professors . . . So, in this period of intellectual and social disintegration of the American college, all unite in football . . . Football has become more than a spectacle; it has become one of the great intangibles not only of college but of our American life. Actually, if you want to look at it on a higher level, football has become the spiritual core of the modern campus.[25]

Pacific would drop football in 1995, though by all accounts it retains a spiritual core.

At the very least, spectator sport has become, in the minds of many administrators, an essential recruiting tool, not only for athletes but for the average student as well. Yet as we shall document, the alleged spillover effects of big-time sports—things like increased donations by alumni and fans to the school in addition to the athletic department, a deluge of applicants, an improvement in the quality of students and faculty due to the higher exposure, greater opportunities for disadvantaged athletes—are mostly illusory. Still, a widespread sense exists, especially in state schools with modest academic reputations, that unless a school fields an FBS football team, or at the very least a Division I basketball team that is theoretically eligible for the NCAA Tournament in that late-winter frenzy known as March Madness, it somehow isn't a real university. Harry Lewis, computer scientist and former dean of the undergraduate Harvard College, observed that college presidents are "worried that sixteen-year-olds won't know who they are without a football team."[26] They'll know what Harvard is, of course, or at least the students Harvard wants to attract will know what Harvard is, but Georgia State and the University of North Carolina at Charlotte are another matter.

J. Douglas Toma, author of *Football U.: Spectator Sports in the Life of the American University* (2003), notes that big-time football is a way for large public universities to brand themselves nationally. Their student bodies may not have the candlepower of those of Stanford or Yale, and they may lack Nobel Prize winners on their faculties, but:

> Where Kansas State, New Mexico, and West Virginia (or Texas Tech, Tennessee, and Connecticut) can compete favorably for institutional prestige, on a

relatively even level with the most prestigious institutions nationally, is in intercollegiate athletics. They may not be able to build a leading chemistry or history department, but they can realistically build a football program of national significance.[27]

And so schools go Division I in football or basketball, their administrators believing that engaging in March Madness or a football bowl game will validate the school as "big time." Football or, to a lesser degree, basketball, are the schools' only real advertisements for themselves; they are, in many cases, the only thing that the overwhelming majority of Americans, or fans, know about UConn or LSU or Alabama.

Football as the "front porch" of a university is a common image, though a front porch is a welcoming, inviting feature, conducive of neighborliness, whereas the athletic department at a big-time sports school, is a massive, arrogant, and bureaucratic obstacle to coming up on the porch unless you have paid prettily for the privilege. Tim Weiser, who had served as athletic director at Kansas State, an erstwhile doormat of the Big 8 and Big 12 that became a football power thanks to—we'll be generous and say *resourceful recruiting*—explained the theory:

> [I]f you drive by a house and you see a front porch that is not well-kept, with shingles falling off, you are likely to draw the conclusion that the rest of the house must also be in bad shape. Conversely, if you have a well-kept front porch, the rest of the university will take on the same image.[28]

What constitutes a shabby athletic front porch? Scuffed rubber baseballs, broken lacrosse sticks, and chain-link basketball nets would do the trick, but there's not an NCAA-level school out there that doesn't equip its athletes better than that. The win-loss record is what the front porch metaphorists are really talking about. Yet does it matter in the least what kind of football or basketball record the teams compile at Williams or Harvard or Princeton or Stanford or MIT? Of course not. The previously named are all private schools, of course, though to a lesser, but still real, extent football wins and losses do not much matter to the reputations of the universities of Wisconsin, Michigan, University of California, Berkeley, or other highly regarded flagship state schools.

Kansas State, on the other hand—perhaps. Former K-State president Jon Wefald said that the blossoming of Kansas State Wildcats—previously mocked as "Mildcats"—football, which was set in motion in 1989 by the hiring of coach Bill Snyder, saved the university. The sport would have been dropped by the early 1990s had the drought continued, Wefald said, and enrollment would have stagnated at around 12,000 instead of the 23,000 students it had when he made the observation in 2003.[29] Contrariwise, K-State vice president for institutional advancement, Pat J. Bosco, told the *Chronicle of Higher Education* in 1999 that the "jury's still out" on the effect football success had on enrollment, and in fact applications actually *declined* in the month after Kansas State won the 1998 Fiesta Bowl, one of the biggest and most publicized victories in the program's history.[30]

Certainly a winning football or basketball team can provide a rallying point for the student and broader communities. They offer up a few pleasant days or nights in the stands or bleachers. They can strengthen a student's identification with his or her school. They can evoke misty water-colored memories of their salad days for alumni. They provide (theoretically) an education for athletes who might otherwise not have had the opportunity to attend college.[31] They fill the college-town bars at night. They give tongue-tied people at parties safe topics on which to discourse.

But what is the cost: financially, through student fees and the diversion of funds from academics to athletics, and in the corruption of the academic mission? Whatever happened to the *educational mission* of higher education? These and other questions are addressed in the pages that follow.

Honesty: a rare policy

An ill-timed joke by Dr. George L. Cross, president of the University of Oklahoma, entered the canon of sports-mania lore. In the early 1950s, Dr. Cross was testifying before a committee of the Oklahoma State Senate. He was dunning the senators for dollars, explaining why the school needed greater taxpayer funding. After an hour-long presentation, a bored senator cut to the chase. "Yes, that's all well and good," the senator told the president. "But what kind of football team are we going to have this year?" Dr. Cross, too quick-witted for his own good, replied, "We want to build a university our football team can be proud of." The wire services picked up Dr. Cross's quote, and within days he and the University of Oklahoma, whose powerhouse football team, coached by legend Bud Wilkinson and the 1950 national champions, were caricatured as jock-worshippers who placed academics a distant second to winning silly games.

Fast forward to 1989. Several Sooners players were in deep trouble for various offenses, ranging from first-degree rape to cocaine dealing to the shooting of a teammate. The program, under the charismatic outlaw coach Barry Switzer, was about to be placed on probation by the NCAA. Ira Berkow of the *New York Times* permitted Dr. Cross to set the record straight. "I remember how all of it started here," said Dr. Cross, then 84, from his office on the Norman, Oklahoma, campus.

> It was 1945 and the war had ended, and here in Oklahoma we were still feeling very depressed from those tough days that Steinbeck wrote about in *The Grapes of Wrath*. At a board of regents meeting, it was suggested to me that I try to get a good football team. It would give Oklahomans a reason to have pride in the state. And it did, but I don't think it was very good for the university.

Jim Tatum, the first coach Dr. Cross hired, was fired for inattention to academics, despite an 8–3 record. Tatum's successor, Bud Wilkinson, turned the Sooners into a national power, and as Dr. Cross said in 1989, "Bud was a class act. Over 90 percent of the football players graduated." But by 1989 the graduation rate had fallen to well under 50 percent and, as Dr. Cross noted, players "became separated from the rest of the student body, and didn't participate in other activities."[32] Football overshadowed the primary purpose of the university. No doubt Dr. Cross was a good and conscientious university president who properly feared the potential of big-time sports, especially football, to corrupt the host institution. But the 1940s and 1950s were no more a golden age of scholar-athletes and sport for the sake of sport than is the second decade of the twenty-first century, in which academic fraud is common, athletic departments operate with open checkbooks, and—perhaps most scandalously, and a central concern of this book—ordinary students, already up to their future ears in student loan debt, are forced to subsidize Division I sports at the vast majority of schools which compete in that top level of intercollegiate competition.

There will be no shortage of high-minded, borderline pious pronouncements about college sports quoted herein. Even the scofflaws and scandalists know just what they are supposed to say, and say it. So as an anticipatory rebuttal to the sententious moderate reformers who wish to preserve big-time college sports but prune them of their unsavory aspects, let us at the outset hear from an unchastened, unregenerate, unapologetic scoundrel: Norm Ellenberger, who was fired as basketball coach at the University of New Mexico in 1979 after compiling an outstanding seven-year win-loss record of 134–62 but also racking up 34 NCAA recruiting violations and conviction in a state court of 21 counts of fraud in what became known as Lobo-gate.

Ellenberger brought swagger to the New Mexico Lobos. Bedecked in "turquoise jewelry and gold chains," he recruited players, as he said, "who never had a book in their homes." Not that he was acting out of altruistic motives, giving underprivileged youths an opportunity to better themselves through diligent study. Building character was not what Norm Ellenberger was about. Instead, his recruits included one player straight out of state prison, another who had "'borrowed' a Cadillac from an Albuquerque showroom," and still others who never bothered to darken a classroom door during their UNM student-athlete days.[33] Ellenberger was not one for sackcloth and ashes. Instead, he defended himself and his ilk:

> What is wrong if a young man pursues a career in professional athletics? We say that people must have goals in life. If the only possible goal for a young man is professional athletics, what is wrong with that? Why degrade that drive within a young man? It is not how many reach the goal that counts. So only two or three percent make it. Well, big deal! How many make it to the top of RCA? How many make it to the top in any profession? It isn't how many make it. It's what they are exposed to along the way, and what kind of people they become as a result.
>
> There is no difference between pursuing athletics and pursuing art, or modern dance, or marching band . . .

It is said that football and basketball programs are for physical activity. But how much physical activity is there for the hundred thousand people in a stadium watching twenty-two guys play football? . . . Sports are the way they are because of the almighty dollar. We have to make money. Somebody, for God's sake, say it! . . .

Somewhere along the line the young man who does not have these advantages has to have help. Who cares whether that person graduates from college? It is not that important. He did not want to go to college in the first place. He is performing a service. He is doing what he is supposed to do. That does not make him a bad person . . . There is no program in any university that he can handle. But he is one hell of an athlete. He can run up and down the basketball court for you. He will bring you money. He will do all these things that people say are so dastardly. But don't you know that that young man is benefiting, that he is learning to be a person, that he is developing, that he is becoming a member of society?[34]

Ellenberger was blunt, and if given free rein he and his kind would utterly corrupt the mission of the academy, but when placed against the sonorous platitudes of the likes of Ohio State president Gordon Gee, he is a breath of foully fresh air. But even his frankness evades the two central questions of this book. Should ordinary students be forced to subsidize big-time athletics at public universities? And how does the sponsorship of such teams impinge on the fundamental function of the university?

Notes

1 Randy R. Grant, John Leadley, and Zenon Zygmont, *The Economics of Intercollegiate Sports* (Singapore: World Scientific Publishing, 2008), p. 215.
2 Janice M. Beyer and David R. Hannah, "The Cultural Significance of Athletics in U.S. Higher Education," *Journal of Sport Management* 14 (2000): 105.
3 Mark Yost, *Varsity Green: A Behind the Scenes Look at Culture and Corruption in College Athletics* (Stanford, CA: Stanford University Press, 2010), p. 27.
4 Frank Pallotta, "ESPN's $7.3 Billion College Football Playoff Gamble Pays Off," *CNN.com*, January 13, 2015.
5 Associated Press, "NCAA Tournament Deal with CBS, Turner Extended through 2032," *espn.com*, April 12, 2016.
6 Welch Suggs, "Sports as the University's 'Front Porch'? The Public Is Skeptical," *Chronicle of Higher Education*, May 2, 2003.
7 Joel G. Maxcy, "The 1997 Restructuring of the NCAA: A Transactions Cost Explanation," in *Economics of College Sports*, edited by John Fizel and Rodney Fort (Westport, CT: Praeger, 2004), p. 15.
8 Ibid., p. 16.
9 Matthew Denhart, Richard Villwock, and Richard Vedder, "The Academics–Athletics Trade-Off," Center for College Affordability and Productivity, April 2009, p. 5.
10 "Football Bowl Subdivision—Membership Requirements: Frequently Asked Questions," http://fs.ncaa.org/Docs/AMA/, accessed September 14, 2017.
11 "About the NAIA," www.naia.org/ViewArticle.dbml?ATCLID=205323019, accessed February 27, 2017.

12 Grant, Leadley, and Zygmont, *The Economics of Intercollegiate Sports*, p. 50.

13 "Scholarships, NCAA," www.ncaa.org/student-athletes/future/scholarships, accessed August 24, 2017.

14 "Estimated Probability of Competing in Professional Athletics," www.ncaa.org/about/resources/research/estimated-probability-competing-professional-athletics, 2016 figures, accessed on January 5, 2017.

15 Evan Comen, Thomas C. Frohlich, and Michael B. Sauter, "The Highest Paid Public Employee in Every State," *247wallstreet.com*, September 20, 2016.

16 "Revenues & Expenses, 2004–2014: NCAA Division I Intercollegiate Athletics Programs Report," National Collegiate Athletic Association, September 2015, p. 8.

17 Steve Berkowitz and Christopher Schnaars, "Colleges are Spending More on Their Athletes Because They Can," *USA Today*, July 6, 2017.

18 Kevin Kiley, "Universities Spend More on Athletics Per Athlete Than on Academics Per Student, Report Finds," *Insider Higher Ed*, January 16, 2013.

19 "College Sports 101," Knight Commission on Intercollegiate Athletics, October 2009, p. 3. Mitch Albom, "Let College Athletes be Like Jodie Foster," *USA Today*, March 16, 2018.

20 Taylor Branch, "The Shame of College Sports," *The Atlantic*, October 2010, www.theatlantic.com.

21 Kiley, "Universities Spend More on Athletics Per Athlete Than on Academics Per Student, Report Finds," *Insider Higher Ed*.

22 "Pope Pius XII Quote on Sport Properly Directed," www.abbeyathletics.com/sport_virtue/pope_pius_xii_quote_on_sport_properly_directed, accessed October 9, 2017.

23 Brian M. Ingrassia, *The Rise of Gridiron University: Higher Education's Uneasy Alliance with Big-Time Football* (Lawrence: University Press of Kansas, 2012), p. 125.

24 Robert Lipsyte, "Varsity Syndrome: The Unkindest Cut," *Annals of the American Academy of Political and Social Science* 445, No. 1 (September 1979): 21.

25 Robert Maynard Hutchins, "College Football Is an Infernal Nuisance," *Sports Illustrated*, October 18, 1954, www.si.com/vault/1954/10/18.

26 Jay Schalin, "College Sports: Foul Ball or Fair Play?" John William Pope Center for Higher Education Policy, November 21, 2008.

27 J. Douglas Toma, *Football U.: Spectator Sports in the Life of the American University* (Ann Arbor, MI: University of Michigan Press, 2003), p. 105.

28 Denhart, Villwock, and Vedder, "The Academics–Athletics Trade-Off," p. 6.

29 Franklin G. Mixon and Len J. Trevino, "From Kickoff to Commencement: The Positive Role of Intercollegiate Athletics in Higher Education," *Economics of Education Review* 24, No. 1 (February 2005): 95.

30 Welch Suggs, "Wins, Losses, and Dollars," *Chronicle of Higher Education*, October 15, 1999.

31 For a defense of the role intercollegiate athletics plays in building school morale, see then-Idaho State provost Gary A. Olson's "Should We Ditch Football?" *Chronicle of Higher Education*, May 5, 2010.

32 Ira Berkow, "The Grapes of Wrath at Oklahoma," *New York Times*, February 18, 1989.

33 Pete Axthelm et al., "The Shame of College Sports," *Newsweek*, September 22, 1980.

34 Norm Ellenberger, "Tell It Like It Is: We Have to Make Money," *The Center Magazine* 15 (January-February 1982): 21–2.

2

FROM BRUTAL GENTLEMEN AMATEURS TO "STUDENT-ATHLETES" ON THE PAYROLL

The development of intercollegiate sports

Sports were alien to college campuses for almost the first two hundred years of American higher education, though by the early nineteenth century, several schools—Harvard, Yale, Amherst, Williams, Brown, Virginia, Dartmouth, and the College of Charleston—had gymnasia at which students trained their bodies.[1] Competitive games were extracurricular, arranged by the students themselves. The idea that schools should sponsor traveling teams that would compete against rival schools was unthought, not to mention unvoiced. Students were the first organizers of collegiate sport, and though this may call to mind Mickey Rooney and Judy Garland and "Hey gang, let's put on a show!" the contests were not problem-free. Ringers, graduates, and transients sometimes padded the rosters. Academic integrity was not paramount, but then these were, after all, just games. They resisted meddling by faculty and administration, spoilsports who wanted to outlaw fun. In time, and not a great deal of time at that, both students and faculty would find themselves relatively powerless to achieve changes in collegiate athletics.

College boys were often mocked as fops, dandies, or skeletal ectomorphs: a far cry from pioneer stock. One writer sneered in the pages of *Harper's Magazine* in 1856 that the lads of America were "an apathetic-brained, a pale pasty-faced, narrow-chested, spindle-shanked, dwarfed race—mere walking manikins to advertise the last cut of the fashionable tailor."[2] They wanted vigor. Perhaps a long walk in the woods would do them good? Yet there was very little cant about the character-building effects of organized sport, or the ways in which participation therein cultivated or brought to the fore certain desirable traits. Sport was play, and play was fun, and if the lads wanted to blow off some steam by knocking each other around on the Elysian Fields, that was fine. Just don't pretend that the game has anything to do with the college's mission. Extracurriculars of the mid-nineteenth century typically consisted of student literary and oratorical societies. The Bucknell student newspaper opined that walking was all the exercise a student needed.[3]

Howard Savage, whose 1929 study of college football marked the high-water point of public scrutiny of the game's ills, speculated that the 1878 agreement between Harvard and Yale to conduct competitions in "public speaking, essay writing, and exercises in Greek, Latin, mathematics, and mental science" was an attempt to "abate some of the enthusiasm that athletics aroused."[4] ESPN emphatically would *not* be interested in covering such tilts.

Though today they maintain a decorous distance from the vulgarity of big-time college sports—or at least they pretend to: Harvard's basketball team was implicated in a cheating scandal in 2012—Harvard and Yale, with a handful of other elite Eastern schools, were the progenitors of intercollegiate athletics. As Ronald A. Smith writes in *Sports & Freedom: The Rise of Big-Time College Athletics*, these venerable institutions "brought forth both commercialized and professionalized athletics. They began the practice of paying professional coaches to turn out winners. They inaugurated the huge, permanent stadiums," and they played a dominant role in establishing the rules of the games, especially football.[5]

The first recorded intercollegiate competition occurred not on gridiron or diamond but on water: specifically, Lake Winnipesaukee in New Hampshire. The catalyst was James Whiton, a Yale junior and member of the Yale Boat Club, which had been established in 1843. (Whiton would go on to be the first American to earn a Ph.D.) In Whiton's account, he fell into a conversation in June 1852 with James N. Elkins, superintendent of the Boston, Concord, and Montreal Railroad. Elkins was looking for ways to promote his new railroad. He told young Whiton, "If you will get up a regatta on [Winnipesaukee] between Yale and Harvard, I will pay all the bills."[6] Thus was born intercollegiate sport—midwifed by commerce.

Whiton anticipated a "jolly lark." The teams, numbering 41 students in all, met at Concord, New Hampshire, on July 30. After observing the Sabbath, getting in some practice, and perhaps a bit of restrained carousing—though "carefulness in diet, such as abstinence from pastry, was observed"—the crews met on a delightful midsummer Tuesday afternoon. Railroad superintendent Elkins had envisioned a nice payday. Competitive rowing was a popular spectator sport of the age, and he hoped that thousands might take his excursion trains to the lake. Hundreds did, which was something of a disappointment, though local businessmen were cheered by the influx. New Hampshire's favorite son, Democratic presidential candidate Franklin Pierce, the Young Hickory of the Granite Hills, was among the onlookers. Harvard won, claiming its prize of "a pair of black-walnut sculls, silver mounted," which were presented to the victors by Franklin Pierce.[7] Quite unintentionally, Pierce had set a presidential, or slightly pre-presidential, precedent for attaching oneself to a popular sporting event. (The railroad would greatly facilitate interregional athletic contests in later years.)

The less than munificent gate discouraged promoters from holding a rematch the following year, but Harvard and Yale's rowers would meet again in 1855 on the Connecticut River near Springfield, Massachusetts. In 1858, Harvard and Yale were joined by Trinity and Brown in forming the College Rowing

Association, the first intercollegiate athletic body. Charles W. Eliot, a member of Harvard's crew team, remarked after an 1858 meet: "I had rather win than not, but it is mighty little matter whether we beat or are beaten—rowing is not my profession, neither is it my love—it is only recreation, fun and health."[8] It was an observation fraught with significance for the debate over athletics several decades hence. Rowing, as Smith notes, had been more a "social activity than a competitive one" at Harvard and Yale.[9] But even to-the-manor-born athletes have a desire to win.

Students had played games informally at Harvard for over a century before the regatta, and on antebellum campuses early versions of both baseball and a rugby- or soccer-like football—were played with great gusto between upper and lower classmen at many colleges. As Ronald A. Smith writes in his classic *Sports & Freedom: The Rise of Big-Time College Athletics* (1988), "These battles on the playing field apparently filled a need for community—not just separate class unity but occasions for the entire student body to take part in an intense experience."[10] A spirit of freedom, of liberation, animated these games, as the young men on the playing field were freed from the often pettifogging rules of decorum that governed the behavior of college students of the era.

By 1875, college regattas, as sports historian Guy Lewis writes, "received front-page treatment in the leading newspapers."[11] Schools of lesser renown found that they could achieve headlines, if not prominence, by demonstrating speed on the water: the 1871 victory of the Massachusetts Agricultural College of Amherst over Harvard and Brown was a prime example.[12] The triumph "gave the agricultural college standing as a real college," in the eyes of some observers.[13]

Harvard and Yale not only competed in that first crew competition of August 3, 1852, but they were also party to the first intercollegiate contests in rugby/football (Harvard-Tufts on June 4, 1875; a year earlier, on May 15, 1874, Harvard had played Canada's McGill to a 0–0 tie); rifle (Harvard-Yale, May 17, 1877); tennis (Harvard, Yale, Amherst, Brown, Trinity on June 7–8, 1883); fencing (Harvard-Columbia, May 5, 1894); ice hockey (Harvard-Brown, February 1895); golf (Yale-Columbia, November 7, 1896); trap shooting (Harvard, Yale, Columbia, Cornell, Penn, Princeton, May 7, 1898); swimming (Yale, Penn, Columbia, March 8, 1899); gymnastics (Harvard, Yale, and 17 other schools, March 24, 1899); and wrestling (Yale, Columbia, Penn, Princeton, April 5, 1905).[14] Intercollegiate sport was blue-blooded at birth; it didn't start with Alabama-Auburn.

The first intercollegiate baseball game pitted Amherst against Williams, though the game, played on July 1, 1859, would have been barely recognizable to twentieth and twenty-first century fans of the sport. Amherst won, 73–32, in a three-and-a-half-hour contest played on a rectangular field under the offense-happy "Massachusetts rules," under which, according to the Society for American Baseball Research, "all ground was fair, runners could be put out by being hit by a thrown ball, and a single out ended each inning." (This hitters' duel lasted 26 innings.) Amherst's secret weapon was the "back hit," whereby a batter would slap the ball to an area behind the catcher, since there was no such thing as foul territory.[15]

The Princeton-Rutgers tilt of November 6, 1869, witnessed by 200 spectators and won by the latter by the now ridiculously anachronistic score of 6–4, is acknowledged as the first intercollegiate football game, for the aforementioned 1875 Harvard-Tufts match was played under much different rules. The pre-Rutgers game bore a greater resemblance to soccer than to what is now known as football. With 25 men to a side, the field teemed with players. But it was not wholly anachronistic: the Rutgers squad included three footballers who were flunking algebra and one who was failing geometry.[16] The faculty declined to hold them out of the game, perhaps setting a precedent for the modern-day Scarlet Knights: in 2015, Rutgers football coach Kyle Flood was suspended for three games and fined $50,000 by the school after an investigation revealed that he had improperly contacted an instructor about a grade for Nadir Barnwell, who was on the verge of academic ineligibility.[17] (During a two-week span, six Rutgers players, including Barnwell, were arrested for various crimes.) After that first game, the two squads met for an evening of merriment and song. The Princeton crests were hardly fallen; Vince Lombardi would have torn his hair out witnessing the gaiety and high spirits of the postgame banquet.

The upperclassmen vs. lowerclassmen football of the mid-nineteenth century was a wild affair of bloody noses and broken bones. Harvard, Yale, Brown, Williams, and West Point faculties all banned the game at one time or another. Many college presidents viewed this new game with alarm. In 1873, Cornell students petitioned the faculty to permit them to play a football game against Michigan in Cleveland, a halfway point. Cornell president Andrew D. White responded: "I will not permit 30 men to travel four hundred miles merely to agitate a bag of wind."[18] The bag of wind, however, would not be deflated. In 1876, an Intercollegiate Football Association was formed, with charter members Harvard, Princeton, and Columbia. (Yale held out for three years due to a disagreement about squad size.) In 1879, the first intercollegiate baseball league, consisting of Harvard, Brown, Amherst, Princeton, and Dartmouth, was formed.

For all the bluster and bluff about sport preparing young men for the trials of adulthood, athletics were largely a student-run affair. Postbellum but pre-twentieth century, intercollegiate athletics were of, by, and for the students. They organized and scheduled the contests, they set the rules, they played the games. It was, in the parlance of a later century, a DIY affair. Intercollegiate sports of all sorts, from rifle and tennis to fencing and golf, largely developed under the leadership of students in the nineteenth century. Few teams had coaches; student captains served as the organizers, the disciplinarians, and strategists. The teams were sponsored by student athletic associations; sports that drew large numbers of spectators were also subsidized by ticket sales. The defenders of the amateur ideal insisted that coaches be drawn from the faculty; others preferred a student coach.

Faculties acted in loco parentis. Students might organize the games, but they were not without oversight. Teams needed (and often were denied) permission to leave campus to play other teams. Faculties could limit schedules and travel; some, for instance Harvard's, forbade competition against professionals, both as a violation of the ideal of amateurism and because men who took money for playing games were déclassé. Students chafed under these strictures. By 1900, athletic committees, composed of faculty, students, and alumni, rose as a kind of middle way between laissez-faire and a stern hand.

Eventually, student control of athletics was wrested away from students by the university. Training became more systematic; equipment more advanced; coaching became more technical and less simply hortatory. Faculties, though, maintained a largely hands-off attitude, permitting the lads to have their fun as long as it didn't interfere with scholarship. As a result, as 1920s reformer Howard Savage wrote, alumni "achieved dominion almost by default."[19] The football team, especially, became the focus of a loyalty comparable in some respects to national patriotism.

Crowds consisting of students, alumni, and those interested outsiders who would be known as "fans," flocked to contests, especially football games, which became spectacles given lavish coverage in newspapers hungry for enticing copy. They also served as rallying points for alumni, a way to stay connected to the alma mater—and, administrators hoped, an inducement for alumni to donate.

Camp football

The game Americans were calling "football" evolved from a soccer-like sport to one more resembling rugby, from which it evolved to a football recognizable by moderns. Yale's Walter Camp, brother-in-law of the laissez-faire sociologist William Graham Sumner, champion of the "forgotten man," was a key player, coach, advisor, and guiding spirit of the Yale squad from 1876–1909, when Yale dominated the football world as no college has before or since. His wife, Alice Sumner Camp, was no genteel eschewer of blocking and tackling: scribbling in her notebook, she managed practices while Walter was away on business.[20] Camp, a New Haven townie who was graduated from Yale in 1880 after having captained its squad for three years, was "the messenger of modernity to college sports."[21] He regularized, timed, rationalized, specialized, codified, and systematized football. Chronometry was Walter Camp's bread and butter—he rose to president of the New Haven Clock Company in 1903—and he sought to introduce clockwork precision into the chaos of the gridiron. Precision and order were his vocation as well as his avocation.

A fixture on the rules committees governing intercollegiate football for almost 50 years, Walter Camp was critical in revising the rules to make the game something more than just a New World variant of the Mother Country's rugby. Camp's innovations included the 11 man team (it had been 15), the down, the requirement that a team gain a specified number of yards in a specified number of downs or else relinquish the ball, the line of scrimmage, the hike, the linked positions of center and quarterback, and the point system for touchdowns, successful kicks, and safeties. Try imagining football without these standards.

As John Stuart Martin relates in his account of Camp the rule-maker, the discussion over his proposal that a gain of five yards be necessary for a new set of downs went like this:

CABOT OF HARVARD: How, Walter, do you propose to tell when five yards have been made?

CAMP: We shall have to rule off the field with horizontal chalked lines every five yards.

PEACE OF PRINCETON: Gracious! The field will look like a gridiron!

CAMP: Precisely.[22]

Football soon became a lightning rod for both praise and damnation of intercollegiate sport. As Ronald Smith writes, "To many it was a cancer because of its brutal side and unethical play; to others it was valued for its promotion of character, virility, and esprit de corps."[23] Punching, kicking, and gouging were not uncommon, and the contrast between the upper-class colleges whose teams excelled at football and the game's ungentlemanly code of conduct was stark. The "flying wedge," devised by advertising man and chess maven Lauren F. Deland for Harvard in 1892, was the most dangerous play. The flying wedge was used for what we now call onside kickoffs: the kicker would touch the ball lightly, pick it up, and be escorted down the field by his blockers, who had lined up many yards behind the ball in a V-formation. They got a running head start and converged at a point several yards down the field, preferably on a single member of the other team. This concentration of force was terrifyingly effective, and perilous, and as a former Harvard manager wrote in 1926, if it had not been banned the sport would not have survived.[24]

Eloquent voices called for banning much more than the flying wedge. They wanted to ban football itself. Men like Theodore Roosevelt mocked as milksops and ineffectual eggheads those who called for banning football. They were unmanly and unsuited for the new world being born. Senator Henry Cabot Lodge (R-MA) told the Harvard Class of 1896: "The time given to athletic contests and the injuries incurred on the playing field are part of the price which the English-speaking race has paid for being world-conquerors."[25] The greater part of that price, of course, was being paid in death and taxes, not broken bones on the fields of play.

There was gold, or at least silver, in them thar bleachers. In 1905, Yale discovered that its student-run athletic department had a reserve fund of $100,000, which was the accumulation of several years-worth of gate receipts. The funds were used, in part, to tutor struggling football players. The growth had been steady. In 1890–1, Yale's football receipts (minus dues and donations) totaled $19,383; they would reach $36,316 in 1893–4 and exceed $50,000 by 1901–2. Harvard first exceeded $50,000 two years later—or 20 years after President Eliot had declared, in his 1882–3 Presidential Report, that Harvard was "opposed to all money-making at intercollegiate contests."[26] (Contrast this with Walter Camp's statement that "Demand should determine ticket prices, and Yale should profit from the attraction."[27] The Yalies had none of Eliot's aristocratic disdain for money-making. They understood that unless one lived on inherited wealth, one needed to be paid for one's labors.)

Yale hired the first professional intercollegiate athletics coach in 1864 to train its crew team. The earliest paid football coaches were frequently alumni of the schools, though they were not immune to pressure to succeed. Yale All-American fullback and coach Frank S. Butterworth wrote in 1904: "Players like to win, but head coaches and especially paid coaches, had to win." In 1905, the Harvard athletic committee and rabid alumni split the $7,000 package that made Bill Reid the highest paid football coach in the country. Reid was "paid nearly double the salary of the average professor at Harvard, 30 percent more than the highest paid professor, and nearly as much as Charles Eliot, Harvard's president since 1869," as Ronald Smith notes.[28] Harvard came late to the professional coaching game: it had taken its cues from England, and the Oxford-Cambridge ideal of amateurism, with its concomitant contempt for professionalism. From one angle this savored of nobility and gentlemanliness; from another it was buoyed by a snobbish disdain for those not to the manor born who actually had to make money to survive. It's all very easy for a man with inherited wealth to turn down an offered salary; it's not so easy, nor so noble, when one has to feed one's family and earn one's daily bread. The widespread American respect for the self-made man, the man making the most of his opportunities in a wide open field of endeavor, and the equalitarian suspicion of upper-class fops and trust-fund dandies ensured that the upper-class British concept of amateurism would not gain purchase in the States.

In defense of the upper-class concept of amateurism, Albert Bushnell Hart told readers of the *Atlantic Monthly* in 1890: "A man who competes from a love of sport prefers not to compete with a man who has gained superior skill by making his sport an occupation."[29] The haughtiness fairly drips from the page. An amateur does not compete or coach for money. It is beneath a gentleman to do so. As Walter Camp said in 1893, "A gentleman does not make his living, however, from his athletic prowess. He does not earn anything by his victories except glory and satisfaction."[30] But not everyone can afford to be an amateur. Nor do gentlemen necessarily make the best athletes. Schools supplied tutors to muscle-bound jocks even in those supposedly halcyon days. They also recruited good athletes whose interest in matters of the mind was limited, to say the least.

Eligibility rules, or lack thereof, would be the envy of many an outlaw coach today. Players often participated for more than four years, and payment of various kinds was not uncommon. Educators willing to bump up grades for star halfbacks were known as "sporty professors."[31] From the University of North Carolina to SUNY Binghamton, as we shall see, their modern analogues are not unknown. "Ringers," often hardy working-class boys whose mugs had never darkened a classroom, were enlisted to play for the dear old alma mater, and in the nineteenth century teams frequently featured graduates of the institution or students in graduate or professional schools. Some athletes skipped from team to team via transfer: they were called "tramp athletes." They'd enroll at State U (or its private school competitor), receive suitable compensation, carry the pigskin all fall while never pushing past a classroom door, and then move on down the road to their next temporary posting. The tangle of rules in effect today was unknown then: there were, at most schools, no limits on length of eligibility, and the idea that one had to be making progress toward a degree was risible. In fact, when in 1855 the Harvard and Yale crews had a rematch of that famous first sporting event, Harvard used Joseph Brown, the same coxswain who had piloted the team to its earlier triumph. Thus the problem of sneaking in ringers, or ineligible players, is conterminous with the entire history of collegiate sport.

The conference is called

The disorderly nature of college football spurred calls for organization. Thus was born the conference, which remains to this day the organizational form of almost all intercollegiate sports. In December 1894, the Southern Intercollegiate Athletic Association was founded by charter members Alabama, Auburn, Georgia, Georgia Tech, North Carolina, University of the South, and Vanderbilt; a year later, Cumberland, Louisiana State, Mississippi, Mississippi State, Tennessee, Texas, and Tulane joined.[32] Football was a sidelight; the association's earliest responsibilities were setting eligibility rules for competition and organizing track meets and basketball tournaments.

The most storied regional athletic association, the Western Conference, later known as the Big Ten, was born at a February 1896 meeting of representatives from the University of Chicago, University of Illinois, University of Michigan, University of Minnesota, Northwestern University, Purdue University, and University of Wisconsin at the Palmer House in Chicago. The state universities of Indiana and Iowa joined in 1899 (making it the Big Nine) and Ohio State University was admitted in 1912.[33]

If football had emerged in the East, it flowered quickly in the Midwest. In 1881, the student newspaper at the University of Wisconsin remarked that football was "more and more fashionable as a college sport" because it was "free from the harshness and danger of our modern base-ball."[34] (Times do change . . .) Wisconsin played its first football game in 1889, or shortly after the resignation of President John Bascom, who regarded intercollegiate sport as "the seat of sin." Charles Adams, who succeeded to the post in 1892, oversaw the flowering—or corruption—of football at UW, which the faculty-created Athletic Council was virtually powerless to supervise. The team won, finishing first in the Western (later Big Ten) Conference in its first two years of existence, 1896 and 1897, but it was plagued by accusations of "bad sportsmanship," "dirty football," and "outright acceptance of money for services on the playing field," according to Michael D. Smith's monograph on the origins of UW athletics.[35]

From the start, the most influential, and often controversial, member of the Big Ten was the University of Michigan. Michigan, under coach Fielding H. Yost, no stickler for observing even loose recruiting rules, won an astounding 55 games in a row from 1901 till late in the 1905 season. The 1901 team outscored its opponents 550–0. Michigan's 55-game streak was broken by the University of Chicago in a 2–0 game. The winning points were scored when Michigan's Dennison Clark was tackled for a safety when returning a punt. Poor Clark was pilloried by the press for his "wretched blunder." He was haunted thereafter by the play, even into middle age, as Fielding Yost recalled. In 1932, Clark shot himself, expressing the hope, in his suicide note, that this "final play" would atone for his error on the field 27 years earlier.[36]

Michigan supplied half of the first pair of teams to play in the Rose Bowl, the original bowl game. The Rose Bowl bloomed in 1902, as a way to promote Pasadena's Tournament of Roses Parade, whose athletic centerpiece had previously been a polo tournament. Its first iteration, on January 1, 1902, was played under the less flowery name of the Tournament East-West Football Game. Fielding Yost's "Point-a-Minute" Michigan team creamed Stanford, 49–0, before a crowd of 8,000 spectators at Tournament Park. (The Rose Bowl stadium would not host its first Rose Bowl game until 1923.) The uncompetitive nature of that first game convinced the organizers to scrap football; a chariot race replaced the gridiron contest in 1903, and not until 1916 would the Tournament of Roses Parade be followed by another football game.[37]

The Big Ten, in its infancy, barred freshmen and graduate students and athletic dorms, and limited coaches' salaries and the season (to five games). Imagine Michigan's Jim Harbaugh living under these rules! In fact, some of these reforms were Michigan-generated, if not necessarily Michigan-approved. In 1906, under the glare of hostile public attention for what was widely regarded as a rogue program, President James Burrill Angell of the University of Michigan persuaded the Big Ten to shorten the season to five games (UM had played 13 the previous season), ban grad students and training tables, reduce eligibility to three years, and require the coach to be full-time. Coach Yost protested those draconian acts. The Big Ten extended the limit to seven games in November 1907, but Yost was unpropitiated. So Michigan's regents withdrew UM from the conference in 1908, and it remained out until 1917. Winning games was paramount for Michigan: as Brian Ingrassia writes, "Many Michigan partisans perceived these rules as a strategy for smaller colleges, like Purdue and Indiana, to limit the Wolverines' ability to train winning teams and garner athletic revenue."[38]

Mr. Eliot objects

That football, a game of brawn and aggression, even violence, that rewards those with a mean streak, should become all the rage in the universities of the American ruling class is among the great ironies of sporting history. Though Princeton and Rutgers played that first recorded intercollegiate game, Yale was the laboratory in which its nineteenth-century iteration was polished with lapidary precision. It was, in the words of Allen L. Sack, the aptly named ex-Notre Dame defensive lineman turned sociologist, "the first football factory in the United States."[39] Sack's thesis is that whereas Harvard "smacked of aristocracy and old wealth" and looked to upper-class British notions of the role sport should play in the life of a gentleman, Yale was "for the sons of the new rich of America's gilded age." To the young aristocrats of Harvard, "To try too hard or to over exaggerate the importance of winning [was] an obvious sign of poor breeding," but to the young individualists of Yale, whose wealth was often the result of success in capitalist competition, there was nothing shameful or embarrassing about striving and winning.[40] In a later study, Sack and David L. Westby found that Yale's trustees over this period had substantially more modest backgrounds than did those of Harvard, who tended to be descended from "an early nineteenth century sea captain or merchant prince."[41]

Cleveland Amory's remark in *The Proper Bostonians* that "undue athletic exertion" was a strong social taboo at Harvard may be one reason why the Crimson won just five of 32 football games against Yale between 1875 and 1911.[42] (Much as we tweak these schools for perceived hypocrisies, they were not using taxpayer monies, and as private institutions it was well within their rights to allocate funds in whatever way the trustees or the governing board saw fit.)

No one exhibited a finer or haughtier scorn for the pigskin game than Charles W. Eliot, president of Harvard from 1869–1909, a tenure stretching from the year of the first intercollegiate football game until the birth of the NCAA. Eliot had proposed a raft of reforms in 1894, among them bans on freshmen and graduate student-players, limiting a student to one sport per year, and holding games only in stadiums owned by the colleges. A decade later, his objections had only deepened. In November 1905, Eliot published "The Evils of College Football" in *The Woman's Home Companion*. "The game of football has become seriously injurious to rational academic life in American schools and colleges," stated the Brahmin. The "lesser objections" to the game, he said, included "publicity, the large proportion of injuries among the players, the absorption of the undergraduate's mind in the subject for two months, and the disproportionate exaltation of the football hero in the college world."[43] Harvard had dropped the game in 1885 at the behest of faculty, but it was reinstated the next season. Eliot was not so sure that this was a wise decision.

> The football hero is useful in a society of young men if he illustrates generous strength and leads a clean life; but his merits of body and mind are usually not of the most promising sort for future service out in the world . . . the mental qualities of the big, brawny athlete are almost certain to be inferior to those of slighter, quicker witted men, whose moral ideals are at least as high as his.[44]

(One guess as to Eliot's physique.)

The "main objection" to the game, however, "lies against its moral quality." Although rules of the time prevented unnecessary roughness, holding, kneeing, kicking, and blows to the head, "the uniform enforcement of these rules is impossible," said Eliot, and they are frequently transgressed because "violations of the rules are in many respects highly profitable toward victory." While such savagery may be justifiable in war, it is unforgivable in a "manly game or sport between friends."[45] Bad habits picked up on the playing fields would be carried over into life outside the lines.

"What then are the sources of the great evils in this sport?" he asked.

> They are (1) The immoderate desire to win intercollegiate games; (2) The frequent collisions in masses which make foul play invisible; (3) The profit from violation of the rules; (4) The misleading assimilation of the game of war as regards its strategy and ethics.[46]

Eliot saw no room for debate on this issue.

> [I]f a college or university is primarily a place for training men for honorable, generous and efficient service to the community at large, there ought not to be more than one opinion on the question whether a game, played under the actual conditions of football, and with the barbarous ethics of warfare, can be a useful element in the training of men for such high service.[47]

Eliot's was a minority view. The primeval appeal of football was captured in an editorial in *The Nation*, of all places:

> The combination of discipline, individual skill, and brute strength which it calls for; the splendid fierceness of the game; the element of personal combat, which delights the savage instinct lingering in the breasts even of the most civilized among us—these qualities account for its growing popularity, and promise a vogue even wider than it now enjoys.[48]

The delightful savagery was almost the game's undoing. The intervention of federal government officials—or, more specifically, the man at the apex of the federal government, the president—"saved"—and altered in significant ways—football.

Modifying the rules of athletic contests is not among the enumerated powers of the president of the United States, but then Theodore Roosevelt was no one's idea of a strict constructionist. He was, however, occupying the White House in 1905, which is perhaps the most critical year in the history of college football. The same press that breathlessly relayed accounts of gridiron heroics metamorphosed overnight into puritanical scolds. Typical was a multipart muckraking series in *Collier's* in 1905. "Buying Football Victories" examined the sordid recruiting practices of several Big Ten (or Big Nine) schools, which were said to have discarded their high ideals in "an insane desire to win."[49] Even more worrisome, though, was the game's violence. The dangers inherent in football had been known prior to 1905, of course. University of Georgia fullback Richard Von Albade Gammon died of a concussion suffered in an October 30, 1897, game against the University of Virginia. The University of Georgia cancelled the remainder of its season, and the Peach State's legislature passed a ban on football.

Gammon's mother appealed to Governor William Atkinson to veto the bill, which would have ended football at Georgia, Georgia Tech, and Mercer.[50] The governor complied, saying that "There is no quality that a nation can less afford to lose than its aggressive manliness."[51]

Eight years later, especially in the Northeast, the outlook was dire. Columbia's Committee on Student Organizations, with the hearty approval of President Nicholas Murray Butler, abolished football in 1905, an abolition that lasted a decade. (Based on its record since, some might say that Columbia never resumed the game.) Football had become an "academic nuisance," said Butler, and the tiny fraction of the student body who participated had no time for studies.[52] Critics might have been flagged for piling on in football's nadir year of 1905. Deaths had not been unknown in football, though they were rare. But in 1905, press accounts tallied 18 (or 32) deaths and 143 serious injuries, and even if these figures were inflated, this was far and away the most dangerous activity sponsored by American colleges.

A new debate, sometimes rancorous, divided campuses. The issue was not U.S. imperialism in the Philippines, the merits of high tariffs versus free trade, or women's suffrage. Rather, it was the existence of football. At the University of Wisconsin, the faculty approved by a vote of 48–25 a resolution to suspend inter-collegiate football for the 1906 and 1907 seasons. Professor Robert M. Bashford of the university's law school told an alumni group that "football has outlived its usefulness." He was supported by Professor Frederick Jackson Turner, progenitor of the famous frontier thesis of American history, who sought to persuade UW's fellow conference members to suspend the game at their schools for two years. Pro-pigskin pressure from Wisconsin students grew intense. Effigies were burned, petitions were circulated, and the faculty retreated. Football at Wisconsin would be placed more firmly in the hands of the faculty, but the upcoming season would not be cancelled. As for faculty control, the never-iron grip of the professoriate quickly weakened. As Michael D. Smith notes, the season was expanded to ten games in 1910, athletes accumulated new privileges, athletic spending rose, and the program became big business, albeit of the state-subsidized variety.[53] The Wisconsin faculty—like perennial Big Ten sad sack Purdue on the field—had been thoroughly routed.

Philosopher Alexander Meiklejohn, dean of Brown University, expounded on the "evils of college athletics" in the pages of *Harper's Weekly*. Meiklejohn was no abolitionist; though he expressed the rather odd view that baseball and football are not "good fun for the participants"—had he, one wondered, ever played either game?—he praised contests between dormitories, classes, or fraternities for their salubrious effects, and he believed that intercollegiate sport, properly administered, built democratic character. Participants, he claimed, learned the value of cooperation, leadership, and the subordination of individual desire to the greater good, and by "fusing together the members of a college community," that intangible thing known as "school spirit" was produced. The problem was that colleges were going about this the wrong way. An emphasis on winning at all costs had given rise to a culture of cheating, or seeking to do harm to opposing players. Good athletes who had no business coming within a mile of a campus were masquerading as students in order to boost win–loss records. Schools had gotten the cockeyed idea that a winning team attracted more students, and put dollars into the purse of alma mater.

Meiklejohn's diagnosis was unremarkable—it would be hard to argue against any of the above propositions—but his solution ran contrary to the regnant progressivist ideology, which held that most situations could be improved by transferring control to experts or trained specialists. On the contrary, Dean Meiklejohn urged a return to the original model of American college sports: "The undergraduates should be given control of their own games." All others—faculty, administration, graduate students—should stay out, though the faculty ought to monitor finances and ensure that seasons do no stretch out unreasonably. Nor should professional coaches be hired; the students should organize and manage their own affairs. This system, argued Meiklejohn, "would call upon one of the strongest elements of the character of American youth—the sense of efficiency and personal responsibility."[54] Well, that dog didn't hunt. That trial balloon sank to earth. But still, what if?

With the proselytizing outdoorsman Teddy Roosevelt in the White House, paeans to the vigorous life were all the rage. Roosevelt had never played the game, but his son Ted was a member of Harvard's freshman team, and anything that got the old blood stirring was fine with the vascular TR. Bucknell president John Harris burbled that his own heart thrilled to:

> [T]he young giants who risk life and limb on the field of strife for the glory of alma mater. This intense struggle for glory other than their own cannot fail to have a beneficial effect on those who take part in the game.[55]

The Bull Moose himself endorsed the roughhouse sport. "Of all games, I personally like foot ball the best," he told Walter Camp in 1895, "and I would rather see my boys play it than see them play any other. I have no patience with the people who declaim against it because it necessitates rough play and occasional injuries."[56] That was before his son Ted broke his nose in the 1905 Harvard-Yale freshmen game.

(When, in the Harvard-Yale varsity game of 1905, umpire Paul Dashiell failed to call a penalty on two Yale men who made a nose-busting tackle on Harvard's Francis Burr, President Roosevelt called Dashiell on the carpet. The umpire wrote a letter of apology to the president, who held up Dashiell's appointment as a chemistry professor at the Naval Academy for six months after Harvard coach Reid told the president he did not "know whether that kind of man was fit to teach the boys at Annapolis."[57] Football and the state had collided—and as usual, TR was the man overseeing the collision.)

In October 1905, President Roosevelt, alarmed by newspaper and magazine reports on the brutality of the college game, as well as his own observations, convened a gathering at the White House of two representatives each from Harvard,

Yale, and Princeton to meet with him and Elihu Root, the secretary of state, to discuss the crisis in college football. (Or alleged crisis: then as now, the media periodically whipped up panics over matters that may or may not have been urgent.) From a distance of a century-plus, the Roosevelt conference seems both bizarre and an augury. Bizarre because, as historian John S. Watterson III notes, its pedigree was patrician: the president's friend Endicott Peabody, headmaster of Groton School and representing a confraternity of exclusive prep schools, had asked the president to take this action. The image of upper-class toffs meeting to save football is amusing in light of the decidedly nonpatrician lineage of many later football stars: surely the likes of Dick Butkus, Ray Nitzschke, Ray Lewis, and Mean Joe Greene would not have been welcome at the Harvard Club.

But Roosevelt's use of the presidency to encourage the modification of the rules of a sport that had nothing to do with the federal government portended a far more activist executive branch to come. As Watterson writes, "That the president who had just resolved the Russo-Japanese War and had earlier intervened in the far more crucial coal strike of 1903 would commit himself to football reform was unprecedented."[58] Roosevelt pioneered the use of the presidency as a Bully Pulpit from which to expound and offer direction on matters that even the loosest constructor of the U.S. Constitution might concede had no basis in that document. At Roosevelt's urging, the participants in the White House meeting produced a statement pledging fealty to the ideals of fair play and good sportsmanship. The imprimatur of the nation's chief executive was on the document, which read:

> In a meeting with the President of the United States it was agreed that we consider an honorable obligation exists to carry out in letter and in spirit the rules of the game of football relating to roughness, holding and foul play and the active coaches of our universities being present with us pledged themselves to so regard it and to do their utmost to carry out that obligation.[59]

The idea was that lesser beings would take their cues from the elite; only a Roosevelt could have believed such. Democrat William Jennings Bryan would not have so assumed, but then the Great Commoner from Nebraska would not have believed that altering the rules of football was within the bailiwick of the president of the United States.

In the aftermath of the president's meeting, the *Princeton Alumni Weekly* noted dolefully that "It has been plain for some time that, unless football is radically reformed, this great American sport is doomed." But these reforms should not only be directed at player safety; the very nature of competitive athletics seemed inconsistent with the university's mission. Football at schools like Princeton had become a form of labor, not recreation, and "if football is no longer a sport, has it any place in college athletics, whose aim, presumably, is to provide a healthful and entertaining means of diversion and physical exercise for young men primarily engaged in intellectual tasks?"[60] In any event, the groundlings failed to take the hint. Vicious hits continued.

Then a right halfback for the Union College squad named William Moore was killed in a November 1905 game against New York University, and reform took on a new imperative. Moore, according to the account in the *Washington Post*, attempted to catapult himself over the NYU defensive line. His head struck something and he fell, limply, to the ground, the ball squirting from his possession. The fans, sensing the severity of the injury, poured onto the field as so many rubberneckers. The referees cleared them off and Moore was carried away to receive medical treatment, to no avail. He died six hours later without having regained consciousness. The game, by the way, resumed; NYU won, 11–0.[61]

NYU Chancellor Henry McCracken, panicked by the death of Moore, telegraphed Harvard President Eliot urging an emergency conference to take drastic steps, possibly including a ban on football. Eliot, the cooler head, told him that "Deaths and injuries are not the strongest argument against football. That cheating and brutality are profitable is the main evil."[62] But McCracken, undeterred, called a conference that representatives of 13 colleges attended on December 8, 1905, at the Murray Hill Hotel in New York. On the question, "Ought the present game of football be abolished?" the votes ran eight nay to five aye. A second conference of 68 schools confirmed the decision in late December, out of which emerged the Intercollegiate Athletic Association of the United States (IAAUS), which in 1910 took the name National Collegiate Athletic Association (NCAA). It set as its task the "regulation and supervision of college athletics throughout the United States," which henceforth would be "maintained on an ethical plane in keeping with the dignity and high purpose of education."[63] This gathering discussed "stringent eligibility rules and methods for enforcement," but this ambitious, perhaps over-reaching, goal was shelved in favor of boilerplate resolutions to maintain "high ideals" and "true amateurism."[64]

President Roosevelt used his considerable influence to effect a merger of the two extant football rules committees in January 1906. The rules changes this new committee produced revolutionized the game: teams got three downs to move the ball ten yards or else they had to turn the ball over to the opponent (the fourth down was born in 1912); they had to have a minimum of six men at the line of scrimmage, so as to limit mass momentum plays; and the forward pass was legalized, albeit with limits on the number of yards a pass could gain and with the albatross of a 15-yard penalty for an incompletion. Speed and quickness were being rewarded over brute bulk. (Forward pass skeptics were not necessarily mossback Neanderthals: Walter Camp was among their number. Though it caught on slowly, the forward pass spread out the field and lessened the incentive for dangerous collisions at the line of scrimmage.) Other reforms and proposed reforms were directed at removing ringers, or mercenaries, from the game, and preventing graduates from playing on teams. One typical 1905 reformer, a professor of surgery at the University of Pennsylvania, urged "a rule which should require all members of athletic teams to be genuine students of the college which they represent and to be satisfactory in their studies."[65] Combined with a four-year eligibility rule and a ban on freshmen participation, these strictures just might have cleaned up the game.

Of course, they didn't. Each of these reforms was at one point adopted (and, in the case of freshmen, dropped), yet the athletic mania, and its warping effect on host institutions, continued unabated. But the game was now firmly in the hands of adults. As J. Douglas Toma writes, institutions had:

> wrested control of college football from students and rank and file alumni. College football was too powerful a force to be left in the control of anyone other than the most important external supporters and the new class of professional administrators taking control of American campuses.[66]

The abolitionist threat passes

Never again would the existence of intercollegiate football be so threatened, though as we shall see, individual schools would drop the sport and be none the worse for wear.[67] Frederick Jackson Turner said in a 1906 speech at an alumni banquet at the University of Wisconsin: "Football has become a business carried out too often by professionals, supported by levies on the public, bringing in vast gate receipts, demoralizing student ethics, and confusing the ideals of sport, manliness, and decency."[68] Faculty at Wisconsin, where Turner taught, sought to cleanse the campus of football. Yet such attempts flew in the face of the exhortations of that commander of the Bully Pulpit, President Theodore Roosevelt, to reject mollycoddlism and the enervated pose of fey youth and embrace masculine endeavor, whether in games or the game of life.

Brian M. Ingrassia, author of *The Rise of Gridiron University: Higher Education's Uneasy Alliance with Big-Time Football,* who taught at Georgia State, "a school with its own intriguing football story" as we shall see, argues that university administrators and others defended and promoted intercollegiate football as a "popular activity intended to make *highbrow* intellectual culture legible, or palatable, to the public." Football would give those outside the rarefied realm of higher education a stake in the enterprise. But it backfired, as it instead "institutionalized athletics as a university-sponsored *lowbrow* cultural ritual with its own permanent place on college campuses."[69] Once lodged, it became almost impossible to dislodge.

Football served as a rallying point for students and alumni; it advertised a college's name far and wide, and—it was assumed, though as we shall see this assumption was shakier than a one-point lead against a Tom Brady-quarterbacked team—encouraged new enrollments. But was football crowding out the central functions of the nation's colleges? *The Nation* noted with some amusement that "the one absorbing question for the graduates and undergraduates of two great institutions of learning is whether eleven Yale boys can beat eleven Princeton boys at football on Thanksgiving day."[70] A Williams alum marveled in 1890 that "you do not remember whether Thornwright was valedictorian or not, but you can never forget the glorious run of his in the football game."[71] Had our great institutions of learning been trivialized?

Woodrow Wilson, the president of Princeton University, had been an assistant coach at Wesleyan, though he never played the game himself. He once jokingly told an alumni club that "Princeton is noted in the wide world for three things: Football, baseball, and collegiate instruction. I suppose the first of these is what you want to hear about."[72] By 1909, however, the sport was once more in the dock. Deaths in the Army-Harvard and Virginia-Georgetown games had spurred renewed calls for its abolition. The press was reporting that football had claimed 32 lives that fall, though an NCAA delegate disputed this, asserting that 18 of those deaths "were not due to football" and another three involved elementary school-boys.[73] And Woodrow Wilson was telling readers of *Scribner's Magazine* that while football ought not to be abolished, it did need to be subordinated to the legitimate tasks of the university:

> All work and no play makes Jack a dull boy, not only, but may make him a vicious boy as well. Amusement, athletic games, the zest of contest and competition . . . these are wholesome means of stimulation, which keep young men from going stale and turning to things that demoralize. But they should not assume the front of the stage where more serious and lasting interests are to be served. Men cannot be prepared by them for modern life.[74]

Football, argued Wilson, was emphatically *not* the front porch of the university, as a later generation of apologists would contend. (Though baseball is the American game, U.S. presidents from TR through the college-football-playing trio of Richard Nixon, Gerald Ford, and Ronald Reagan have tended to have closer personal ties to football.) William Howard Taft, who in a later era would have made a fine and immovable nose tackle, enthused in 1915 that "the feeling of solidarity and loyalty in the student body that intercollegiate contests develop is a good thing; it outlasts every contest and it continues in the heart and soul of every graduate as long as he lives."[75]

Representatives of 28 schools had attended the first IAAUS convention in December 1906. (Thirty-nine schools were members.) Harvard, Yale, Chicago, and Princeton did not deign to join, and only Vanderbilt and the University of North Carolina joined from the South. The Pacific Coast was wholly unrepresented. Most members were smaller private schools of the East; the large public universities of Middle America were out, but then many already belonged to the Big Ten. By 1909, the IAAUS, soon to be the NCAA, numbered 57, with notable exceptions including Harvard, Yale, Princeton, Cornell, and Columbia. By 1911 it was up to 95 members, among them Harvard and Chicago. Yale didn't join the NCAA until 1915. Not their kind of people. And in fact, the elite Eastern schools were wary of association with the public universities of the American inland. It seems odd today, when the huge public universities of states like Alabama and Ohio and Texas rule the collegiate sporting world, to think that a century ago elite private schools sat atop the sporting pyramid.

The first president of the NCAA, Captain Palmer Pierce of West Point, was sharply critical of shady recruiting practices and tramp athletes, not just the violence of the game, which after all was amenable to mere rule changes. Its first convention in 1906 approved a resolution that, if followed, would have obviated so much of the mess and moil to come in big-time football:

> *Resolved*, That interclass games and intra-mural athletics in general should be fostered, to the end that a larger number of students may receive the benefits, and that intercollegiate competitions should be made rather an incident than the main end of college and university athletic sports.[76]

This resolution stands as the road not taken.

From the first, the emphasis of the NCAA was on the ideal of amateurism. That is, one played for the love of the game, not for remuneration. Member schools agreed not to offer inducements to students based on athletic ability. Nor were freshmen or those not taking a full schedule of classes eligible for participation. But given that the members themselves were responsible for enforcement, these rules were enforced more with laxity than stringency. The language of the early years of the NCAA has a charmingly anachronistic ring. For instance:

> There can be no question but that a boy or young man, who is habituated to the endeavor to win games by means, some of which he knows to be unfair and against the rules, later will play the game of life with the same ethical standards.[77]

Cheat at football; cheat at business. Reform would serve as a perpetual will-of-the-wisp, always envisioned but never achieved. Sport had insinuated—or barged—its way into the curriculum.

Physical education gave a gloss of academic respectability to college athletics, though the goals of physical educators—especially women, who dominated the field—were sometimes antithetical to those of coaches and boosters.[78] Physical education got a boost from the federal government during the First World War. President Wilson's Secretary of War, Newton Baker, told the NCAA's Executive Committee in August 1917 that:

> What the nation requires is that all our young men attending school shall have the benefit of physical training so as to develop their bodies and make them proper material for filling the armies of the country in the present emergency.

Just as the argot of football, with its blitzes and bombs, would echo warfare, so would the practice of football ready young men for actual warfare. The NCAA concurred with Secretary of War Baker, resolving at its December 1917 convention that "athletic sports be made subservient to the work of military preparation, and be made therefore an essential factor in military training."[79] In accordance with

the National Defense Act of 1916, colleges had established rifle clubs and competitive shooting. Athletic coaches were dispatched to military training camps, led by,
fittingly, Walter Camp.

Outside the academy, the Young Men's Christian Association (YMCA) and
other social outreach organizations emphasized sport as a means of uplift and an
antidote to juvenile delinquency. More than half of secondary school students took
physical education, or "gym," by 1934, and some colleges and universities made
such classes mandatory, to the everlasting dismay of nonathletic boys and girls.[80]
The first four-year course of study in athletic coaching was offered at the University of Illinois in 1919, with other schools following this lead in the 1920s.[81] By
the teens and 1920s, sport had moved colleges from the periphery of popular
consciousness toward its center. The ivory tower remained out of reach for most
Americans, foreign and inaccessible, but the Fighting Irish and the Wolverines and
the Trojans were as real as gridiron dirt and as close as the nearest sports page or
radio. "Well-intentioned progressives had . . . made sport permanent by creating
athletic departments, constructing concrete stadiums, and hiring a corps of professional athletic experts," writes Brian Ingrassia.[82] There was no going back. Or at
least there *seemed* to be no going back.

The athletic department was a virtual King Kong in some schools. Not at tiny
Amherst, although Alexander Meiklejohn, then president of Amherst College,
lamented in a 1922 letter to A. Lawrence Lowell, then president of Harvard:

> Our games are no longer the play of undergraduates. The players tend to
> become puppets in the hands of coaches and boards of control who represent
> the "institutions" in their public contests for victory. These coaches and sys-
> tems are, to say the best of them, highly specialized in point of view. In gen-
> eral they have very little understanding of the genuine purposes of a college.
> And yet they tend, more and more, to become independent bodies, respon-
> sible only to the public which is interested in the winning of victories.[83]

Breathless newspaper accounts made celebrities of 19-year-old halfbacks; the
introduction of player numbers by the University of Pittsburgh in 1915 had helped
to individualize and distinguish the 22 figures engaged in the on-field ruction
below. Though the famed American apostle of the arts and crafts movement,
Elbert Hubbard, may have scoffed that "Football bears the same relation to education that a bull-fight does to agriculture," the sport's appeal expanded apace,
much to the disgust of many intellectuals and the professoriate.[84] And some of
them fought back. Glenn E. Hoover, professor of economics at Mills College,
spoke for the anti-gridiron forces in the *New Republic*. The sport, he wrote in 1926:

> has now degenerated into a series of gigantic public spectacles, absorbing the
> interest of the average student, who, for one-third of the school year, marches,
> shouts, sings, rallies and roots, but never takes part in the contest itself, any
> more than he would at a horse race.

Hoover is just warming up. He absolves the callow college boys, for they are merely children, and saves his real venom for the alumnus, who lives and dies with Good Old State U's football fortunes. Yet:

> He never drains a glass to her discoveries in science or her contributions in art, but his ego expands in her hour of triumph, for he thinks himself a part of the winning machine. He is fat now and short-winded; he does not play the game and never did, but he attends the rallies, held on the very steps of Science Hall, where learned professors, enjoying a brief hysterical lapse, maintain in all seriousness that Pep and Spirit, drilled, pumped and ballyhooed into the Rooting Section, will win the game.[85]

What is to be done? Hoover, an explicator of the land economist Henry George, disclaims any affiliation with the "prohibiting cult," so he does not call for abolition of the sport. He does express a wistful wish that perhaps "we could trim the salary and dignity of the professional coach, that Colossus of the Campus, and make him at least a little lower than the president."[86] (From the distance of four score and ten years, University of Alabama football coach Nick Saban, with his new $11 million-plus contract extension in 2017, making him the highest-paid public employee in America, bats an eyelash in mild amusement.[87] Well, to give credit where credit is due, at least one man batted an eyelash back. In 2007, when the University of Alabama gave Saban an eight-year, $32 million contract—long since superseded—university trustee emeritus Gary Neil Drummond, an engineer and president of a family coal-mining concern, blasted the package as "CEO pay ... one of the worst things we have ever done." Drummond asked, "What are we about as a university? Football is a big part of it, but paying the dollars we are talking about here is more than anyone else is getting."[88] Alas, by conceding the first part of that last sentence, the late Mr. Drummond had given away the game.)

Back to 1926. Glenn Hoover saw a light at the end of the tunnel: professional football, he predicted, "would do for college football what it has done for college baseball, to wit, remove it from the spot light, render it an innocuous thing and plunge it into oblivion." Not exactly. Even as, in our day, the National Football League is toppling from its perch, weakened by overexposure and national anthem protests and the inevitable concussion lawsuits, the college game remains strong. But then rumors (or dreams) of college football's death have always been greatly exaggerated.[89]

The Carnegie Foundation suits up

The prospect of big-time football pervasively corrupting American higher education grew so large in the collective mind of the intelligentsia that the Carnegie Foundation for the Advancement of Teaching issued a series of reports, or bulletins, in the 1920s and early 1930s, capped by Bulletin 23, *American College Athletics*, which was sent to the printers on June 29, 1929, and by coincidence was released to the public on October 24, 1929, the day the stock market began its historic crash. This would seem to be an ill omen, but for the report's author or subjects?

Howard J. Savage authored the 347-page *American College Athletics*, which was issued under the unprepossessing tag "Bulletin Number Twenty-Three." Let no one accuse the Carnegie Foundation of sensationalism in marketing its products! Product of a three-year study, relying on personal interviews instead of questionnaires, employing five investigators who personally visited 130 colleges and universities, the Carnegie report "is often considered the most significant historical reform document in intercollegiate athletics."[90] Savage's report occasioned a brief spasm of soul-searching and considerable defensiveness on the part of the big-time football schools.

Despite his surname, Savage was relatively mild in tone. His prime villain was commercialism, which had distorted the values upon which college life ought to be based and encouraged sedentary habits in the vast majority of students who are not at play on the fields of glory. The answer? Less glamour, more participation! He also recommended:

> —faculty control of intercollegiate athletics, which he concedes has been regarded as a panacea in the past, often existing in name only, with faculty having little responsibility beyond assessing athletes for academic eligibility.
> —a balancing of intercollegiate with intramural athletics, with an upgrade of facilities for the latter. Today this reads like a pipe dream, but the Savage study found that 50–63 percent of students in the schools under study played intramural sports, which in some cases were compulsory.[91]
> —a reduction of the extravagant facilities, budgets, and publicity lavished on athletes, especially football players. (This wasn't just a nonstarter: it didn't even suit up!)

Dr. Henry S. Pritchett, president of the Carnegie Foundation, supplied a lengthy introduction whose tone was markedly harsher than that of Savage. Pritchett laid out the two questions that the Carnegie investigators sought to answer: First, "What relation has this astonishing athletic display to the work of an intellectual agency like a university?" And second, "How do students, devoted to study, find either the time or the money to stage so costly a performance?" Pritchett goes on to ask:

> [W]hether an institution in the social order whose primary purpose is the development of the intellectual life can at the same time serve as an agency to promote business, industry, journalism, salesmanship, and organized athletics on an extensive commercial basis . . . How far can an agency, whose function is intellectual, go in the development of other causes without danger to its

primary purpose? Can a university teach equally well philosophy and sales-manship? Can it both sponsor genuine education and at the same time train raw recruits for minor vocations? Can it concentrate its attention on securing teams that win, without impairing the sincerity and vigor of its intellectual purpose?[92]

These questions could have been asked, with equal relevance, yesterday.

The professionalization of the college game through coaching and advanced training methods has robbed it of innocence, argues Pritchett. No more a student-run enterprise, football is now a "highly profitable" and hyperorganized spectacle in which "little if any personal initiative" has been left to the player. The joy and pleasure of play has been transmogrified into drudgery performed "for the glory and, too often, for the financial profit of the college."[93] His cogent points com-mingle with a soupçon, or maybe even a full dollop, of fuddy-duddyism. Pritchett dislikes intensely the publicity attendant on college football, and the press-box poets who make gods of broad-shouldered 19-year-olds. This is "demoralizing" for the youths, an assertion contradicted by every scrapbook ever compiled. Pritchett also rode a favorite hobbyhorse: lavish pay for coaches. While college coaches in the 1920s were achieving a celebrity that in some—though not all—cases dwarfed that of college presidents (who, today, outside academe, can name even *one* college president?), the salaries were nowhere near Nick Saban land. The report stated:

> At over one hundred universities and colleges the highest salary paid to a dean was $15,000, the median $6,000, the average $6,409. The highest-paid full professor received a salary of $12,000, while the median among such professors was $5,000, and the average $5,158. Among eighty-three directors of physical education or graduate managers, the highest salary was $14,000, the lowest $1,000 for part-time work, the median $4,800, and the average $5,095. Of ninety-six head football coaches, the highest paid drew a salary of $14,000, and the lowest $1,800, while the median salary was $6,000, and the average $6,107.[94]

So the median salary for a football coach equalled that of a dean and exceeded that of full professors and directors of physical education. Pritchett stirringly concludes:

> The paid coach, the gate receipts, the special training tables, the costly sweaters and extensive journeys in special Pullman cars, the recruiting from the high school, the demoralizing publicity showered on the players, the devotion of an undue proportion of time to training, the devices for putting a desirable ath-lete, but a weak scholar, across the hurdles of the examinations—these ought to stop and the inter-college and intramural sports be brought back to a stage in which they can be enjoyed by large numbers of students and where they do not involve an expenditure of time and money wholly at variance with any ideal of honest study.[95]

This sounds, at once, charmingly naïve and jarringly contemporary. Same as it ever was, as the song goes. But that Pullman car left the station long ago. Responsibility for restoring the allegedly Edenic era of precommercialized and professionalized college sport rested with the presidents and faculty, who would prove not up to the job.

Howard Savage was less sweeping than Dr. Henry S. Pritchett in his criticism, preferring to concentrate his fire on the warping effects of commercialism. "Monetary and material returns from intercollegiate athletics" have paid for fine buildings, he concedes, but at the cost of "things of the spirit or the mind."[96] If Pritchett's view of the salaried college coach was jaundiced, Savage's was almost roseate. He did not deny that these instructors of the gridiron were well paid: the Carnegie researchers found that at the 58 large colleges in their survey, the median maximum salary for coaches was $6,500, and for full professors, $6,000. The average maximum salary of the head coaches was $6,926, or $611 higher than the average maximum salary of the highest-paid full professors, which was $6,315. So the schools apparently valued football coaches more than full professors. But on the bright side, wrote Savage, "the tenure of the football coach is coming less and less to depend on victory," as institutions "are becoming less and less subject to the pressure for victory from a few rabid enthusiasts."[97] Well, that forecast sure didn't pan out. He was accurate, however, as we shall see, in his assessment that a winning team does not "affect registration appreciably."[98]

Savage opined that recruiting was less squalid than it had been at the dawn of the century. Indeed, although 81 of the 112 institutions under study engaged in some form of recruiting, "there can be little doubt that the evils of soliciting and subsidizing athletes have diminished over the last twenty-five, twenty, or even fifteen years."[99] While he did not condemn professionals who play for pay, he believed that admitting and then subsidizing "students" whose primary purpose is to labor on the fields of play degraded scholarship and discredited schools. Classes must be dumbed down to meet these hulks on their level, he said, and the concatenation of concessions—in testing, grading, attendance, and otherwise—"disunifies the student body" as it subordinates the intellectual integrity of the school to the requirements of a handful of athletes.[100]

Savage also bemoaned the fact that money-hungry schools had jettisoned rivalries for more lucrative opportunities. He instanced the rupture of the New York University-Syracuse and Ohio State-University of Iowa battles—the former gone with the wind; the latter to be resumed, though between 1929 and 1943 they played only once. But Savage hadn't seen nuthin' yet. The conference realignments of the 1990s and early twenty-first century saw the surcease of some of the most storied rivalries in the game: Penn State-Pitt, Nebraska-Oklahoma, Pitt-West Virginia, and Michigan-Notre Dame, among others, as the top-heavy Power Five conferences (Atlantic Coast, Big Ten, Big 12, Pac-12, and Southeastern) swallowed up schools whose loyalty had a price.

Savage was more sanguine than preface-writer Pritchett. Intramural sport he praised for its healthy effects, and even big-time football, despite the rampant commercialism, the fallacy that a successful team lends prestige to a school, and the sordidness of recruiting and pay for play, was not irredeemable. The past 30 years of college athletics, he wrote, had seen a marked improvement morally, physically, and spiritually. "[T]here can be no question of abolishing college athletics, nor should there be," he lectured. "What can be looked for is a gradual establishment through concrete action of a few general principles, to which all men would agree in the abstract."[101] Those principles included the diminution of "commercialism," which, since it presumably entails a curtailment of media coverage of the sport, would be unworkable and unconstitutional, and a vague commitment to "challenge the best intellectual capabilities of the undergraduate," which is so vaporous and insubstantial as to vanish into thin air.[102]

"Give the game back to the boys," urged Savage, though of course the student-run football programs of the nineteenth century had not exactly been idylls played on Elysian fields.[103] In any event, the game was not given back to the boys. Despite the publicity given to the Savage report, the games were further professionalized and commercialized. Athletic departments became more numerous, and more powerful.

Though Savage denied even the possibility of ending college athletics, there had been discussion, and even action, in the direction of abolishing intercollegiate football during the decade in which the Carnegie investigators spelunked through the caverns of football. In 1925, the 65 newspapers constituting the North American Newspaper Alliance sponsored a series of articles asking whether or not the sport should be nixed at the intercollegiate level. Herein we see a cleavage developing between taxpayer-supported public schools and private schools. Football may have first gained its toehold in the latter, but by the 1920s the expense and the compromises attendant on a serious football program were causing second, third, and even final thoughts among private school presidents. For instance, Gettysburg College president Dr. Henry W.A. Hanson called the sport "a disgrace to modern college life." The relative handful of football players "crowds the overwhelming majority of the student body into the grandstand," so that the bulk of the studentry is sedentary, except for "exercise of the vocal organs."[104]

Gettysburg never did drop the sport, but Antioch College of Ohio did, and in later years Antioch students wore T-shirts reading "No football team since 1927."[105] (Football had the last laugh: Antioch closed its doors in 2008, though it reopened in 2011.) In 1925, Antioch president Dr. Arthur E. Morgan praised the then-temporary suspension of football as a spur to physical activity for the generality of students: "Today all of our students are in athletics, and the elimination of football has made possible a normal distribution of interests in athletic sports."[106]

Presidents of other small private schools—Berea College of Kentucky, Stevens Institute of Technology in Hoboken, New Jersey—also expressed satisfaction with their decisions to drop football. Dr. Karl F. Wettstone of the University of Dubuque, a largely German Presbyterian school, said:

We abolished intercollegiate athletics as a stand against commercialization. In the old days, a college was known as a seat of learning, where athletics were but an incident. Today, however, athletics have become the most important factor. The vast amount of attention given to athletic activities by the general public has led administrators and college executives to use the athletic reputation of the institution as a means of securing appropriations from State boards and endowments from wealthy individuals.

"For the present deplorable situation," said President Wettstone, "I blame the State universities. When these institutions, backed by public funds, began to develop expert teams in various departments of athletics, the older and smaller schools realized that they must follow suit or lose their hold."[107] Dubuque refused to follow suit; it dropped football after a 1–6 season in 1924. In fact, it dropped all intercollegiate sports. President Wettstone made his stand. He had inherited a school whose football players "skipped class, ditched chapel, cursed, smoked, and drank heavily. They accepted money from boosters and threatened to take their talents elsewhere for richer benefits," according to Baylor professor of history Elesha Coffman in his superbly titled history "You Cannot Serve God and Gridiron." During the 1924 season, players had thrown a prostitute out of a dorm window "without paying her." Whereupon she paid a call on the then-president of the school, Cornelius M. Steffens, and demanded payment.[108] This was all too much for the staunch German Presbyterians whose contributions maintained the University of Dubuque. Steffens was out; young Karl Wettstone was in. He took the bull by the horns, abolishing intercollegiate sports in his first year. His action drew national attention, but Wettstone was gone by 1927, sport returned in 1928, and football was reinstated in 1929. The team plays on to this day. Gridiron 7, God 0.

Resentment of Savage's Carnegie report was widespread in the South and Midwest. As education historian John R. Thelin writes, "the Carnegie Foundation report was depicted as a product of the East Coast establishment."[109] The Big Ten, riddled with dubious recruiting practices and a win–at–all–costs mentality, was sharply criticized in the Carnegie report: only the Universities of Chicago and Illinois escaped some form of censure. The Big Ten's response was immediate—perhaps too immediate. Major John L. Griffith, league commissioner of athletics, admitted on October 23, the day before the Carnegie study's issuance, that "I have not had an opportunity to read the report." Nevertheless, he asserted confidently that:

I don't believe the Carnegie investigators have given a fair picture of Big Ten conditions. We have nothing to be ashamed of. I think that I am better informed of Big Ten athletic conditions than any investigator for the Carnegie Foundation. And I honestly believe that the Western Intercollegiate Conference [Big Ten] universities are cleaner in regard to proselyting and subsidizing athletes than are any other ten universities any one may name.[110]

The Big Ten also played, not without merit, the regional card. University of Michigan law professor Ralph W. Aigler, chairman of the board in control of UM athletics, told the faculty senate that the Carnegie report was "almost vicious" in its assault on the integrity of Midwestern football. Savage, he implied, regarded the outlanders of Middle America as small-s savages:

> In a number of places in the bulletin the Western Conference [Big Ten] is referred to and, curiously, almost always with a sort of half-veiled sneer. The truth apparently is that the bulletin was written from the point of view of the Eastern athletic man, who has it pretty firmly fixed in mind that, athletically, things are pretty raw in the territory west of the Allegheny Mountains.[111]

Besides, the league was willing to enforce rules against errant members, as evidenced by its recent disciplining of the University of Iowa. Was Iowa really that egregious a transgressor, or were the Hawkeyes merely a scapegoat, a burnt offering to Howard Savage and the Carnegie Report? Although the Big Ten suspended the University of Iowa in May 1929, or five months before the release of Bulletin 23, Raymond Schmidt of the College Football Historical Society notes the widespread suspicion that the Big Ten's anathema upon Iowa was a preemptive strike, as conference officials knew that harsh criticism from Carnegie was in the offing. (The aforementioned law professor Ralph W. Aigler of the University of Michigan found conditions at Iowa "almost shocking.")[112] Iowa alumni were notorious for maintaining slush funds with which to subsidize athletes, "the money being channeled through local businessmen." This violated Big Ten policy, which forbade scholarships or aid "on a basis of athletic skill."[113] Overseeing the operation was an athletic director (AD) with a reputation for truculence; when the school president forced his resignation in April 1929, the AD departed, along with sheaves of potentially incriminating documents.

The Big Ten faculty committee, which was not, in contrast to today's faculty committees, wholly impuissant, suspended athletic relations with Iowa. Investigators found a long trail of illegally recruited and supported players. Still, it didn't seem particularly sordid: one source of athlete subvention was the sale of school yearbooks, which seems almost quaint. Other instances were straightforward pay-for-play arrangements. For instance, Tom Stidham, a talented lineman from Haskell Indian Institute, was offered $75 per month to join the Iowa team. Stidham said he wouldn't take a penny under $100, so a Dr. White and a Mr. Williams agreed to meet his demand, and the deal was done.[114] Alas, the deal raised red flags, and Stidham never played a down for the Hawkeyes. He did, eventually, coach the Oklahoma Sooners, who could have taught the University of Iowa a thing or two about bending the rules. The recruiting violations for which Iowa was briefly booted from the Big Ten strike our ears as mild, in some cases even sensible. Alumni organized a "Labor Fund" through which players were paid to work at local businesses. In some cases these were no-show jobs, but for the most part the footballers at least showed up.[115]

Curiously, specifics relating to Iowa were largely absent from the Carnegie Report, so if the Big Ten intended to make an example of the Hawkeyes, it may have jumped the gun. As for Iowa, the school suspended those athletes whose recruitment was the primary cause of its temporary excommunication from the Big Ten, and in February 1930 the school reentered the conference, perhaps chastened.

Pacific Coast football schools, which as W. Burlette Carter notes were mostly "large universities that depended on governmental support of their athletics programs," were unmoved by the report's criticism of commercialism. One NCAA representative from the Pacific district pooh-poohed "the attitude of some of our Eastern brethren," arguing that big crowds conduced to a clean sport.[116] The enhancement of school spirit and alumni loyalty, not to mention support from state legislators, were a gift, and big-time football was the giver.

Although college football's cradle was in the Northeast, the South became its hotbed. "College football became a primary means of reasserting a Southern sense of identity and superiority," argues Wes Borucki. The Civil War remained a potent memory; in Borucki's account, the victories in the 1920s and 1930s by teams like the University of Alabama's Crimson Tide over Northern football powerhouses were a source of pride and honor.[117] As is still the case today, Southern teams consisted overwhelmingly of Southern-born and bred players: a team of carpetbagging outsiders would not have packed quite the same symbolic punch.

Southern schools largely ignored the Carnegie bulletin. When, in early 1931, the Associated Press asked faculty advisors and publicity directors of several colleges and universities below the Mason-Dixon Line what changes in subsidizing football and recruiting players they had instituted since the publication of the Savage report, the most frequent answer was a terse "none." Whether flagship state universities (Georgia, Kentucky, Maryland, South Carolina, Tennessee), public colleges (Virginia Military Institute, Alabama Poly [later renamed Auburn]), or private schools (Vanderbilt, Oglethorpe, Centenary, Tulane), the unanimous response to the Associated Press poll was somewhere between a yawn and a sneer. And when the Associated Press asked if football was "overemphasized," the answer was a resounding "No!"[118] The clerisy locked in their ivory towers may have been furrowing their brows over the football madness infecting institutions of higher learning, but the residents of those institutions were, by and large, unconcerned.

Harry Stuhldreher, one quarter of the legendary Four Horsemen of the 1924 Notre Dame backfield, and by 1931 the head coach at Villanova, attributed football reformism to jealousy. The complainers, he noted, were concentrated in the East. They were "only envious of [football's] popularity." He scoffed at those who bemoaned the high salaries pulled down by top coaches, making the irrelevant argument that "They talk about limiting the salary of a coach to the size of a college president's. I coach at a religious institution whose president is a clergyman and receives no salary. Where would I get off?" Stuhldreher defended intersectional games, which critics said cost too much money, too much travel time, and weakened natural and local rivalries. These are "good for the country," he said, as they "cement the unity of the United States, helping the youth of one section to become acquainted with the youth of other sections." A new Civil War, by this means, could be averted. The method of acquaintance, of course, was bashing each other's heads in, but hey, it's a start. And as for spring practice, also decried by reformers, "No football player is compelled to participate in Spring practice."[119] (Unless he wants to play in the fall, Coach Stuhldreher could have added, but did not.)

In a follow-up report for Carnegie two years later, Savage and his coauthors confidently asseverated that "the deflation of American football has begun . . . The road to a more sincere appreciation of the values of sport and sportsmanship is under way."[120] Surely this ranks as one of the worst prophecies this side of the *Literary Digest* predicting that Alf Landon would defeat Franklin Delano Roosevelt in 1936. (FDR eked out an electoral college victory, 523–8.) Savage had been misled by colleges reacting to straitened economic circumstances. Depression was, briefly, the mother of belt-tightening.[121]

In a 1950 memoir, Savage insisted that the report "at no point proposed or favored the abolition of college athletics." Rather, he said, it sought to rein in commercialism and encourage good sportsmanship and honesty. Savage expressed regret that Henry S. Pritchett trained his fire on the professional coach as "the root of all athletic abuses."[122] Savage was proud of the effect his bulletin had, noting that by 1930, the season subsequent to the study's release, gate receipts from college football had dipped, student interest seemed to be declining, and a few colleges had even dropped or deemphasized the sport. He wrote in 1953, "Observers attributed this development in part to undergraduate revulsion over the subsidizing of athletes, in part to a more serious student attitude toward academic work, in part to high prices for admission to contests."[123] Left out of this curiously incomplete list is the Great Depression!

This would not be the last time football reformers permitted the wish to be father to the thought.

Notes

1 Guy Lewis, "The Beginning of Organized Collegiate Sport," *American Quarterly* 22, No. 2 (Summer 1970): 223.
2 Ibid.: 225.
3 Bruce Leslie, "The Response of Four Colleges to the Rise of Intercollegiate Athletics 1865–1915," *Journal of Sport History* 3, No. 3, (Winter 1976): 214.
4 Howard J. Savage, *American College Athletics*, with a preface by Henry S. Pritchett (New York: Carnegie Foundation, 1929), www.thecoia.org/wp-content/uploads/2014/09/Carnegie-Commission-1929-excerpts-1.pdf, p. 9.
5 Ronald A. Smith, *Sports & Freedom: The Rise of Big-Time College Athletics* (New York: Oxford University Press, 1988), p. ix.
6 James M. Whiton, "The First Harvard-Yale Regatta (1852)," *The Outlook* 68 (June 1, 1901): 286.
7 Ibid.: 287.
8 David L. Westby and Allen Sack, "The Commercialization and Functional Rationalization of College Football: Its Origins," *Journal of Higher Education* 47, No. 6 (November–December 1976): 643.

9 Smith, *Sports & Freedom: The Rise of Big-Time College Athletics*, p. 26.

10 Ibid., p. 21.

11 Lewis, "The Beginning of Organized Collegiate Sport," *American Quarterly*: 228.

12 Ronald D. Flowers, "Institutionalized Hypocrisy: The Myth of Intercollegiate Athletics," *American Educational History Journal* 36, No. 2 (2009): 349.

13 Gregory S. Sojka, "Evolution of the Student-Athlete in America," *Journal of Popular Culture* 16, Issue 3 (1983): 56.

14 Smith, *Sports & Freedom: The Rise of Big-Time College Athletics*, pp. 219–20.

15 Jim Overmyer, "July 1, 1859: Baseball Goes to College," Society for American Baseball Research, http://sabr.org/gamesproj/game/july-1-1859-baseball-goes-college, accessed February 1, 2017.

16 Smith, *Sports & Freedom: The Rise of Big-Time College Athletics*, p. 71.

17 Ryan Dunleavy, "Kyle Flood Suspended 3 Games, Fined $50K by Rutgers," *Asbury Park Press*, September 16, 2015, www.app.com/story/sports/college/rutgers/2015/09/16/kyle-flood-suspended-fined-rutgers/32512487/.

18 Smith, *Sports & Freedom: The Rise of Big-Time College Athletics*, pp. 69, 74.

19 Savage, *American College Athletics*, p. 10.

20 John Stuart Martin, "Walter Camp and His Gridiron Game," *American Heritage* 12, No. 6 (October 1961), www.americanheritage.com.

21 Nand Hart-Nibbrig and Clement Cottingham, *The Political Economy of College Sports* (Washington, DC: Lexington Books, 1986), p. 21.

22 Martin, "Walter Camp and His Gridiron Game," *American Heritage*. Not everyone revered Walter Camp: Harvard President Eliot said in 1905 that he was "deficient in moral sensibility—a trouble not likely to be cured at his age." Smith, *Sports & Freedom: The Rise of Big-Time College Athletics*, p. 200.

23 Ibid., p. 83.

24 S. deJ. Osborne, "Flying Wedge First Used in 1892 by Deland Coached Harvard Team," *Harvard Crimson*, November 5, 1926, www.thecrimson.com/article/1926/11/5/flying-wedge-first-used-in-1892/.

25 Smith, *Sports & Freedom: The Rise of Big-Time College Athletics*, p. 96.

26 Westby and Sack, "The Commercialization and Functional Rationalization of College Football: Its Origins," *Journal of Higher Education*: 630, 642.

27 Ibid.: 644.

28 Smith, *Sports & Freedom: The Rise of Big-Time College Athletics*, p. 147, 156.

29 Albert Bushnell Hart, "The Status of Athletics in American Colleges," *Atlantic Monthly* 66 (1890): 64–5.

30 Eric T. Vanover and Michael M. DeBowes, "The Impact of Intercollegiate Athletics in Higher Education," *Academic Perspectives in Higher Education Journal* 1, Issue 1 (2013), http://digitalcommons.odu.edu/aphe/vol1/iss1/1.

31 W. Burlette Carter, "The Age of Innocence: The First 25 Years of the National Collegiate Athletic Association, 1906 to 1931," *Vanderbilt Journal of Entertainment and Technology Law* 8, No. 2 (Spring 2006): 235.

32 Roger Saylor, Southern Intercollegiate Athletic Association, http://library.la84.org/SportsLibrary/CFHSN/CFHSNv06/CFHSNv06n2g.pdf, accessed February 25, 2017.

33 "Big Ten Membership History," www.bigten.org/genrel/061110aag.html. "The 1890s were a critical time for American collegiate sports. Big name universities were determined to win at any cost and were committing bigger and bigger excesses to do so. Professional baseball pitchers were becoming campus stars. Coaches were inserting nonstudents for football games and putting themselves in their own line ups. Jam-packed college grandstands went wild rooting for 'heroes' who attended school only during baseball and football seasons . . . Collegiate sports were at a critical crossroads and might have been set back many years—or even abolished—had it not been for the urgent and historic meeting" which laid the groundwork for what would one day be known far and wide as the Big Ten. Joanna Davenport, "From Crew to Commercialism—The Paradox of Sport in Higher Education," in *Sport and Higher Education*,

edited by Donald Chu, Jeffrey O. Segrave, and Beverly J. Becker (Champaign, IL: Human Kinetics Publishers, 1985), p. 9.

34 Michael D. Smith, "Origins of Faculty Attitudes toward Intercollegiate Athletics: The University of Wisconsin," *Canadian Journal of History of Sport and Physical Education* 2, No. 2 (December 1971): 61.

35 Ibid.: 62, 66.

36 Robin Lester, "Michigan-Chicago 1905: The First Greatest Game of the Century," *Journal of Sport History* 18, No. 2 (Summer 1991): 272–3.

37 "Michigan's Bowl Game History: 1902 Rose Bowl," Bentley Historical Library, http://bentley.umich.edu/athdept/football/bowls/1902rose.htm.

38 Ingrassia, *The Rise of Gridiron University: Higher Education's Uneasy Alliance with Big-Time Football*, p. 63.

39 Allen L. Sack, "Yale 29–Harvard 4: The Professionalization of College Football," *Quest* 19, Issue 1 (1973): 24.

40 Ibid.: 26–7.

41 Westby and Sack, "The Commercialization and Functional Rationalization of College Football: Its Origins," *Journal of Higher Education*: 634.

42 Sack, "Yale 29–Harvard 4: The Professionalization of College Football," *Quest*: 24; Cleveland Amory, *The Proper Bostonians* (Boston: Dutton, 1947), p. 299.

43 *Charles W. Eliot: The Man and His Beliefs*, edited by William Allan Neilson (New York: Harper & Brothers, 1926), p.115.

44 Ibid., p. 116.

45 Ibid., p. 117.

46 Ibid., p. 118.

47 Ibid., p. 119.

48 "The Future of Football," *The Nation*, November 20, 1890.

49 Edward S. Jordan, "Buying Football Victories," *Collier's*, November 25, 1905: 21.

50 William Hanford Edwards, *Football Days: Memories of the Game and of the Men Behind the Ball* (New York: Moffat, Yard and Company, 1916), pp. 244–5.

51 Ingrassia, *The Rise of Gridiron University: Higher Education's Uneasy Alliance with Big-Time Football*, p. 51.

52 Nicholas Murray Butler, "Should Football Be Ended or Mended? Why Columbia Has Abolished the Game," *Review of Reviews* 33, No. 1 (January 1906): 71.

53 Smith, "Origins of Faculty Attitudes Toward Intercollegiate Athletics: The University of Wisconsin," *Canadian Journal of History of Sport and Physical Education*: 67, 69.

54 Alexander Meiklejohn, "The Evils of College Athletics," *Harper's Weekly*, December 2, 1905, http://app.harpweek.com.

55 Leslie, "The Response of Four Colleges to the Rise of Intercollegiate Athletics 1865–1915," *Journal of Sport History*: 218.

56 John S. Watterson III, "Political Football: Theodore Roosevelt, Woodrow Wilson, and the Gridiron Reform Movement," *Presidential Studies Quarterly* 25, No. 3 (Summer 1995): 557.

57 Smith, *Sports & Freedom: The Rise of Big-Time College Athletics*, p. 197.

58 Watterson III, "Political Football: Theodore Roosevelt, Woodrow Wilson, and the Gridiron Reform Movement," *Presidential Studies Quarterly*: 559.

59 Carter, "The Age of Innocence: The First 25 Years of The National Collegiate Athletic Association, 1906 to 1931," *Vanderbilt Journal of Entertainment and Technology Law*: 216.

60 "Reform in Football: Must Come or the Game Is Doomed, It Is Declared," *Washington Post*, October 15, 1905.

61 "Football Player Killed: William Moore, of Union College, Dies from Blow on Head," *Washington Post*, November 26, 1905. Moore's forename is given as both William and Harold in accounts of his death.

62 Smith, *Sports & Freedom: The Rise of Big-Time College Athletics*, p. 199.

63 Carter, "The Age of Innocence: The First 25 Years of The National Collegiate Athletic Association, 1906 to 1931," *Vanderbilt Journal of Entertainment and Technology Law*: 221.

64 D.A. Sargent, "History of the Administration of Intercollegiate Athletics in the United States," *American Physical Education Review* 15 (1910): 258.

65 J. William White, "Football and Its Critics," *The Outlook* 81 (November 18, 1905): 668.

66 Toma, *Football U.: Spectator Sports in the Life of the American University*, p. 19.

67 In 1907, Miss Anna Jeanes, a Quaker, left a sizeable bequest to Swarthmore if the school would terminate its intercollegiate athletics program. The matter was debated, but the bequest was rejected, though as Bruce Leslie notes, Swarthmore did drop football and basketball for one year as part of a cleansing process. Leslie, "The Response of Four Colleges to the Rise of Intercollegiate Athletics 1865–1915," *Journal of Sport History*: 221.

68 Ronald A. Smith, *Pay for Play: A History of Big-Time College Athletic Reform* (Urbana: University of Illinois Press, 2011), p. 28.

69 Ingrassia, *The Rise of Gridiron University: Higher Education's Uneasy Alliance with Big-Time Football*, pp. xi, 4.

70 "The Future of Football," *The Nation*, November 20, 1890.

71 Gregory S. Sojka, "The Evolution of the Student-Athlete in America: From the Divinity to the Divine" in *Sport and Higher Education*, p. 20.

72 Watterson III, "Political Football: Theodore Roosevelt, Woodrow Wilson, and the Gridiron Reform Movement," *Presidential Studies Quarterly*: 556.

73 Carter, "The Age of Innocence: The First 25 Years of the National Collegiate Athletic Association, 1906 to 1931," *Vanderbilt Journal of Entertainment and Technology Law*: 239–40.

74 Woodrow Wilson, "What Is a College For?" *Scribner's Magazine*, November 1909: 576.

75 Flowers, "Institutionalized Hypocrisy: The Myth of Intercollegiate Athletics," *American Educational History Journal*: 352.

76 Carter, "The Age of Innocence: The First 25 Years of the National Collegiate Athletic Association, 1906 to 1931," *Vanderbilt Journal of Entertainment and Technology Law*: 220.

77 Ibid.: 229.

78 For a 1930s argument that physical educators should return to biological objectives such as development of strength and adequate physical development rather than athletics and recreation, see C.H. McCloy, "Forgotten Objectives of Physical Education," *Journal of Health and Physical Education* 8, Issue 8 (September 1937): 458–61, 512–3.

79 Carter, "The Age of Innocence: The First 25 Years of the National Collegiate Athletic Association, 1906 to 1931," *Vanderbilt Journal of Entertainment and Technology Law*: 245–6.

80 Guy M. Lewis, "Adoption of the Sports Program, 1906–39: The Role of Accommodation in the Transformation of Physical Education," *Quest* 12, No. 1 (1969): 38.

81 Ibid.: 39.

82 Ingrassia, *The Rise of Gridiron University: Higher Education's Uneasy Alliance with Big-Time Football,* p. 171.

83 Ibid., p. 181.

84 *Selected Writings of Elbert Hubbard*, Volume 1 (New York: Wm. H. Wise & Co., 1922), p. 412.

85 Glenn E. Hoover, "College Football," *New Republic*, April 14, 1926: 256.

86 Ibid.: 257.

87 Steve Berkowitz, "Nick Saban to Be Paid $11.125 Million this Season after Alabama Contract Extension," *USA Today*, May 2, 2017.

88 Russell Hubbard, "Saban Pay Too Steep, Says Ex-UA Trustee," *Birmingham News*, January 4, 2007.

89 Hoover, "College Football," *New Republic*: 257.

90   Smith, *Pay for Play: A History of Big-Time College Athletic Reform,* p. 60.
91   W.H. Cowley, "Athletics in American Colleges," *Journal of Higher Education* 70, No. 5 (September–October 1999/originally published 1930): 498.
92   Henry S. Pritchett, *American College Athletics,* Preface; Cowley, "Athletics in American Colleges," *Journal of Higher Education*: 494–5.
93   Pritchett, *American College Athletics,* Preface.
94   Cowley, "Athletics in American Colleges," *Journal of Higher Education:* 499.
95   Pritchett, *American College Athletics,* Preface.
96   Savage, *American College Athletics,* pp. 17, 34.
97   Ibid., p. 23.
98   Ibid., p. 30.
99   Cowley, "Athletics in American Colleges," *Journal of Higher Education*: 500.
100 Savage, *American College Athletics,* p. 32.
101 Cowley, "Athletics in American Colleges," *Journal of Higher Education*: 501.
102 Savage, *American College Athletics,* p. 37.
103 John R. Thelin, *Games Colleges Play: Scandal and Reform in Intercollegiate Athletics* (Baltimore, MD: Johns Hopkins University Press, 1994), p. 39.
104 "Shall Intercollegiate Football Be Abolished?" *Literary Digest,* October 10, 1925: 69.
105 Kevin McMullin, "Antioch College," *Collegewise,* October 25, 2006, http://wiseli keus.com/collegewise/2006/10/antioch_college.html.
106 "Shall Intercollegiate Football Be Abolished?" *Literary Digest*: 69.
107 Ibid.: 70.
108 Elesha Coffman, "You Cannot Serve God and Gridiron," *Religion in American History,* July 2014, http://usreligion.blogspot.com/2014/07/you-cannot-serve-god-and-grid iron.html.
109 Thelin, *Games Colleges Play: Scandal and Reform in Intercollegiate Athletics,* p. 44. Mark Schlabach, "FBI Wiretaps Show Sean Miller Discussed $100K Payment to Lock Recruit," *espn.com,* February 25, 2018. Will Hobson and Jesse Dougherty, "Should Federal Resources Be Used to Enforce NCAA Rules?" *Washington Post,* March 11, 2018.
110 "Defends Big Ten Policies," *New York Times,* October 23, 1929.
111 "Defends Michigan on Its Athletics," *New York Times,* January 21, 1930.
112 Ibid.
113 Raymond Schmidt, "The 1929 Iowa Football Scandal: Paying Tribute to the Carnegie Report?" *Journal of Sport History* 34, No. 3 (Fall 2007): 344, 345.
114 Ibid.: 346, 347.
115 Ibid.: 347–8.
116 Carter, "The Age of Innocence: The First 25 Years of the National Collegiate Athletic Association, 1906 to 1931," *Vanderbilt Journal of Entertainment and Technology Law:* 269.
117 Wes Borucki, "'You're Dixie's Football Pride': American College Football and the Resurgence of Southern Identity," *Identities: Global Studies in Culture and Power* 10 (2003): 477. The University of Alabama's first football team, the Cadets, played its inaugural game against Birmingham High School on November 11, 1892, and won 56–0—the same score today's Crimson Tide roll up against the Mercers and Florida Internationals of the football world. The game was introduced to Alabama by William G. Little, who had learned the sport at a northern prep school. The UA teams were not denominated the Crimson Tide until 1907. Donna R. Causey, "The University of Alabama football team was represented by the Alabama Cadets in 1892," http://alabamapioneers.com/alabama-cadets-represented-university-alabama -football-team-1892/.
118 "Carnegie Report Called Fruitless," *New York Times,* January 14, 1931.
119 "Envy of Football's Popularity is Cited by Stuhldreher as Reason for Criticism," *New York Times,* February 28, 1931.
120 Thelin, *Games Colleges Play: Scandal and Reform in Intercollegiate Athletics,* p. 40.

121 See also Howard J. Savage, "The Carnegie Foundation's Study of American College Athletics—Three Years Later," *Research Quarterly of the American Physical Education Association* 4, No. 1 (1933): 15–25.

122 Howard J. Savage, *Fruit of an Impulse: Forty-Five Years of the Carnegie Foundation, 1905–1950* (New York: Harcourt, Brace and Company, 1953), p. 158.

123 Ibid., p. 159.

3

STOPPING FOOTBALL IN ITS TRACKS—
OR GETTING RUN OVER

Firing a football coach could be hazardous to a school president's career—unless, that is, the coach was on a losing streak, in which case his dismissal would be met with hurrahs. In the case of the University of Pittsburgh of the 1930s, a coach and a chancellor collided, each represented by a massive edifice: Pitt Stadium, home of the football team, and the 42-story Cathedral of Learning, a Gothic monument to Pitt's academic aspirations. The coach was Jock Sutherland, a dentist (bridge and crown work was his specialty) who guided Pitt to five national championships and a record of 111–20–12 between 1924 and 1938.[1] The chancellor was John Gabbert Bowman, whom the *Saturday Evening Post* described as "an extremely ambitious educator" with "a certain amount of poetic idealism."[2]

Pitt, then a partially public institution, which received one-third of its income from the state of Pennsylvania, had been disparaged by Upton Sinclair as "the only high school in the country that gives a degree." Chancellor Bowman determined to improve its reputation. The Cathedral of Learning would be a mighty symbol of the preeminence of academics at Pitt. First, however, came Pitt Stadium, which was completed in 1925 at a cost of $2.1 million, financed by a bond issue. The Cathedral, on the other hand, had to rely on private financing. It would "lift the eyes of drab Pittsburgh from earth to heaven," proclaimed Bowman, and perhaps it is no wonder that the men of wealth in Pittsburgh were reluctant to pony up for a building that seemed to be a towering rebuke to them. It would not be dedicated until 1937.[3]

By then, as Francis Wallace wrote in the *Saturday Evening Post*, the Cathedral of Learning, which despite its skyscraping had languished in the shadow of Pitt Stadium, was reversing roles with the football program. The excesses of the latter were becoming an embarrassment. The payment of athletes at Pitt became an open secret: From 1929–32, members of the team were paid $650, spread over ten equal payments, with additional provision for books and tuition. At this rate, the players were living high on the hog during the Depression, so in 1933 the football salary dropped to $400, to be boosted to $480 the next year.[4]

Teams became reluctant to schedule Pitt. Snide remarks flew. A graduate manager of the University of California sneered that Cal would prefer to play "a school of equal academic standard" in the Rose Bowl following the 1937 season—and he almost got his wish when Pitt's players voted 16–15 to reject the Rose Bowl invite, perhaps, as rumor had it, because the school refused their demand of $200 per player for the game.[5] (*Almost* because the University of Alabama was Cal's opponent that year.)

Chancellor Bowman sought to bring the football program to heel. In February 1938, Pitt adopted the Code Bowman, which left benefits for upperclassmen untouched but required sophomores to work two hours a day for their $480 and forced freshmen not only to work, but also to pay their $300 tuition. In November of that year, the 30 freshmen footballers revealed that they had been assured by an assistant athletic director that this was all for show, and that none was really expected to pay tuition. The administration, of course, denied that this was the case, and things came to a head when student demonstrators, led by those same freshmen, marched on the chancellor's office, protesting the Code Bowman and demanding free tuition, among other things.[6] Coach Sutherland resigned, citing "intolerable" conditions. Student protests roiled the campus, at least until a philosophy professor, Dr. Charlesworth, exchanged blows with students who had disrupted a class on Plato's *Republic*. "I simply believe that philosophers should take action once in a while. I don't believe the schools should be run by self-appointed and noisy groups," explained the not-so-mild-mannered don.[7] Would that he had a thousand heirs!

Jock Sutherland never returned as coach. Chancellor Bowman eliminated all payments to athletes. Henceforth, he said proudly, the shoulder-padded and helmet-garbed Panthers who took the field for Pitt would be real students. Pitt paid the price for reform. The team collapsed into ineptitude and it took years to recover. In 1940, the team finished under .500 (3–4–1) for the first time since 1912. They would not again win more games than they lost until 1948.

Frank Porter Graham, president of the consolidated University of North Carolina, had even less luck than Chancellor Bowman in reining in football. In November 1935, as UNC was winding up a crackerjack football season, Graham was drawing up a proposal to ban any and all recruiting of athletes, as well as any preferential treatment in the awarding of scholarships, jobs, or loans. Freshmen would be barred from competition, as would academically marginal students. Bowl games would be out. This was no theoretical or abstract cause for Graham: UNC was beset during the 1935–6 academic year by a "widespread and highly organized cheating ring" whose members included football players.[8] At season's end, Graham presented his plan to meetings of the National Association of State Universities and the Southern Athletic Conference, whose members included UNC and North Carolina State. Several of Graham's planks were approved by the Southern

Conference by the slim margin of 6–4, with Graham (who voted for both UNC and NC State) putting it over the top. Rejected proposals included those to ban teams from participating in bowl games or tournaments and the granting of academic tenure to coaches.[9]

The response from the home folks was harsh and immediate. Alumni were outraged; donations would be withheld, Graham was warned. A friend of President Graham's wrote him in December 1935 that:

> [I]f your policy is adopted and as a result of same the University of North Carolina has a third- and fourth-rate team when its competitors, such as Georgia and Tennessee, have first-rate teams, the alumni are going to rise up in their wrath.[10]

His critics, said Graham, "opened up [with] machine guns, and in some cases . . . poison gas." The fact that his was a taxpayer-supported system made Graham especially vulnerable to criticism. As Richard Stone observes in his study of the ill-fated Graham plan, "he had alienated countless football enthusiasts among the university's alumni at a time when the institution had lost already about 40 percent of its normal state appropriation as a result of austere depression-era budgets."[11] Public universities are, almost by definition, politicized. The alumni chapters that protested the Graham plan consisted of taxpayers who paid Graham's salary and voters to whom state legislators and the governor had to answer. Alumni pleaded with Graham to understand that a winning team that the entire state could get behind surely would help to boost state appropriations.

Law professor W. Burlette Carter has made this point in his history of the early years of the NCAA. "State-supported institutions," he writes:

> had to satisfy governments that provided their funding. In areas where other forms of recreation were scarce, governments actively supported and encouraged the development of intercollegiate athletics because the events were popular with the people, and governments felt they served a public purpose.[12]

Although not quite bread and circuses, it was taxpayer-supported entertainment with a thin educational veneer.

The UNC battle was hardly a case of black and white hats having it out: as Duke coach Wallace Wade, a sharp critic of the Graham plan, argued, prohibiting special aid to athletes would make football a game for the sons of rich or well-off men. Graham's friend Charles W. Tillett, Jr., a Charlotte lawyer, told him that:

> [T]here is nothing inherently wrong in an alumnus helping a boy to get an education even though the motive of the alumnus is to provide a good player for the home team . . . What you are doing . . . for the sake of curbing excess, which is evil . . . [is] prohibiting moderation, which is not evil.[13]

Indeed, "During the 1930s and early 1940s, it was not uncommon for an alumnus to adopt a local high school athlete and 'put him through college,'" writes Walter Byers, former NCAA executive director. This came to be frowned on and interdicted, but the ban also prohibited such private acts of altruism as certainly happened under this practice.[14] Should generosity really be censured?

President Graham had hoped that the rest of the nation's colleges would follow the lead of the Southern Athletic Conference; they didn't. The specter of unilateral disarmament was raised. Moreover, the Graham Plan was being breached around the league. So after a few months' worth of reflection and public reaction, the SAC reversed itself. The ban on preferential scholarship treatment for athletes was dropped by the SAC, and the whole thing fell of its own weight. The Graham Plan was tossed atop the scrap heap of idealistic reforms that a football-mad world was never going to adopt. Graham learned his lesson; although he continued in his post until 1949, "he never again placed himself at the head of a major crusade to purify college athletic programs."[15]

Stone concluded his account of Graham's quixotic venture with a statement that has not aged well, given the massive scandal surrounding UNC athletics in the twenty-first century (and which is discussed later). He wrote that:

> [T]here is also a stern expectation among the various components of the UNC community that success will be garnered in "the right way" and that Carolina's teams will operate within the rules of the day, remain free of scandal, and project a positive image for the institution.

Despite the failure of the Graham plan, the president "managed to implant a bit of his southern Presbyterian conscience into his university, and that influence has survived until the present day."[16] Well—not quite.

By the 1930s, the most eloquent, sometimes infuriatingly haughty voice against King Football belonged to Robert Maynard Hutchins, president of the University of Chicago. The University of Chicago was a product of the late Gilded Age; its financial angel was that symbol of late nineteenth-century American capitalism, John D. Rockefeller. William Rainey Harper, the school's first president, regarded football as a tremendously effective way to nurture a relationship with the surrounding community. In 1892, he hired Amos Alonzo Stagg, one of the giants of early football, as Director of Physical Culture and Athletics, a position thitherto unknown in American education. (As Hal A. Lawson and Alan G. Ingham point out in an essay on Chicago athletics in the *Journal of Sport History*, Harper had been Stagg's professor of Biblical literature at Yale Divinity School. Football coaches were men of greater complexity way back when.)[17]

Amos Alonzo Stagg, son of a cobbler and disciple of Walter Camp, was proud of his vocation. He called the coaching profession "one of the noblest and most far-reaching in building manhood. No man is too good to be the athletic coach for youth."[18] His mentor Camp, choosing an unfortunate metaphor, was a bit more clinical: "Coaching football is the most engrossing thing in the world. It is playing chess with human pawns."[19] Stagg believed that intercollegiate competition, and the training therefore, cultivated mind, body, and soul. Harper dispensed with all that moralistic guff, writing Stagg: "I want you to develop teams which we can send around the country and knock out all the colleges." Thus encouraged, Stagg was not scrupulous as regards methods: his Chicago teams recruited professionals and other ineligible players and put them up in special athletic dorms, claiming that their "injuries and bruises . . . would prevent men making long walks to their classes."[20] Football made a national name for the university, which won seven Big Ten titles between 1899 and 1924. Harper gave Stagg a lifetime appointment; unlike the vast majority of football coaches, who had no faculty status and were under short-term contracts, he felt no win-or-else pressures.

Robert Maynard Hutchins, a product of Oberlin College and Yale Law School, assumed the presidency of the University of Chicago in 1929, 23 years after Harper's death. Hutchins cared not a whit that the Chicago Maroons might knock out other colleges. Athletics were an ancillary function of a college, if that, in his view. He and the college faculty annulled the school's physical education requirement, which had long served to help Stagg identify promising players, and they began emphasizing intramural sport at the expense of intercollegiate sport. Coach Stagg dug in his heels, but Hutchins would not be intimidated by a mere football coach. He proposed that Stagg accept a public relations job, a demotion the proud coach rejected. There was no venom in the relationship, just a conflict of visions. (For an explication of Hutchins's educational philosophy, see Robert Maynard Hutchins, *No Friendly Voice* [1936]).[21]

The team staggered through the 1930s. Hutchins lost no sleep over their fortunes. "A college racing stable makes as much sense as college football," said Hutchins. "The jockey could carry the college colors; the students could cheer; the alumni could bet; and the horse wouldn't have to pass a history test."[22] His indifference to football was seconded by William H. McNeill, editor of the University of Chicago's *Daily Maroon*, who wrote in 1937: "It is a depraved system which has to depend on the prestige of eleven men to attract students to the university to uphold the university's name." Yet McNeill's crusade found little support among students, only 6.8 percent of whom favored the "abolition of intercollegiate athletics" at Chicago in a 1937 poll.[23]

After the 1938 season, in which the Maroons posted a record of 1–6–1, Hutchins penned "Gate Receipts and Glory," an article for the *Saturday Evening Post*. If there had been any doubt about where Robert Maynard Hutchins stood on the question of whether or not big-time football and serious academics were compatible, this piece was the great dispeller. "Since the primary task of colleges and universities is the development of the mind, young people who are more interested in their bodies than in their minds should not go to college," stated Hutchins, flatly. He rejected as myth the claims by "apologists of athleticism" that athletics elevates moral character and brings out leadership qualities. Nor did he believe that ticket sales build libraries, or that winning teams attract worthwhile students.[24] "In many American colleges it is possible for a boy to win twelve letters without learning to write one," said Hutchins, who could turn a phrase. Like all critics of football rampant, Hutchins had his pet reforms. He praised Harvard president Lowell's quondam suggestion that teams play but a single game each season, and that against their natural rival.[25] Sensing a non-starter when he saw one, Hutchins proposed, instead, to "take money out of athletics." He called for a nonuple of elite colleges, mostly but not all private—Harvard, Yale, Chicago, Dartmouth, Michigan, California, Amherst, Williams, and Stanford—to: (1) "Reduce admission [to football games] to ten cents." and (2) "Give the director of athletics and the major coaches" academic tenure so that "their jobs depend on their ability as instructors and their character," not their win-loss record.

On a parallel track, Hutchins called for an expansion of intramural athletics, and a renewed stress on "fun and health." Broad participation of the student body was the ideal; its antithesis was 50,000 sedentary fans sitting on benches for three hours watching 22 brawny men slug it out. He also suggested an emphasis on lifelong sports—tennis, golf, skating, and even touch football.[26] Failing the enactment of these reforms, Hutchins hoped that professional football would soon supplant the college game, rather as professional baseball had done for college baseball. Little did he know that the two varieties of the 100-yard game, college and pro, would grow apace, almost in tandem.

But the writing was on the wall at Chicago. The problem was that Chicago required its football players to take the same classes as the rest of the student body, and there just weren't enough easy-A, jock-cosseting professors. Coveted young football heroes avoided the University of Chicago like they avoided upper-level physics. In 1939, stumbling en route to a 2–6 record, the Maroons lost, consecutively, to Harvard (61–0), Michigan (85–0), Virginia (47–0), and Ohio State (61–0), and were also shut out by the University of Illinois (46–0) and Beloit (6–0). They did beat weaklings Wabash and Oberlin, but then the Little Sisters of the Poor could have played Oberlin to a tie.

The defeats were demoralizing to many backers of the athletic program, though outside observers found silver linings. *Look* magazine chose the Maroons' starting lineup as its 1939 All-American team as a puckish protest against the professionalization of college sport:

> Working on the naïve assumption that college football is an amateur sport, this writer has chosen an amateur All-American team . . . I name the University of Chicago varsity eleven. This team is unique in that it is composed of students who look on football as recreation . . . There isn't a single hired hand on this eleven. From end to end, from quarterback to fullback, the players are unsalaried and unsullied. Not one of them has an athletic scholarship. None is majoring in poultry husbandry, appreciation of music, butter and egg judging, blacksmithing or tire vulcanizing.[27]

The columnist Heywood Broun asserted that having a good football team was "a priori evidence of stupidity."[28] Alumni were not propitiated by backhanded compliments. One alumnus huffily wrote Hutchins:

> I do not suppose you are interested in the feelings of University of Chicago Alumni: my guess is that you will not even know what those feelings are until you are disappointed by the results of the drive of alumni contributions for 1940 or 1941.

He demanded, "Either fish or cut bait!" Hutchins shot back:

> If fishing requires us to buy a football team, I am not prepared to fish . . . If the alumni are so hysterical and so lacking in an adequate conception of what a university is that they cannot look on football as a game, then we may be forced to cut bait.[29]

Say this for Hutchins: The man was constitutionally incapable of glad-handing.

Since Chicago did not wish to start bidding for players, or admitting athletes who could not do the work required of other students, its choices indeed came down to two, according to Robin Lester's history of Chicago football, *Stagg's University*. The options were to drop down in class, playing nonpowerhouse teams, or to drop football entirely. There was substantial support for the former option, but President Hutchins said that it would be "worse to be beaten by Beloit and Oberlin" than to lose by 85 points to Michigan and that "We do not like to be classed with Monmouth and Illinois Wesleyan."[30] (As Lester notes, this was inconsistent of Hutchins, who had often declared that the success or failure of a football team had nothing to do with academic quality.) Hutchins also rejected a proposed Midwestern football conference, much lower-key than the Big Ten, to consist of Chicago, Butler, Toledo, Western Reserve, Xavier, and others.[31]

Adding to the urgency of the situation were reports that UC alumni were trying to revive the program by enticing promising players to matriculate with the promise of jobs and financial aid. So in December 1939, Hutchins told the university's trustees:

> Since we cannot hope to win against our present competition and since we cannot profitably change our competition, only two courses are open to us: to subsidize players or to discontinue intercollegiate football. We cannot subsidize players or encourage our alumni to do so without departing from our principles and losing our self-respect. We must therefore discontinue the game.[32]

The trustees, after vigorous discussion, approved the request on December 21, 1939. Chicago euthanized football. The university had arranged to announce "a spate of gifts" at the same time as it pronounced football dead, so as to allay any alumni fears that dropping football would harm the university's financial profile. Highbrows across the country praised Chicago and Hutchins, as did newspaper editorialists, though the hometown *Chicago Tribune* was critical, recalling days of yore when the Maroons were dominant, "men were men, and the University of Chicago wasn't afraid of competition."[33]

A portion of the student body was upset, but no effigies went up, and no buildings burned down. Hutchins explained his decision in a speech to students on January 12, 1940:

> I hope that it is not necessary for me or anyone else to tell you that this is an educational institution, that education is primarily concerned with the training of the mind, and that athletics and social life, though they may contribute to it, are not the heart of it and cannot be permitted to interfere with it.[34]

The Maroons locker room would be converted to house the Manhattan Project laboratory, giving new meaning to the phrase *long bomb*.

Après Hutchins—there was no deluge. No other Big Ten—or big-time—school copied UC. As Ronald Smith writes, "Chicago and Hutchins became icons not for athletic reform, but more for athletic eccentricity and intellectual elitism."[35]

William H. McNeill, historian and long-time University of Chicago professor, who as a student editor had crusaded against football, called the dropping of football a "significant loss for the university," as it severed the link between the university and the city, between "town and gown." Hutchins missed an opportunity to take the radical but sensible step, argues McNeill, of forging an affiliation of the university with the professional Chicago Bears football team. The players would have been paid, the pretense of "student-athlete" dropped, the Bears would have played on campus at Stagg Field, and a "graduate football team for a graduate university might have turned into a very profitable marriage for both parties." This might have served as the road out of the hypocrisy of big-time college football. As it was, McNeill characterizes Hutchins's failure to connect with the Bears "a missed opportunity of monumental proportions."[36] For the National Football League (NFL), which began life as the American Professional Football Association in 1920, presented the alternative of frank, unapologetic professionalism. It had no need for hypocrisy, forged transcripts, or under the table pay for play. There was no pretense that the middle linebacker of the Chicago Bears burned the midnight oil boning up on European history.

Robert Maynard Hutchins was not a man afflicted by second thoughts. In 1954, 15 years after the Chicago Maroons had left big-time football, Hutchins took to the pages of *Sports Illustrated*, of all unlikely venues, to argue against its reinstatement at Chicago. He was unrepentant. The university, argued Hutchins:

> should devote itself to education, research and scholarship. Intercollegiate football has little to do with any of these things and an institution that is to do well in them will have to concentrate on them and rid itself of irrelevancies,

no matter how attractive or profitable. Football has no place in the kind of institution Chicago aspires to be.

"The university hoped to prove that 'normal' young Americans could get excited about the life of the mind," continued Hutchins, who marveled that "we Americans are the only people in human history who ever got sport mixed up with higher education. No other country looks to its universities as a prime source of athletic entertainment."

American exceptionalism? Not for Hutchins. He called football "an infernal nuisance" for "anybody seriously interested in education" and denied that "there are any conditions under which intercollegiate football can be an asset to a college or university."[37] Far better for the school to offer intramurals at which students of all skill levels can partake of salubrious physical activity. But, in 1969, the University of Chicago once more fielded a varsity football team, settling into the Division III level in 1973. Hutchins died in 1977, his handiwork having been undone, if only partially.[38]

Fox, meet henhouse

There was no looking back. In the flush period following the World War II, college football reached new heights, as cavernous stadia were built or expanded and attendance hit 14.7 million in 1947–8. Ethical concerns still attached to the big-time sports, but they were pushed to the margins. As education historian John R. Thelin relates, in 1947 the governor of Kentucky commissioned a Chicago-based consulting firm, Griffenhagen Associates, to assess the future of the University of Kentucky. The Griffenhagen Report raised red flags about one method of funding the football and basketball programs—the former helmed by a young supercoach, Paul "Bear" Bryant, the latter a nationally renowned contingent coached by the legendary Adolph Rupp. Athletic grants-in-aid were partially subsidized by student fees, which struck the authors of the Griffenhagen Report as unfair, given that athletics were purely for entertainment and had no real connection to UK's educational purpose. Professionalized athletics of the kind existing at the University of Kentucky has "no worthy place in a university," concluded the report, which recommended that UK "should return intercollegiate athletics to its amateur standing."[39]

The university's board of trustees objected to this sweeping conclusion as well as the Griffenhagen Report's criticism of the use of mandatory student fees to support athletic teams. "The student is not, as a matter of fact, compelled to pay a fee for athletics," the trustees nitpicked.

> He pays a general incidental fee for which he receives a great many privileges beyond direct instruction. One of these is that of attending athletic contests. It does not seem practical to make one part of this general incidental fee optional.

Student fees were not a negligible part of the UK athletic budget: in 1953, they totaled $62,716, or 15 percent of the total income of the University of Kentucky Athletic Association.[40] Taxing the general student body to subsidize the jocks and their fiefdom was sacrosanct. No such purity existed within Kentucky's athletic department, however. The university's powerhouse Rupp-coached basketball team was riddled with point-shavers; the NCAA gave UK a death penalty in 1953, the program to be resurrected the following year.

Meanwhile, in the Northeast, the quondam giants of the gridiron—now reduced to mortal size and shrinking, athletically, by the year—issued proclamations from the high ground of moral certitude. For instance, in October 1951, the presidents of Harvard, Yale, and Princeton published a joint statement in opposition to the granting of athletic scholarships. "A student takes part in college athletics because of the value of the experience for him," declared the presidents, "and he has the same obligation as other students to assume responsibility for solving his educational problems." [*Educational problems* is an anemic synonym for *paying high tuition bills despite hailing from a modest economic background.*] "Any other view seems to us a distortion of educational and moral values." They continued: "The athletic program exists for the welfare of the student, for the contribution it can make to his healthy educational experience, not for the glorification of the individual or the prestige or profit of the college." [They sure were singing a different tune half a century earlier.]

The upshot of all this sanctimonious huffing? "No athletic scholarships or special subsidies of any sort for athletes are given by Harvard, Yale, or Princeton." They awarded such aid solely on the basis of financial need to athletes on the same terms as other students.[41] In 1951, spurred in part by point-shaving scandals in college basketball as well as reports of the slush funds through which alumni paid players and picked up expenses for many top football teams, the American Council on Education (ACE), a coordinating body for the nation's college and university presidents, was next up to the plate. Its Special Committee on Athletic Policy, consisting of eleven university presidents or chancellors, met and heard testimony between December 1951 and February 1952. The entire council approved, amid fanfare and bright hopes for the future, the report of the Special Committee on Athletic Policy, which discouraged bowl games and spring practices and unethical recruiting.

This was advertised as an act of resurgent reform, an updating and reinforcement of the thrust of the Carnegie report, and this time it bore the imprimatur of the nation's higher education mandarins. Surely this betokened salutary change. It didn't. In fact, it was compromised at birth. For college presidents, while good at lip service, have never been in the vanguard of intercollegiate athletic reform. The ten members and the chairman of the Special Committee on Athletic Policy represented a reasonably diverse range of athletic programs, split between powerhouses (and aspiring powerhouses) such as Notre Dame, Southern Methodist, and the universities of Mississippi, Nebraska, Utah, and Washington; and academically prestigious schools that took their football seriously (Furman, Wesleyan, Western

Reserve—the only Ohio school that owns a lifetime winning record against Ohio State—and Yale). The chairman was John A. Hannah, president of Michigan State from 1941–69, during which time he presided over MSU's ascent—or descent—into big-time, ethical-corners-cutting football. Hannah was hardly in a position to lecture anyone, given goings-on at his school.

Michigan State, formerly the Michigan Agricultural College, has always played a distant second fiddle in the Great Lakes State to the University of Michigan. Football was seen as one way to even the score. In the 1930s the team enjoyed success under head coach "Sleepy Jim" Crowley, who had been another quarter of Notre Dame's legendary Four Horsemen. Crowley began a booster club through which his players could be paid to play; Michigan State College, as it was then called, was chided for "an over-emphasis on intercollegiate athletics" in 1933 by the North Central Association, the regional accrediting organization.[42] John Hannah, then secretary to the Board of Agriculture at Michigan State, converted a sizeable bequest from a local philanthropist into a scholarship fund covering tuition, books, room, and board for athletes who maintained at least a C average.

Hannah became president of Michigan State in 1941; as Beth Shapiro notes in her account of Hannah's presidency, when he assumed the position MSC was "a small agricultural college with less than 6,000 students and an annual budget of $4 million." When he departed in 1969, MSU was "a mega-university of more than 40,000 students, with an annual budget of more than $100 million." It had become, as the conservative man of letters Russell Kirk, an MSC grad, called it, "Behemoth University." Hannah was a builder; a believer that big is better than small, and that Michigan State was no mere cow college but a big-time institution of higher education. Football could help make that ambition a reality. He told head coach Charlie Bachman, "Michigan State is a diamond in the rough; all it needs is a football victory over Michigan—no, two victories—so people will not say it was a fluke, and the College will become a great educational institution."[43]

The teams played an annual rivalry game, usually won by Michigan, but Hannah wanted to make them conference rivals as well. Admission to the Big Ten would certify Michigan State's status as a major college. The University of Chicago's withdrawal had left an opening, but there was just one problem: the University of Michigan did not want Michigan State to achieve that kind of parity. It opposed Michigan State's efforts to join the conference throughout the 1940s, and was bolstered by fellow Big Ten schools that objected to Michigan State's athletic scholarship program.

Hannah offered to scrap the scholarships and expand the stadium. Big Brother in Ann Arbor worried that it would now have a serious rival for the best in-state players, but in 1948 the schools of the Big Ten unanimously extended an invitation to Michigan State. The educational philosophy of the leadership of this tenth member of the Big Ten could not have been more different than that of the school it replaced. The Spartans joined the Big Ten in 1950 and won the national championship in 1951. That year Michigan State football coach "Biggie" Munn unburdened himself of this gem: "I would rather have my son be a football player than a Phi Beta Kappa" because "you learn democracy and Americanism in the game of football."[44]

That same year, 1951, saw John Hannah appointed chairman of ACE's Special Committee on Athletic Policy. No sooner had the committee released its report in early 1952 than the Big Ten launched an investigation of the Spartan Foundation, a booster club that was believed to be subsidizing athletes. The foundation was dissolved and Michigan State was placed on a year's probation by its new conference. Allegations of unethical behavior would dog MSU throughout Hannah's tenure. Harold Tukey, faculty representative from 1956–9, said that Hannah had one code of ethics "which dealt with athletics and one which dealt with life." Among the transgressions he overlooked were "grade fixing, drug use, and slush funds."[45] So you'll have to excuse the athletic directors and coaches of America if they were underwhelmed when in February 1952 Hannah's Special Committee on Athletic Policy unveiled a report filled with sonorities and platitudes. It began:

> American colleges and universities engage in intercollegiate athletics because of a deep conviction that when properly administered they make an important contribution to the total educational services of the institution. There is an increasingly widespread awareness, however, that athletics may become so severely infected with proselyting, subterfuge, and distorted purpose as to neutralize their benefits. Certainly the abuses and suspicion of abuse now associated with the conduct of intercollegiate athletics foster moral apathy and cynicism in our students—those young men and women who increasingly share responsibility for this country's strength and freedom.[46]

There it is: that echo of the Cold War which can be found in every ringing proclamation of the 1950s, from calls to build a federal interstate highway system to proposals for federal aid to education. For "the strength of our free society depends not only upon armaments but also upon the integrity of our institutions and our people."[47] If John Hannah was conscious of his hypocrisy, he didn't show it. Instead, he urged greater powers for "the faculty and central administration," though not, we can assume, troublemaking Michigan State professors like faculty rep Tukey. The Special Committee recommended several staples of the reform diet, among them:

> —[C]oaches should not be paid salaries in excess of those paid to those full-time members of the faculty.
> —Admission standards . . . should apply to all students, athletes and non-athletes alike.
> —[T]o be eligible for intercollegiate competition, a student should be enrolled in an academic program leading to a recognized degree, and should be making normal progress . . . toward the degree.
> —Freshmen shall be ineligible to participate on varsity teams.[48]

The ACE recommendations were widely praised but not so highly praised as to achieve their enforcement anywhere. Each of the above recommendations, while coming from an establishment rather than a radical or abolitionist point of view, strikes modern ears as hopelessly naïve. Certainly John Calipari and the University of Kentucky basketball team, famous for its "one and done" phenoms who go to class about as often as Venus transits the sun, would have a good laugh over them. Although Hannah was a believer in athletic scholarships, his committee sternly lectured that while superior athletic performance might be considered as a secondary factor in the awarding of grants-in-aid, it "should never be the sole factor or even the primary one."[49]

The committee also called for a clear delineation of athletic seasons, so that football practices and games are limited to a period between September 1 and December 15, and basketball games and practices take place between November 1 and March 15. Today's distended schedules, which include spring football practice, games beginning even before the first day of class in August, and bowl games as late as January 10, reveals how pitifully little influence the 1952 reformers had. And one wonders just how serious John Hannah was about abolishing bowl games, which the committee proposed, given that Michigan State had just won the national championship and would, after the 1953 and 1955 seasons, be headed to the Rose Bowl.[50] So President Hannah was not, shall we say, a fanatic on these issues. Flexibility was the watchword.[51]

The miracle in Columbus

Echoing the earlier cited wisecrack of University of Oklahoma president, Dr. George L. Cross, Ohio State president Howard Bevis, referring to the success of the volatile Woody Hayes's football teams in the mid-1950s, said, "we should have a university of which the football team can be proud."[52] Bevis's joke was reprised, to even less laughter, by OSU president Gordon Gee in 2011, when he was discussing football coach Jim Tressel's two-game suspension and $250,000 fine as a result of violations of NCAA player eligibility rules. Gee, asked about firing Tressel, joked, "Let me be very clear. I'm just hoping the coach doesn't dismiss me."[53] In a humorless age, such jokes are dangerous. Yet Ohio State was the site of one of the most astounding revolts against the hegemony of major-college football since President Hutchins deflated Chicago's ball. The Buckeyes actually tried, for one brief fleeting moment, to put one of John Hannah's recommendations into effect.

In what Professor James E. Odenkirk of Arizona State University would later call, in the pages of the *Journal of Sport History*, the "eighth wonder of the world," on November 28, 1961, the Ohio State Faculty Council voted 28–25 to keep Ohio State from accepting a Rose Bowl invitation because faculty were concerned that the Buckeyes were too dominant a presence on campus and football was out of control.[54] Try to imagine this happening today at Alabama or Clemson. Actually, don't try; your head will explode.

The 1961 edition of the Buckeyes had dominated their opponents, their only blemish a 7–7 tie in the season opener against Texas Christian University. After demolishing archrival Michigan, 50–20, in their finale, the Buckeyes awaited the chance to accept the inevitable bid to the Rose Bowl to play UCLA, the champion of the Athletic Association of Western Universities (later known as the Pac-10) Conference.

This was a mere formality, of course. Except it was not. As Odenkirk relates in his monograph on the episode, in 1957 Ohio State, responding to the football team being placed on probation for funneling money to players in violation of NCAA rules, had transferred control of athletics from the university administration to the faculty council. This might have seemed to be a cosmetic bureaucratic maneuver; Woody Hayes ruled the roost at OSU, and in matters pigskin, the faculty council was assumed to be about as influential as a junior high student council is in the operations of its school.

But Hayes's volatility, combined with the perception that academics were taking a distinct back seat to football and basketball, set the stage for an event that seems, in retrospect, extraordinary—the stunning first shot in a revolution that never did come to pass. The faculty council, with students, professors, and members of the media packing the faculty club lounge as onlookers, debated the invitation. Supporters of a Rose Bowl trip argued that the game was a merited reward for an excellent season, that the national publicity would be of value, and that academics remained preeminent at OSU. Opponents charged that football was running, and perhaps even ruining, the university, and that under the quarter system, wherein classes began January 2, game-bound students and football players would miss the first few days of class.

Football critics had one influential ally: Jack Fullen, secretary of the Ohio State Alumni Association, who frequently derogated Coach Hayes and insisted that "The football tail is wagging the college dog."[55] Fullen had an ally in Professor Bruce Bennett, a member of the Department of Athletics and prominent figure in the North American Society of Sport History. Bennett added another reason to reject the bid: the Rose Bowl trip would be "an enormous boondoggle for the athletic administration and their families, administrative personnel, state legislators, city officials, and prominent alumni who were guests of the university." At a time when the state legislature was viewing OSU appropriations with a skeptical eye, should taxpayer dollars really be expended on a Pasadena vacation for dozens of hangers-on?[56] To the astonishment of the sporting world and the consternation of OSU football fans, the faculty council declined the Rose Bowl invite by a vote of 28–25. The Rose Bowl then extended an invite to Minnesota to serve as the Big Ten representative; the Gophers eagerly accepted.

Students, or at least those who lived and died with the fortunes of the Buckeyes, erupted in anger. They marched on the state capitol. Jack Fullen, faculty council members, and the university president were hanged in effigy. Cars were damaged. Windows were broken. The Columbus *Dispatch* published the names and addresses of those faculty council members who had voted to spurn the Rose Bowl.

Unpleasant phone calls ensued. The football team emerged as the voice of reason. Coach Woody Hayes, addressing 1,000 alumni in Cleveland, said, "I may not agree with those 28 'No' votes but I respect the integrity of the men who cast them, if not their intelligence. I would not want football to drive a line of cleavage in our university."[57] On the second day of protests, co-captain Mike Ingram, speaking through a bullhorn, told the crowd, "They're not going to change their minds. We might as well face it. We're not going to the Rose Bowl. Go home before somebody gets hurt." When some students jeered, Ingram shouted, "The team did all the damn work! If they can accept the decision, you certainly can."[58]

The victory of the eggheads was brief. The faculty council was then stacked with more pliable members, and in 1962 it voted 36–20 to accept the next Rose Bowl bid, whenever that might be. (It turned out to be the January 1, 1969 game.) Jack Fullen, the alumni association secretary who had taken on Woody Hayes, later lamented, "[W]e lost the battle to scale down the program . . . The big loser is Ohio State University . . . the sideshow is still the main attraction and the stuff under the tent is of secondary importance."[59]

Fast forward to the NCAA's 2011 investigation into improprieties at Ohio State. Eight football players were found to have traded memorabilia—jerseys, footballs, cleats, rings—for cash with a tattoo parlor owner (somehow the nature of his business added the necessary sprinkling of sleaze), and nine players had either received payments for no-show jobs or cash to attend charity events. The Ohio State administration, trying to stay ahead of the game, slapped its own wrist with minor forfeitures of revenue and scholarships and the imposition of probation, but the NCAA handed down substantially stiffer penalties—a longer period of probation, more lost scholarships, ineligibility for a 2012 bowl game, and a five-year "show cause" penalty that made it exceedingly difficult for Jim Tressel to take a head coaching job during that period. (Instead, Tressel eventually became president of Youngstown State University.) Ohio State's athletic director said he was "surprised and disappointed" by the severity of the NCAA ruling.[60] One might ask why these young men, who were receiving no payment for their services other than the chance to attend classes in which they had little interest, should be forbidden to sell their jerseys or bowl-game rings for cash.

Build it, and they will pay

Football's edifice complex also had its roots in academically elite institutions. Harvard built its horseshoe-shaped steel-reinforced concrete 40,000-seat stadium in 1903, gift of the Class of 1879.[61] It was the first permanent concrete football stadium in America. Now, you might think this inconsistent with Dr. Eliot's scoffing reference to the "enfeebling theory that no team can do its best except in the presence of applauding friends," but the stadium went up during the last years of Eliot's presidency. The Brahmin had fought football, and lost.[62]

Harvard set the pace, though a decade later its chief rival constructed the Yale Bowl, with a capacity of over 70,000. But it would take a couple of decades before the stadium-building boom hit. The 1920s saw cavernous stadia rise from the ground from Columbus to Los Angeles. One of the earliest public university arenas, California Memorial Stadium in Berkeley, was funded by public subscription: its $1 million price tag was covered by "the sale of 10,000 preferential seats at a cost of $100 each, in the space of 10 days."[63] Berkeleyites of the Roaring Twenties were not unanimously enthusiastic about the stadium; one critic complained that athletics "as conducted now in our large arenas is but for the few picked teams while the many students who need physical development the most become stoop-shouldered from rooting from backless bleachers."[64] America was becoming a nation of watchers.

Cal, envious of the new arenas built for private school rivals Stanford (Stanford Stadium) and USC (the Rose Bowl), began playing in its new digs in 1923, within the same lustrum as other enormous football stadiums also funded by public subscription and the sale of preferred seating at Ohio State (1922) and the universities of Illinois (1923) and Michigan (1927). Schools with less rabid or affluent fan bases financed construction through bonds and gate receipts in addition to subscriptions. The emplacement of these structures on college campuses was a vivid reminder of just how significant a role football had come to play in the lives of the schools. Rare was the science lab or history department that caught the eye or imagination in quite the same way that a 75,000-seat concrete bowl did.

Fast forward eight decades. The faculty at Cal, perhaps in keeping with the school's counterculture reputation, has not shied from taking on the athletic department. In November 2009, the UC Berkeley division of the Academic Senate voted by 91–68 for an "Academics First" proposal that recommended to Chancellor Robert Birgeneau the immediate cessation of direct financial support (including from student fees) of athletics. Ultimately, the Academic Senate's action was wholly impuissant—about as effective as a high school student council asking the principal for Fridays off.

The immediate spur for the resolution was the revelation that the administration had forgiven $31 million in loans the athletics department had taken out over the years to cover its chronic shortfalls. Coming on the heels of a budget squeeze that had ended such traditional practices as the library staying open 24 hours a day during exam time, news of this free pass to the sports program nettled. Brian Barsky, a professor of computer science and persistent critic of Berkeley's emphasis on big-time sports, said:

> Apparently the chancellor couldn't find the funds to keep the library open even though the cost was a fraction of 1 percent of what he takes out of his discretionary funds to subsidize Intercollegiate athletics. The amount was less than what the football team pays to the local luxury hotel where it stays on the eve of each home game. What does that say about the priorities of this great institution, the best public university in the country?

(Michigan and North Carolina clear their throats.)

"Will our world-class public university put entertainment ahead of education?" asked professor of anthropology Laura Nader.[65] Football coach Jeff Tedford's $2.8 million salary, which made him the highest paid public employee in the Golden State, ought to have answered that question. (Just a few years earlier, in 1992, Chancellor Chang-Lin Tien refused to enter a bidding war against Arizona State and double the salary of Cal football coach Bruce Snyder to $500,000 because he did not "believe that a football coach should make more than the highest paid faculty member.")[66]

Cal's administration met "Academics First!" with an even more powerful retort: *Safety First.* A kick returner bringing one back 100 yards could trace the course of the Hayward Fault, whose last quake, which registered a 6.8 on the Richter Scale, came in 1868. The U.S. Geological Survey "reports a 31 percent probability of a magnitude 6.7 or greater" earthquake on the Hayward Fault by 2035.[67] So in 2008 the UC Board of Regents, following the lead of chairman Richard Blum (husband of U.S. Senator Dianne Feinstein), ordered Cal to perform a seismic retrofit to fortify venerable Memorial Stadium or play elsewhere beginning in 2011. Estimated cost: $321 million, on top of another $150 million designated for the Barclay Simpson Student Athlete High Performance Center, named for the Cal-supporting philanthropist who had helmed a $3.3 billion capital campaign.

To repay the bulk of the $464 million renovation of athletic facilities, the Cal athletic department embarked on an Endowment Seating Program (ESP), which permitted well-heeled fans—surely there were a few Silicon Valley billionaires who had passed through Berkeley— to pay from $40,000 to $225,000 to secure their seats by making tax-deductible "charitable contributions" ranging from $2,741 annually for 30 years for the "cheap seats" to one-time upfront fees of $225,000 for the prime vantage spots.[68] Memorial Stadium had been constructed with funds raised from public subscription; why not do it again?

Luxury boxes, which had proven windfalls to other programs, were out, as surveys of Cal alumni revealed that they did not want to be segregated from the hoi polloi.[69] (This was in contrast to the University of Michigan. Michigan's $226 million 2008 renovation of its stadium, colloquially known as the Big House, was paid for, in large part, by revenue from the sale of luxury boxes, though Michigan athletic director Bill Martin preferred the euphemism "enclosed seating." Spirited opponents of the plan included former UM president James Duderstadt; Fielding H. Yost III, grandson of the point-a-minute coach; and a former Bill Clinton speechwriter named John Pollack, who claimed that to "enshrine wealth and power in glass and steel at the leading public institution totally undermines the values of the university itself." But perhaps those values had been undermined long ago in UM's complete and total embrace of the big-time sports model. The luxury boxes, or enclosed seating, were built, just as they had been at Ohio State, Penn State, Wisconsin, and Michigan's other Big Ten rivals. One advantage of these isolated suites, explained the Ohio State senior director of ticketing, is that "you don't have every Tom, Dick and Harry walking down the hall just trying to see who they know."[70] The hoi polloi know their place in Columbus.)

Cal's ESP program gave wishful thinking a bad name. After all, the Golden Bears hadn't been to the Rose Bowl since 1959, and sell-outs of Memorial Stadium were about as common as Republican professors in the Berkeley sociology department. Despite Berkeley's academic reputation, it lacked the donor base of its old Bay Area football rival Stanford. Borrowing almost $500 million was "apparently an unprecedented amount for a college-sports project," observed the *Wall Street Journal*, as it dwarfed previous stadium-borrowing sums of $220 million by the University of Minnesota, $200 million by the University of Washington, and $148 million by the University of Michigan—all public universities.

Three years into the campaign, the school had just $31 million of the $270 million ESP target in hand, with another $113 million in nonbinding ESP agreements from which pledgers can walk away at any time and for any reason—including lousy football.[71] More than 80 percent of the seat purchasers were buying on the 30-year payment plan, which minimized upfront money. This was far shy of projections. Although only 2,902 seats fell under the Endowment Seating Program, Bears fans, never among the most rabid in the country, failed to pony up in sufficient numbers. Coincidentally, a similar plan for the University of Kansas, whose football fans are also nonrabid, to raise money through seat licenses to renovate its own Memorial Stadium, flopped and was junked in 2010. Cal's plans had to be revised. But construction went on, financed by long-term bonds, and after a one-year closure for renovations, the stadium reopened in 2012. By mid-2013, less than two-thirds of the ESP seats had been sold.

Brian Barsky became the eloquent and voluble voice of the opposition. "Why on earth are we going into such debt?" he asked. "If we really must go into debt, then at least it should be for the academic program, please, and not for a football stadium."[72] Adding injury to insult, Barsky noted that in 2016 the Cal athletic department paid out $4.75 million to settle a wrongful death lawsuit prompted by the death of a Cal Golden Bears player in 2014. The player, Ted Agu, had collapsed during an off-season drill under the direction of a strength and conditioning coach notorious for his brutality. The coach received not a pink slip but two contract renewals in subsequent years.[73]

The Cal athletic department posted a $21.76 million deficit in 2016, and a deficit of approximately $16 million in 2017.[74] And the department is giving new meaning to the phrase "long-term debt." Eben Novy-Williams, writing in *Bloomberg*, notes that "annual payments will be $18 million until 2032, when they jump to $26 million. They'll peak at $37 million a year in 2039. The school plans to pay off the full sum by 2053, though the loan extends to 2112."[75] Perhaps by then the California Golden Bears will have appeared once more in the Rose Bowl.

In the meantime, the $20 million-plus that Cal receives from the Pac-12's TV deal is available to help retire the debt, though other schools use that money for recruiting, salaries, and the support of low-revenue "Olympic" sports.[76] Naming rights to the field were sold to Kabam, a video game manufacturer, for $18 million over 15 years, and a deal with Under Armour, maker of athletic gear, will bring in $86 million over ten years. Still, the sale of ESP seats remains the linchpin of the stadium financing plan, and that, as associate chancellor and chief-of-staff emeritus John Cummins wrote in his thorough survey of the issue, depends on "a consistent, highly successful football program."[77]

In 2016, the Bears went 5–7, after which they fired coach Sonny Dykes, who was still owed $5.88 million. In 2017, new coach Justin Wilcox led the Bears to a 5–7 record, followed by a 7–6 record in 2018. The 2017–18 season also marked the inauguration of a new policy, approved by the UC Berkeley Academic Senate, requiring that 80 percent of incoming scholarship athletes have achieved at least a 3.0 GPA in high school, which is the floor for all nonathletes. This standard applies to each sport, discretely; just because the fencing team, say, has no recruits below 3.0 doesn't mean the basketball team gets a break. Under the rule, the football team is limited to five special sub-3.0 admits with each class. The chair of the Academic Senate expressed confidence when the rule was adopted in 2014 that even though a majority of that year's Golden Bears squad had failed to score a 3.0 in high school, better student-athletes could be recruited if Cal focused on the "national level." Whether that is a proper focus for a state-supported school went unsaid.[78]

As John Cummins sums up the last couple of decades at Cal:

> Budgets and deficits have skyrocketed, the salaries of senior athletic administrators and revenue sports coaches have done the same, graduation rates in these same sports have been mediocre at best, and embarrassing scandals have materialized from time to time.[79]

(When it comes to football, the Berkeley administration is no more laid-back and mellow than that of Ohio State. In the midst of the 2009–10 budget crisis, the school ripped up "the lovely grass surface of Witter Rugby Field and replace[d] it with artificial turf," as *California Watch* reported. The reason? The football team wanted a new practice field. So the rugby squad, which had won 24 national championships, or 24 more than the football team had ever won, was out of luck. That's the way it goes for so-called minor sports.)[80]

Cal is not swimming alone in the Red Ink Sea. *Bloomberg*'s Eben-Novy Williams found that the athletic departments of at least 13 schools have debt obligations exceeding $150 million—typically incurred due to construction or renovation of football-related facilities. Private fundraising is seldom if ever sufficient; the sale of bonds frequently finances stadium construction, and these become "a significant portion of many athletics departments' budgets," as the Knight Commission observes.[81] The ten most debt-heavy schools (all public; figures for private schools were not available) are, in order, California, Texas A&M, Washington, Illinois, Georgia Tech, Texas, Oregon, Michigan, Minnesota, and LSU.[82]

If things continue as they are—and as economist Herbert Stein used to say, things that can't go on forever, won't—powerhouses such as LSU, Michigan, and Texas will remain more than solvent, but perennial doormat Illinois and chronically mediocre football programs like Minnesota and Georgia Tech will have no choice but to look to their state legislatures or further squeeze fees from their students. And that is the subject of Chapter 4.

Notes

1 "Jock Sutherland: Never a Losing Season," www.225.pitt.edu/story/jock-sutherland-never-losing-season, accessed June 13, 2017.
2 Francis Wallace, "Test Case at Pitt: The Facts about College Football Play for Pay," *Saturday Evening Post*, October 28, 1939: 14.
3 Ibid.: 15, 47.
4 Ibid.: 49.
5 Ibid.: 51.
6 Francis Wallace, "The Football Laboratory Explodes," *Saturday Evening Post*, November 4, 1939: 21.
7 Ibid.: 80, 82.
8 Richard Stone, "The Graham Plan of 1935: An Aborted Crusade to De-Emphasize College Athletics," *North Carolina Historical Review* 64, No. 3 (July 1987): 283.
9 Ibid.: 279.
10 Allen L. Sack and Ellen J. Staurowsky, *College Athletes for Hire: The Evolution and Legacy of the NCAA's Amateur Myth* (Praeger: Westport, CT, 1998), p. 41.
11 Stone, "The Graham Plan of 1935: An Aborted Crusade to De-Emphasize College Athletics," *North Carolina Historical Review*. 281.
12 Carter, "The Age of Innocence: The First 25 Years of The National Collegiate Athletic Association, 1906 to 1931," *Vanderbilt Journal of Entertainment and Technology Law*. 270.
13 Stone, "The Graham Plan of 1935: An Aborted Crusade to De-Emphasize College Athletics," *North Carolina Historical Review*. 286.
14 Walter Byers with Charles Hammer, *Unsportsmanlike Conduct: Exploiting College Athletes* (Ann Arbor: University of Michigan Press, 1995), p. 65.
15 Stone, "The Graham Plan of 1935: An Aborted Crusade to De-Emphasize College Athletics," *North Carolina Historical Review*. 282.
16 Ibid.: 292, 293.
17 Hal A. Lawson and Alan G. Ingham, "Conflicting Ideologies Concerning the University and Intercollegiate Athletics: Harper and Hutchins at Chicago, 1892–1940," *Journal of Sport History* 7, No. 3 (Winter 1980): 41–2.
18 Ingrassia, *The Rise of Gridiron University: Higher Education's Uneasy Alliance with Big-Time Football*, p. 117.
19 Rick Telander, *The Hundred Yard Lie: The Corruption of College Football and What We Can Do to Stop It* (New York: Simon and Schuster, 1989), p. 117.
20 Lawson and Ingham, "Conflicting Ideologies Concerning the University and Intercollegiate Athletics: Harper and Hutchins at Chicago, 1892–1940," *Journal of Sport History*: 42, 43.
21 Robert Maynard Hutchins, *No Friendly Voice* (Chicago: University of Chicago Press, 1936).
22 Toma, *Football U.: Spectator Sports in the Life of the American University*, p. 120.
23 Robin Lester, *Stagg's University: The Rise, Decline, and Fall of Big-Time Football at Chicago* (Urbana: University of Illinois Press, 1995), p. 174.
24 Robert M. Hutchins, "Gate Receipts and Glory," *Saturday Evening Post*, December 3, 1938: 23.
25 Ibid.: 73, 76.
26 Ibid.: 76–7.
27 Lester, *Stagg's University: The Rise, Decline, and Fall of Big-Time Football at Chicago*, p. 182.
28 Ibid., p. 172.

29 Lawson and Ingham, "Conflicting Ideologies Concerning the University and Inter-collegiate Athletics: Harper and Hutchins at Chicago, 1892–1940," *Journal of Sport History*: 56.
30 Lester, *Stagg's University: The Rise, Decline, and Fall of Big-Time Football at Chicago,* pp. 183, 185.
31 Lawson and Ingham, "Conflicting Ideologies Concerning the University and Inter-collegiate Athletics: Harper and Hutchins at Chicago, 1892–1940," *Journal of Sport History*: 58.
32 Lester, *Stagg's University: The Rise, Decline, and Fall of Big-Time Football at Chicago,* p. 185.
33 Ibid., pp. 187, 190.
34 Lawson and Ingham, "Conflicting Ideologies Concerning the University and Inter-collegiate Athletics: Harper and Hutchins at Chicago, 1892–1940," *Journal of Sport History*: 59.
35 Smith, *Pay for Play: A History of Big-Time College Athletic Reform,* p. 77.
36 William H. McNeill, *Hutchins' University* (Chicago: University of Chicago Press, 1991), pp. 97–8.
37 Hutchins, "College Football is an Infernal Nuisance," *Sports Illustrated.*
38 Barry Bearak, "Where Football and Higher Education Mix," *New York Times*, September 16, 2011.
39 Thelin, *Games Colleges Play: Scandal and Reform in Intercollegiate Athletics,* p. 119.
40 Ibid., p. 120.
41 "3 Colleges Assail Athletic Subsidy," *New York Times*, October 29, 1951.
42 Beth J. Shapiro, "John Hannah and the Growth of Big-Time Intercollegiate Athletics at Michigan State University," *Journal of Sport History* 10, No. 3 (Winter 1983): 28.
43 Ibid.: 29.
44 Thelin, *Games Colleges Play: Scandal and Reform in Intercollegiate Athletics,* p. 109.
45 Ibid., p. 36.
46 "Report of the Special Committee on Athletic Policy," *The Educational Record* (February 16, 1952): 246–7.
47 Ibid.: 247.
48 Ibid.: 247–50.
49 Ibid.: 250.
50 Ibid.: 252.
51 The American Council on Education, fortified by grants from the Carnegie Corporation and the Ford Foundation, took up these issues again in the 1970s, also to little effect.
52 John Lombardo, *A Fire to Win: The Life and Times of Woody Hayes* (New York: St. Martin's, 2005), p. 125.
53 Seth Wickersham, "Is Gordon Gee Serious?" *ESPN: The Magazine*, August 22, 2011, www.espn.com.
54 James E. Odenkirk, "The Eighth Wonder of the World: Ohio State University's Rejection of a Rose Bowl Bid in 1961," *Journal of Sport History* 34, No. 3 (Fall 2007): 389.
55 Ibid.: 391.
56 Bruce L. Bennett, "An Analysis of Why Ohio State Did Not Go to the Rose Bowl in 1962 and the Spirited Aftermath," *North American Society of Sport History*, 1994 proceedings, http://library.la84.org/SportsLibrary/NASSH_Proceedings/NP1994/NP1994zza.pdf.
57 Ibid.
58 "Agony Instead of Roses in Columbus," *Sports Illustrated*, December 11, 1961, www.si.com/vault/1961/12/11/621635/agony-instead-of-roses-in-columbus.
59 Odenkirk, "The Eighth Wonder of the World: Ohio State University's Rejection of a Rose Bowl Bid in 1961," *Journal of Sport History*: 394.
60 Jeff Benedict and Armen Keteyian, *The System: The Glory and Scandal of Big-Time College Football* (New York: Anchor, 2014), p. 112.
61 "Harvard Stadium Football History," www.gocrimson.com/information/facilities/Harvard_Stadium_Football_History.

62 Quoted in J. William White, "Football and Its Critics," *The Outlook* 81 (November 18, 1905): 663.

63 "The House that Andy Built: The Making of Memorial Stadium," December 16, 2010, www.californiagoldenblogs.com/2010/12/15/1865216/the-house-that-andy-built-the-making-of-memorial-stadium.

64 Sojka, "Evolution of the Student-Athlete in America," *Journal of Popular Culture*: 56.

65 Zach E.J. Williams, "Resolution Urges End to Campus Athletic Funding," *Daily Californian*, November 6, 2009.

66 John Cummins, "A Cautionary Analysis of a Billion Dollar Athletic Expenditure: The History of the Renovation of California Memorial Stadium and the Construction of the Barclay Simpson Student Athlete High Performance Center," Center for Studies in Higher Education, Research & Occasional Paper Series, February 2017, p. 5.

67 Brian Barsky, "UC Berkeley's Endowment Seating Program Doesn't Quite Add Up," *Daily Californian*, January 25, 2011.

68 Natasha Osborne, "Quarterly Report Shows Slow Memorial Stadium Luxury Seat Sales," *Daily Californian*, February 20, 2013, www.dailycal.org/2013/02/20/quarterly-report-shows-slow-luxury-seat-sales/; Football Premium Seating, www.calbears.com/sports/2014/4/15/209272816.aspx, accessed February 23, 2017.

69 Ryan Phillips, Lowell Bergman, Kara Platoni, and John Cummins, "On the Line," UC Berkeley Graduate School of Journalism, August 1, 2011, http://escholarship.org/uc/item/8nm6467t.

70 Joe LaPointe, "For the People or the Powerful? Skybox Plan Divides Michigan," *New York Times*, April 9, 2006.

71 Rachel Bachman, "Cal's Football Stadium Gamble," *Wall Street Journal*, April 20, 2012.

72 Phillips, Bergman, Platoni, and Cummins, "On the Line."

73 Brian Barsky, "Power Harassment and Winning at Any Cost, Financial and Human," Ucbfa.org, undated.

74 Jon Wilner, "Cal Athletics' $20 Million Question: Will Sports Need to Be Axed?" *San Jose Mercury News*, September 30, 2016. Brent Schrotenboer, Steve Berkowitz and Christopher Schnaars, "Deficits a Rising Concern for Some Pac-12 Schools," *USA Today*, June 29, 2018.

75 Eben Novy-Williams, "College Football's Top Teams Are Built on Crippling Debt," *Bloomberg*, January 4, 2017, www.bloomberg.com/news/features/2017-01-04/college-football-s-top-teams-are-built-on-crippling-debt.

76 Jon Wilner, "New Cal Stadium Not a Hot Ticket," *San Jose Mercury News*, June 25, 2013.

77 Cummins, "A Cautionary Analysis of a Billion Dollar Athletic Expenditure: The History of the Renovation of California Memorial Stadium and the Construction of the Barclay Simpson Student Athlete High Performance Center," pp. 20, 22.

78 Jeff Faraudo, "80 Percent of Cal Recruits Must Have 3.0 GPA by 2017–18," *San Jose Mercury News*, October 29, 2014.

79 Cummins, "A Cautionary Analysis of a Billion Dollar Athletic Expenditure: The History of the Renovation of California Memorial Stadium and the Construction of the Barclay Simpson Student Athlete High Performance Center," p. 23.

80 Lance Williams, "Amid Fiscal Crisis, UC Berkeley Commits $320 Million to Football," *California Watch*, February 17, 2010, http://californiawatch.org/dailyreport/amid-fiscal-crisis-uc-berkeley-commits-320-million-football-1114.

81 "College Sports 101," Knight Commission on Intercollegiate Athletics, p. 16.

82 Novy-Williams, "College Football's Top Teams Are Built on Crippling Debt," *Bloomberg*.

4

ATHLETIC FEES ROUT HAPLESS STUDENTS

The college sports scandal that never makes the headlines

Student fees are the most controversial component of athletic subsidies, and they would be far more controversial if those being bilked knew what was going on. The NCAA defines as *athletic subsidies* anything that is not generated by the athletic department itself. These are generally in the form of either institutional support or student athletic fees. Most of those who have to pay these fees barely notice them on the invoice. Tuition, room, and board are the big-ticket items; the assorted fees often seem like incidentals—a few bucks a year so the activities committee can bring a washed-up boy band of your youth to campus for a nostalgia-soaked concert, or a couple of hundred dollars for health services. Sometimes these various charges are lumped together in one single fee, so that only by diligent research can one separate out exactly what is being covered. The athletic component of student fees can constitute as much as three-quarters of the total. That's not the chess club or the tall flags you're subsidizing, kids.

Such fees are one of four primary sources of revenue for the athletic department, the others being governmental support (usually from the state, though some states restrict the use of public funds for intercollegiate athletics), direct support from the institution itself, and indirect support for facilities and administration. One major study found that 81 percent of Division I public schools "allocate student fees directly to athletics," with an average student fee subsidy per school of $3.53 million.[1] Student fees, or what J.D. Glater in the *New York Times* called a "back door tuition increase," are not new; as long ago as 1875 the University of Wisconsin charged a student activity fee for heating public rooms and hallways. This was a definitional stretch, though activity surely took place in these settings.[2]

In general, state legislatures have limited the permissible fee recipients of state-subsidized colleges and universities to the following student activities: health services, social centers, debt service on facilities, publications or student government, recreational programs, cultural programs, and intercollegiate athletics.[3] According to the exhaustive data compiled by *USA Today*, in the most recent school year for which figures are available (2015–16), just 13 of the 230 public-school Division I NCAA athletic departments received no institutional or student fee subsidy. This baker's dozen, and their total annual athletics revenue, consisted of Texas A&M ($194.39 million), Texas ($187.98 million), Ohio State ($170.79 million), Oklahoma ($150.37 million), LSU ($141.65 million), Tennessee ($140.45 million), Penn State ($132.25 million), Kentucky ($132.18 million), Arkansas ($124.98 million), South Carolina ($122.33 million), Nebraska ($112.14 million), Mississippi State ($94.9 million), and Purdue ($78.70 million). (The very latest figures show the two Lone Star State schools still atop the athletic revenue list, with the University of Texas earning $214.8 million and Texas A&M $212 million.)[4] The majority of these schools (seven) play in the Southeastern Conference (SEC); ten of them rank in the top 14 revenue-producers. The outlier here is Purdue, with the 47th highest revenue, and a tradition of poor football—but relative frugality.

The biggest subsidy for any school in the Revenue Top Ten was granted Auburn ($140.07 million revenue, $5.44 million subsidy, for a subsidy of 3.38 percent). Virginia is the first high revenue school ($103.27 million) with a subsidy ($13.73 million) exceeding 10 percent of revenue (13.3 percent). In fact, UVA has hiked its annual athletics fee paid by students from $388 to $657 over the past ten years; as the *Washington Post* noted, athletics spending at Mr. Jefferson's university zoomed from $50.3 million in 2004 to $87.4 million in 2014.[5] The most subsidized D-I athletics programs among the top 50 in revenue belong to hapless Rutgers ($83.97 million revenue, $28.61 million subsidy, 34.07 percent subsidized) and the University of Connecticut ($79.23 million revenue, $35.27 million subsidy, 44.52 percent subsidized).

Beyond the top 50 we enter a world in which athletic programs would not exist in anything like their current form without massive subsidies. We find schools in which subsidies constitute more than three-fourths of the sports budget. In descending order of total revenue, the members of this three-quarters club are: James Madison, University of Massachusetts, Delaware, UC Davis, SUNY Stony Brook, Eastern Michigan, Florida International, George Mason, Georgia State, Towson, Sacramento State, Rhode Island, Coastal Carolina, Kennesaw State, SUNY Albany, College of Charleston, UC Irvine, UC Santa Barbara, Lamar, UMASS Lowell, UC Riverside, East Tennessee State, University of Illinois at Chicago, Stephen F. Austin, Northern Arizona, Central Connecticut, Cal State Fullerton, New Jersey Tech, SUNY Binghamton, Maryland-Baltimore County, UNC Greensboro, Oakland, Cal State Northridge, Alabama State, Indiana State, Tennessee Tech, Delaware State, Texas-Rio Grande Valley, Missouri-Kansas City, Radford, Wisconsin-Milwaukee, Texas-Arlington, Northern Kentucky, Morehead State, Utah Valley, Tennessee State, Norfolk State, Texas A&M-Corpus Christi, Cleveland State, Winthrop, Prairie View A&M, Southern Utah, Indiana-Purdue Fort Wayne, Texas Southern, Wright State, Morgan State, Longwood, Indiana-Purdue Indianapolis, Southern Illinois Edwardsville, South Carolina Upstate, Chicago State, Maryland-Eastern Shore, New Orleans, and Coppin State. Certain of these names appear in this book again and again.

The above-mentioned are almost all schools that play Division I basketball but are not members of the Football Bowl Subdivision. The exceptions are the University of Massachusetts, a school without a conference (it left the Mid-American Conference after the 2015 season) and Eastern Michigan of the MAC, or Mid-American Conference. The good old reliable MAC is predictably subsidy-dependent. Besides departing Massachusetts, the MAC schools racked up these numbers:

Western Michigan $37.6 million revenue, $24.25 million subsidy, 64.4 percent
Akron $34.59 million, $23.81 million, 68.85 percent
Buffalo $34.27 million, $24.81 million, 72.40 percent
Miami (Ohio) $33.66 million, $23.77 million, 70.62 percent
Ohio $31.88 million, $20.26 million, 63.56 percent
Central Michigan $31.15 million, $21.73 million, 69.74 percent
Eastern Michigan $30.21 million, $24.31 million, 80.46 percent
Northern Illinois $28.52 million, $17.66 million, 61.93 percent
Toledo $27.91 million, $14.76 million, 52.88 percent
Kent State $26.02 million, $19.29 million, 74.13 percent
Ball State $25.54 million, $18.33 million, 71.75 percent
Bowling Green $22.84 million, $12.53 million, 54.86 percent.[6]

The chumps at the bottom of the Division I or FBS food chain, desperate to rise and be considered among the elite—the Gonzaga Bulldogs and Boise State Broncos are their patron saints—subsidize their teams primarily with student fees and university general support, though their spokespeople sometimes reassure reporters that self-sufficiency is just around the corner. Ticket sales are meager, television revenue is almost nonexistent, and their conferences make little from tournament appearances, but the *ignis fatuus* of big-time basketball or football success leads them on.

As Matthew Denhart, Robert Villwock, and Richard Vedder observe in a report for the Center for College Affordability and Productivity, "Playing intercollegiate sports is a bit like playing the lottery—most lose money, but sometimes a school gets a nice payoff."[7] Alas, those MAC schools have been buying lottery tickets for a long time now, and they haven't hit a winner yet.

You hide it well

On occasion, the athletic fee is itemized on a tuition bill; more often it is hidden within a general fee that supports the aforementioned activities as well. As a result, student awareness of these fees is limited, and schools are happy to conceal what amounts to a tax on behalf of athletics. Given that most students not engaged in intercollegiate athletics are less than thrilled by fees that can total well above $1,000 annually, transparency is distinctly a secondary consideration for many schools.

Virginia and Tennessee each require state-subsidized schools to disclose the purposes to which student fees are put, but as Steve Berkowitz reported for *USA Today*, some of those schools affected do the bare minimum toward compliance. Virginia prohibits the expenditure of public funds or tuition money for athletics, which leaves student fees as a prime source of revenue for the hungry athletics departments. As a result, the athletics fee can constitute fully 23 percent of a student's bill in Virginia. Berkowitz found that only three of Virginia's eleven publicly supported Division I schools (Virginia, Virginia Tech, William & Mary) provided an activity by activity breakdown of student fee disbursements on their websites.[8] The other schools were at best unclear in their exposition, at worst obfuscatory. Concealment was getting the better part of transparency. One team of researchers charged, "Deception makes it appear as if the university prefers the public to be ignorant."[9]

The prime sponsor of the Virginia transparency law, House of Delegates member Robert G. Marshall, explained his advocacy:

> A fee is a fee. A tax is a tax. I'd like to know what I'm being charged and what I get for it. I think that the students and the parents who are paying for this want to know. I get almost as many complaints about fees going up as I do about tuition.

Responding to Berkowitz's *USA Today* piece, Delegate Marshall accused the schools of being "embarrassed" by the high fees, and therefore "covering [their] tracks." And time is on their side: a student is ephemeral, transitory, here today and gone in four years, but a taxpayer-supported institution—that's forever.[10] Virginia took the next step with a 2015 law capping the percentage of a state school's athletic budget that comes from student fees and school funds to 20 percent for FBS schools (the University of Virginia and Virginia Tech), 55 percent for FBS newcomer Old Dominion, 70 percent for FCS schools (such as William and Mary and the Virginia Military Institute), 78 percent for Division I basketball schools without football teams (such as George Mason and Virginia Commonwealth), and 92 percent for Division III schools without football. Schools were given five years (Old Dominion got ten) to slip under the ceiling.[11] The total athletic budgets of the universities without football teams are considerably smaller.

Yet statutory limitations on the percentage of student fee contributions to the athletic program are well-meaning but ultimately ineffective, because such money is fungible, and by a simple legerdemainic sleight of hand the school can shift funds so that the percentage shrinks to below whatever the threshold might be. *Knowledge is good*, as the infamous motto of *Animal House*'s Faber College declared, but in the wrong hands—or rather the wrong minds—it can lead to criticism of institutions whose practices are laid bare. As Richard Vedder, a premier scholar of the economics of education, archly observes, universities, putatively in the business of disseminating knowledge, are given to "secrecy" and even "deception" in the matter of student fees.[12] Vedder's fellow Ohio University professor David Ridpath adds:

Most students and parents have no idea what goes into fees, and bills are not itemized. If athletics is so important to overall health and promotion of the institution, why not be transparent about the bill and what students are paying?[13]

Gleaning information about athletic fees from schools in the Mid-American Conference, which includes Ohio University, "proved exasperating," says David Ridpath.[14] The exasperation is a feature, not a bug. The consumers who pay these bills might prove a mite more resistant if they knew exactly what it is they were paying for. Brit Kirwan, then-chancellor of the University of Maryland system, opined that transparency "is a way of bringing pressure to bear" on runaway expenditures; it might even begin to "put a hold on, or tamp down, the rate" of spending on intercollegiate athletics. (Amusingly, Towson, a school within Chancellor Kirwan's domain, did not itemize fees on its website when Kirwan was quoted in the media; shortly after the story appeared, it did.)[15]

State schools in Florida finesse the transparency requirements, or at least dim the lights, by calculating the athletic fee per credit hour. Thus Florida State, with annual athletic revenue of $113.74 million, lists an athletic fee of just $7.90 per credit hour. Heck, that's less than the cost of a movie ticket! But given that the typical annual course load at FSU is 30 hours, the athletic fee is $237 per student.[16]

The case for fee obfuscation was made by Jack Boyle, Cleveland State's vice president for business affairs and finance, who when asked by *USA Today* why the school did not advertise its athletics fee, replied, "Why would you?" He elaborated:

> Whenever we spell something out, somebody decides they don't want that service. We don't spell out in tuition that 1.8 percent of it goes to run the religion department. "I'm an atheist. Why should I pay for them? I'd never go to any of their courses."

Besides, Boyle added, if you don't want to shell out for sports teams, sign up with the University of Phoenix or another online school.[17] To which Jeff Smith of the University of South Carolina Upstate supplies a riposte:

> If you're not driving at a university, you don't pay a parking fee. If you don't use the lab, you don't pay a fee. Maybe there should be a choice for students who don't want to pay an athletics fee. Maybe somehow it can be legislated. Schools created the problem, but they're not trying to fix it.[18]

The poor get poorer

The schools hardest hit by the explosion in athletic costs—the losers in this arms race—are those with, to use a charitable word, modest athletic reputations. As Richard Vedder and Matthew Denhart put it in a seminal 2010 paper on the subject, "schools that are, on average, poorer, less prestigious, and athletically more marginal have been clobbered."[19] A Knight Commission study found that the top-level FBS schools "generate revenues that are 14 times higher than the programs at the bottom level."[20] Moreover, there is evidence that for schools in the top quarter of total athletic operating expenditures, each additional dollar spent generates more than a dollar of revenue, but for the other three-quarters of schools, each additional dollar spent "generates significantly *less* than one dollar of revenue."[21] So the rich get richer, the poor get poorer, and the kid driving a 1997 Accord with a leaky radiator to his MAC school has to fork over more in student athletic fees.

Relatively purse poor, lacking the gate receipts, the TV revenue, the bowl game or tournament purses, and the well-heeled and football-obsessed alumni whose checkbooks are always open, the lower-tier FBS and basketball-only schools choose to rely instead on a dreary compound of student fees and institutional—usually taxpayer-supported—subsidies. Athletic subsides, argue Vedder and Denhart, "are a tax on other revenues, a tax diverting resources from traditional academic purposes, and this tax is highly regressive, hitting the poor more than the rich."[22]

Parsing data from the NCAA, *USA Today*, and the Department of Education's Integrated Postsecondary Education Data System, Vedder and Denhart examined the 99 FBS public schools, which include the three major military academies, known to sports fans as Army, Navy, and Air Force. By the 2008–9 academic year, the epicenter of their study, subsidies constituted 31.01 percent of the total operating revenues of the athletic departments under review. The "athletics tax," or average subsidy per full-time equivalent (FTE) student, had risen from $395 in the 2004–5 academic year to $506 in 2008–9. But these numbers mask a stark disparity between the athletics haves and have-nots. While schools within the power conferences are largely self-financed (though many of them also nick students for fees), their less-favored cousins in the more unfashionable precincts of Athleticdom beggar their young scholars at an astonishing rate. For instance, the subsidy per FTE student was $67 in the Big Ten, yet $1,177 per FTE in the Mountain West Conference.[23]

The differences per conference in the average subsidy as a percentage of total intercollegiate athletic operating revenue—what Vedder and Denhart dub the "tuition tax"—give new meaning to the word *inequality*. The authors break it down as follows (with "tuition tax" per FTE in parentheses):

Mid-American Conference: 72.3 percent ($915)
Sun Belt Conference: 60.7 percent ($559)
Western Athletic Conference: 47.5 percent ($718)
Conference USA: 46.2 percent ($697)
Mountain West Conference: 43.0 percent ($1,177)
Big East: 25.6 percent ($491)
Atlantic Coast Conference: 13.3 percent ($327)

Pac-10: 12.7 percent ($242)
Big 12: 6.0 percent ($130)
Southeast Conference: 5.4 percent ($168)
Big Ten: 3.6 percent ($67).[24]

Student fees are not regressive because they disproportionately affect those who attend schools with mediocre football programs, unfortunate as that may be for the Sun Belt Conference booster. Rather, they are regressive because the young men and women enrolled in these institutions are, on average, from less well-off families. The authors use the percentage of students receiving Pell Grants as a proxy for relative wealth, or lack thereof, of attendees. They found that the most Pell Grant-dependent conference student bodies were among those with the highest tuition taxes: Conference USA (34.54 percent of students receiving Pell Grants), Western Athletic (30.47 percent), Sun Belt (30.41 percent), and MAC (26.95 percent); while the four least Pell Grant-dependent student bodies attended the schools with the lowest tuition tax: Atlantic Coast Conference (14.87 percent of students receiving Pell Grants), Big 12 (16.42 percent), Big Ten (16.44 percent), and Southeast Conference (19.13 percent). Vedder and Denhart contrast the neighboring schools of the University of Michigan and Eastern Michigan University, whose stadia are but 6.3 miles apart, though in the football universe they may as well be the Sun and Pluto. Almost 40 percent of EMU students receive Pell Grants, which is thrice the percentage of UM Pell recipients.[25]

The authors view the reduction or elimination of such subsidies as a transpartisan issue. Conservatives, argue Vedder and Denhart, should be disturbed by the misallocation of resources and the coercive nature of sports subsidies. The "bundling of services" does not permit a student to pick and choose which extracurricular activities—or in this case entertainment—he or she wishes to support.[26] The sheer unfairness of the system also rankles. Natalia Abrams, director of Student Debt Crisis, a nonprofit organization, says, "These students are being forced to pay for something that they may or may not take advantage of, and then they have to bundle this into student loans they'll be repaying for 10 or 20 years."[27] Liberals, say Vedder and Denhart, ought to be outraged by the regressive nature of athletic fees, and the greater burden they lay on poor students and colleges. As Vedder has written elsewhere, fees are regressive because they are "more onerous for lower-income students than for the more affluent, who are able to attend schools where athletic fees are lower."[28] Drawing on work by Professor Jeff Smith of the University of South Carolina Upstate—a Division I school in all but football; athletic subsidy per full-time equivalent student was $1,235[29]—Vedder notes that schools in the lower-fee conferences have, on average, superior academic reputations to those in the higher-fee conferences. Not counting such prestigious private schools as Stanford, Vanderbilt, and Duke, the low-fee conferences boast the well-regarded public universities of Michigan, North Carolina, Virginia, and California (Berkeley and UCLA), while typical high-fee FBS conference schools include Kent State, Middle Tennessee State, and Georgia Southern.

The conference with by far the highest per-student athletic subsidy is the Big South, which consists of such public institutions as the University of North Carolina Asheville and Radford (VA), as well as private religious schools such as Liberty University and Campbell University. In 2010–11, the Big South's per-student athletic subsidy was $1,512, or 25 times higher than the Big Ten's figure of $61.[30] As Vedder notes, the $1,512 average student athletic fee, if multiplied by five (most Big South students do not graduate in four years), adds about $7,500 to the average student's post-college debt load. And it is no dig at UNC Asheville to say that a diploma therefrom will not—except in certain areas—open as many doors as will one from a low-fee Big Ten school.

The top 10 conferences in terms of per-student athletic subsidy in the study reveal the folly of relying on D-I basketball as a path to riches. They were, in order, the Big South ($1,512), the Northeast ($1,161), the Mid-Eastern Athletic Conference ($1,059), the America East Conference ($969), the Colonial Athletic Association ($951), the Mountain West ($936), the Southwestern Athletic Conference ($910), the Atlantic-10 ($885), the Ohio Valley ($874), and the MAC ($831). Only two of these—the Mountain West and the MAC—compete in FBS football; the flagship sport of the other eight is Division I basketball. Paralleling the work of Vedder and Denhart, the five conferences with the smallest such subsidy were the Big Ten ($61), the SEC ($109), the Big 12 ($136), the Pac-12 ($235), and the Atlantic Coast Conference ($304).[31]

If the MAC is on the fringes of the big-time football world, it is dead center in the debate—the incipient debate, or the debate we *ought* to be having—over student subsidy of major college athletics. Richard Vedder, director of the invaluable Center for College Affordability and Productivity, which has done so much to drag these oft-hidden subsidies into the light, is a Distinguished Professor of Economics Emeritus at MAC stalwart Ohio University; B. David Ridpath, who has also done excellent work on the subject, is Vedder's colleague.

Not coincidentally, the OHIO faculty has been harshly critical of the school in this regard. In May 2010, the Faculty Senate resolved that "the current funding model for intercollegiate athletics is incompatible with the academic mission of higher education" and urged the administration to "seek rapid and meaningful alternatives." Noting that in 2008–9, Ohio University's athletic revenues of $19.5 million were propped up by $14.6 million in institutional subsidies—or 75 percent of the total, the fourth-highest in the FBS—the faculty encouraged a significant reduction in the institutional subsidy.

The Student Senate, however, took the opposite tack, approving a resolution calling for an increase in the general student fee, about half of which goes to support athletics. Student Senate president Robert Leary—a classics major, so this was no jock-bedazzled Joe College—explained:

> I know [OHIO] doesn't have the most prestigious athletics program, but having a Division I sports program does contribute to the overall experience here at the university. I know a lot of students who are supporting athletics through all this.[32]

The athletic supporters got their wish.

Following up on the Vedder-Denhart study, Denhart teamed with OHIO's David Ridpath to produce "Funding the Arms Race: A Case Study of Student Athletic Fees," a January 2011 publication of the Center for College Affordability and Productivity. Again, the focus is on Ohio University, a large (20,000 or so undergraduates) public university of middling reputation whose teams play in the Mid-American Conference, a so-called mid-major basketball conference and one of the weakest of the FBS football conferences. The MAC excels in one regard, however: it consistently boasts the highest student athletics fees in the FBS. Ball State, for example, may not be able to compete well with Alabama or Texas on the football field, but its student body sure pays for the privilege of trying.

Denhart and Ridpath conducted an online survey of OHIO graduate and undergraduate students in the fall of 2010. They received 910 complete responses. Women were overrepresented (61 percent, as opposed to 51 percent of the student body) in the sample, as were graduate students (32 percent). The goal was to determine the awareness and approval of the existence and extent of fees dedicated to intercollegiate athletics. The vast majority (84.1 percent) of respondents were aware that OHIO charged a general activities fee. Just over one in five (21.3) estimated that fee within 5 percent of its actual amount, which was $531 per quarter. Most (54.4 percent) underestimated by a median amount of $231 per quarter. Most (54.4 percent, again), however, were aware that a portion—in fact a significant portion—of this general fee was funneled to sports teams.[33]

Although intercollegiate athletics consumes the lion's share (40.8 percent) of monies raised by the general fee, a plurality of students (19.8) gave it a ranking of 8—that is, the lowest score on a 1–8 scale—when asked how deserving the various fee recipients were of funds. The next most common rankings also indicated the low value students placed on intercollegiate athletics: 18.4 percent rated it a 7, 18.0 percent rated it a 6, and 14.5 percent rated it a 5. That is, almost 70 percent of OU respondents said that funding intercollegiate athletics should be a low priority. Over a third (35 percent) reported attending zero athletic events per year, even though admission is "free" due to the general fee. The mean number of inter-collegiate athletic events attended per year was 5.8, which, as Denhart and Ridpath note, works out to about $130 per event.[34] Now *that's* a pricey ticket for, say, an Akron-Western Michigan men's soccer game or a Central Michigan-Buffalo women's basketball tilt.

Ah, but a strong sports program acts as the university's front porch, luring on-the-fence applicants across the threshold, right? Not at OHIO. Asked how important a factor OHIO's intercollegiate athletics reputation was in influencing their college decision, 53.7 percent answered "extremely unimportant" and 24.8 percent chose "unimportant." Just 4.5 percent answered "important" and a min-uscule 2.1 percent pegged it as "extremely important." Not surprisingly, there was little appetite for a fee increase. Sixty-three percent of survey participants preferred a reduction in the intercollegiate athletics fee, 18 percent selected the option "remain the same," and the rest expressed a willingness to pay more, the most popular choice being between an additional one cent and $15 dollars annually.[35]

The MAC was the subject of a second major study in this newly expanding field of research. B. David Ripdath of OHIO, Jeff Smith of the University of South Carolina Upstate, and Daniel Garrett and Jonathan Robe of the Center for College Affordability and Productivity collaborated on a study of student perceptions of athletic fees at MAC schools. This quartet chose the 13 member institutions of the MAC, which they characterized as "one of the highest subsidized conferences in NCAA Division I," as their object of study.[36] Through emails and phone calls, the researchers assembled a survey population of 3,258 full-time students from ten of the MAC schools. (Western Michigan, the University of Akron, and the University of Buffalo either did not cooperate or had response rates too low to be usable.) The respondents skewed female (60 percent), with a 75–25 split between undergraduates and graduate students.

The researchers found little support among MAC students for higher fees. About half (49 percent) of the respondents agreed with the statement "I desire the fee for intercollegiate athletics be reduced in the future," while 25 percent desired the fee "to remain the same in the future." Of the quarter of the sample willing to pay higher fees, a plurality (8 percent) was willing to go only as high as $.01–$15 per semester.[37] Similarly, just under half (46 percent) of the sample ranked intercollegiate athletics "extremely unimportant" as a priority, and 27 percent called it "unimportant." Another 19 percent answered "slightly unimportant" or "slightly important," while just 9 percent ranked college sports as "important" or "extremely important."[38]

Given the opportunity to comment, survey participants took aim at MAC fees:

—This survey actually shocked me and I was just so surprised because I feel like that is a lot of extra money per year. I can barely afford college as is and finding out that I have to pay about $1,500 more just for some of the stuff mentioned . . . made me mad.
—Absolutely ridiculous! I had no idea this was going on.
—I understand that athletics are important to some, but I feel that a learning institution such as a college should focus on academics and the teaching/ learning experience. I would prefer to go to a college that has a Division I-type status in some sort of knowledge-based competition.[39]

Staying within the MAC, specifically at the University of Toledo, a public school, a master's thesis by Katherine Ott investigated the extent to which those who pay the student fee at Toledo approve of those organizations funded thereby, and, more fundamentally, whether they are even aware of its existence.[40] Toledo's mandatory activity fee dates to 1920–1, when students were charged $1 a semester, in return for which they received a weekly student newspaper, *The Teaser*, and membership in the school's athletic association. The levy inched upwards over the years; by the time of Ott's study in 2008–9, it was the considerable sum of $555.60

per semester, or $1,111.20 a year.[41] But do Toledoans even know they are paying this fee, or what it is used for? Ott employed an online survey of full-time students in the spring of 2009 to find out. Her sample size consisted of 760 valid responses that skewed female (58.1 percent of respondents as opposed to a female UT population of 49.5 percent). More than nine in ten (91.3 percent) were aware of the activity fee, although, perhaps predictably, less than half (42.5 percent) knew the approximate dollar amount ($501–$700). A plurality (43 percent) estimated the fee to be less—often quite a bit less—than was the case.[42]

Respondents were asked to rank the five most important activities and organizations funded through the Toledo fee. The top choices were the Student Recreation Center (70.2 percent), the Student Medical Center (64.3 percent), the Student Union (63.2 percent), the Computer Learning Resource Center (54.0 percent), and Academic Enrichment (51.7 percent). Athletics and Cheerleading were ranked *Important* by only 20.9 percent of respondents; a pathetic 6.0 percent esteemed the Larimer [Athletic] Team Facility as *Important*. The five recipients of activity fee funds ranked least important were the Marching Band (51.3 percent pegged them as one of the five least important), the Larimer Team Facility (49.7 percent), the Morse Center YMCA (49.1 percent), the Child Care Facility (41.1 percent), and Athletics and Cheerleading (38.7 percent).[43] Yet despite its relative unpopularity, Athletics and Cheerleading "received more general fee dollars than any other organization in 2008 ($9,309,270)."[44] You pay for this but they give you that, as a rock star once sang.

Not to pick on the MAC, whose teams often display an appealing underdog feistiness, but it was once again on the vivisection table when a team of young investigative reporters from the University of Cincinnati examined the extent to which Ohio public-school collegians subsidize their college teams. Writing in 2015 and using figures from 2013, the student journalists found that MAC schools dominated the upper rungs of the subsidy ladder. The athletics subsidy per student at Ohio's eight public FBS schools was: Miami (Ohio), $1,226; University of Akron, $1,095; University of Cincinnati, $1,024; Kent State, $998; Bowling Green, $990; Ohio University, $830; University of Toledo, $724; and Ohio State, $0.[45] Six of the eight schools are members of the MAC. Ohio State, of course, is in the Big Ten, and the University of Cincinnati, which has bounced around over the years, was in the Big East through 2013, after which it joined the American Athletic Conference.

The student journalists created something of a local splash with the story. University of Cincinnati president Santa Ono, whose official biography boasted that he "has gained a reputation as a chief executive who is accessible and responsive to the university's wide range of constituents," refused to comment, but Professor Jeff Smith of South Carolina Upstate said that this was "Robin Hood in reverse," as the less affluent student bodies paid high fees, while the more affluent student body of Ohio State paid nothing.

The situation at Cincinnati was especially raw. A 2010 university task force on the future of UC sports reported an athletic department deficit of $24 million and festering, largely due to "a historical lack of interest in UC sports." A survey conducted under the task force's auspices seemed to back this up: asked to rank ten facets of campus life in terms of importance, academics came first and athletics last. So what did the task force recommend? Dumping more and more money into the athletics pit, and jacking up the student athletics fee—this despite the fact that between 2005–8, athletic subsides had grown at a greater rate at UC than at any other public FBS school. An $86 million upgrade of the football stadium and an $87 million renovation of the basketball arena were made priorities.

The faculty had voiced its opposition to the emphasis on athletics; they were ignored. The young journalists quoted several UC students making similar points: "I didn't come to UC for sports. I came for an education." "I did not choose UC for its sports programs." "Students aren't paying for sports. They're paying to get an education." "Why should I be paying $1,000 in athletic fees? I could be spending it on a semester's worth of books."

Thomas Humes, a developer and UC's board chair, rebutted with an old familiar tune. Major-college sports, he said, are "something everybody can identify with. It drives emotions and excitement and spirit and attitude. It's our common rallying point."[46] Student government president Tim Lolli made a similar point in 2010, telling *USA Today* that as a result of sporting success, "Student involvement is up on campus. There's a better feeling on campus, more pride for the university. It's something that connects students to the university other than going to class."[47] Not a single UC student interviewed by the journalists cited athletics as a reason to attend the school, though surely—despite athletics ranking tenth out of ten university features in popularity—there is some student, somewhere, who came to Cincinnati to watch the Bearcats, whose basketball teams often hover somewhere in the Top 20.

Ohio State, which, excepting its rejection of the 1962 Rose Bowl invite, has never exactly subordinated athletics to education, came out smelling like roses compared to the other Ohio schools. Its administrators were not above emitting whiffs of sanctimony. "There is nothing more important than academics," pontificated OSU athletic director Gene Smith, who served as AD during the scandals that led to the ouster of football coach Jim Tressel. "When we recruit young people to come here, our priority commitment is to help them get their degree." Smith, noting that the athletic department contributed $9 million to a library renovation project, added piously, "We never think about how much money we spend on the academic part of our responsibility, because there is nothing more important than that. We just do it."[48]

Welcome to the big time; now pay up

Student journalists are often in the vanguard of fee critics. Writing in the Georgia State *Signal*, Alex Graham told his fellow GSU students that they "pay some of the highest athletic fees in the country and a good chunk of those fund the university's football program."[49] As Graham explains, GSU derives a whopping 68 percent of its athletic funding from the annual $550 athletic fee for any student taking at least six credit hours.[50] This exceeds the 65 percent cap established by the University System of Georgia's Board of Trustees; GSU has until 2020 to come into compliance. (By contrast, the annual fee at the University of Georgia, the state's football powerhouse, is $106.) When you include direct assistance from the institution, 84 percent of the Georgia State athletics budget is subsidized—a dubious distinction that put them at #14 on the *Huffington Post/Chronicle of Higher Education* list of the athletic department most dependent on subsidies. (Number one was the New Jersey Institute of Technology at 90 percent; Georgia State was the most subsidized of FBS schools, barely edging out Eastern Michigan University and its 83 percent.)[51]

The GSU community can't say it wasn't warned. A 2006 study of the feasibility of launching a Panther football program admitted that "the only practical model . . . available to fund the incremental expenses [due to a football team] is an increase in student fees." These were already $284 annually, but football here, as elsewhere, would eventually constitute the single largest piece of the athletic pie—a quarter of the 2016 athletic department budget of $27.6 million.[52] The feasibility study, conducted by C.H. Johnson Consulting of Chicago, spoke of the "many intangible benefits" of a football team, in particular a heightened sense of school spirit at what was, and still is, primarily a commuter school with about 30,000 students and what the *New York Times* termed "an indifferent alumni base in town."[53] (Three-quarters of the students enrolled commute.) Down the road, it was hoped, some grateful and sentimental and wealthy graduate would remember the good times at Panthers games by making a sizeable charitable donation to good old GSU.

Mike Huckaby—Chancellor of the University System of Georgia, not the Arkansas politico—envisioned a bright future for the Panthers, albeit ungrammatically: "Unlike my time as a student at Georgia State, football has become part of the student experience now, and I expect this will continue to grow just as Georgia State continues to advance as a leading urban research institution." Mark Becker, Georgia State University president, is also sanguine: "Before Georgia State started playing football, it was uncommon to see students wearing Georgia State's clothing, and school pride was considerably less than it is today. That literally changed with our first game in 2010." Becker heard the buzz, or what he hopefully believed to be the buzz. Neither gentleman mentioned fees, though the students Graham quoted were not as reticent. "If they want us to pay this much in student fees, I don't want it to go to football," said junior Katherine Hunter, who suggested instead that it be spent on homecoming. Similarly, Audrey Marime objected to her fees "funding . . . this sport I don't even play," though her preference was that the fee go to more general student activities. More condemnatory was Zainab Babalola, who scoffed, "People barely go to the games, especially football games because our team is awful." With a 6–5 record in 2017, including a 56–0 loss to Penn State, the Panthers show no sign of being weaned from student fees any time soon.

The GSU administration knew there would be growing pains. The consulting company's report made it clear that Georgia State would heavily depend on student fees, at least at first. But no one is more delusional—or perhaps we should say exuberantly optimistic—than a football fan. Surely the fees were a temporary burden whose weight would lessen as the years went on. In 2009, on the eve of GSU's maiden voyage into the turbulent seas of college football, the incoming student body president conceded that those students who knew about the fees were unhappy about them, and many more had no idea that their bills had been inflated due to football, but he said, sunnily, "Nobody will question it 10 years from now when they're sitting in the stands and cheering." That ten years is just about up. And the cheers are hard to hear.

Georgia State made a splash by hiring Bill Curry, former NFL star and University of Alabama coach, as the man to guide the Panthers from the FCS, which it joined in 2010, into the FBS in 2013—a move that contradicted former school president Carl V. Patton's 2009 assertion that "We could never, at this time, raise the kind of money we'd need for D-I [FBS]. Not in my lifetime."[54] At press time, President Emeritus Patton was still among the living. Alas, Coach Curry left just before GSU made the big leap to the FBS. The team struggled out of the gate—0–12 in 2013, 1–11 in 2014. But GSU, especially its football-mad president Mark Becker, doubled down. In 2016 the school purchased for $22.8 million the 67-acre site that had formerly been the home of major league baseball's Atlanta Braves. GSU is in the process of converting it to a 30,000 seat football stadium. Though the conversion will be spaced over a number of years, the Panthers began play at Georgia State Stadium in 2017. The school promises that this will be "transformational."[55] In Georgia State's first game in the new stadium, it lost to a team from the lower FCS division, Tennessee State, by a score of 17–10. Transformations take time.

The imbalance between Georgia State's sparse crowds and FBS standing—it routinely ranks in the bottom ten or 20 teams—and its robust fees points to an inequity articulated by a foursome of writers from the *Huffington Post* and the *Chronicle of Higher Education*: "students who have the least interest in their college's sports teams are often required to pay the most to support them." In the case of Georgia State, fully 59 percent of the population is eligible for Pell Grants, so this is a relatively nonaffluent student body being hit up for the sake of big-time football. Brea Woods, a 20-year-old GSU junior who had already borrowed $19,000 for her education, when she learned that she was paying that $550 athletics fee, huffed, "That makes me mad because I'm not an athlete."[56] But Brea was just a year from graduating and leaving GSU, continuing the cycle in which students, shortly after becoming aware that they are paying this fee, cease being students and cease paying the fee. No sooner do they get worked up over it than they are sent padding out into the world, diplomas in hand and deeply in hock.

If having an FBS team is the pass key to being a "real university," and if creating such a team de novo is on a par with kicking a 105-yard field goal, and if the overwhelming majority of schools in such a position are relatively new, without much tradition, lacking billionaire alumni, then there's one fail-safe source of revenue with which to build your own football team: student fees.

Administrators tend to be apologetic about student athletic fees, in the manner of a gentlemanly thief who is obviously embarrassed about taking your money but not so embarrassed as to let you keep it; no, he prefers contrition after the fact. There are, however, those who feel no compunction whatsoever about mulcting ordinary students for the benefit of cosseted athletes. Some even offer advice as to the most effective means of getting these students to tax themselves. One such, Robert T. Bronzan, planning consultant for major athletic facilities, told readers of the journal *Athletic Business* (audience: those responsible for "planning, financing and operating athletic/recreation/fitness programs and facilities") that when traditional revenue sources—especially state financing—dry up, the savvy builder of stadia, arenas, and practice facilities looks to clueless students for help. Though it may sound challenging, raising money through "self-assessment of student fees" is doable if you play your cards (and the chumps) right.[57]

It's a four-year process, says Dr. Bronzan. The first three years require planning, or what he calls *incubation*. The administration needs to "implant in each of the three successive freshman classes" the necessity of new facilities, which can only be financed, or so it should be claimed, through student fees. All the while, you are cultivating a vanguard class: "student leaders who appear to recognize and favor student financing of facilities are identified and nurtured in a low-key manner." This low-key manner, we assume, differs from the higher-key approach that Division I schools often take in recruiting football and male basketball players with comely hostesses and prodigious partying opportunities. In the fourth year, these nurtured students form the "nucleus" of a campaign to convince their fellow students to tax themselves to build a new athletic facility.[58] Timing is key. There are two optimal periods for a campus-wide vote, says Dr. Bronzan. The first is six to eight weeks into the fall semester, when the excitement of a new year is yet to wear off, and students are enjoying the football season, and it's early enough that "the available time for the opposition to become organized is limited." Keeping the campaign brief is advised no matter when the election is held, for a disorganized opposition is ideal.

The other good time is late in the year, perhaps three or four weeks before final exams. The advantages here are that 1) "impending course examinations interfere with the opposition's efforts to organize a counterattack": who has time to write anti-fee op-eds for the student newspaper when that Organic Chemistry final is just around the corner?; and 2) "senior students are more likely to vote in favor of an assessment since it will not apply to them."[59] (Even better is to saddle future students with the burden, as North Texas did with a 2008 vote for a fee that would not go into effect until 2011, and Bowling Green students did with a vote in 2009 to impose an additional $60 fee per semester beginning in 2011 to help fund an arena.) Does this seem, ah, unseemly? No matter. Edifices are complex. And if you need to rig the game, well, as Vince Lombardi said, winning isn't everything; it's the only thing.

Bronzan's advice, proffered in 1984, has become conventional wisdom. For instance, when the University of Texas at San Antonio sought to double its student athletic fees in order to help finance an ambitious launch of a football program, it scheduled the student referendum for September 11 and 12, 2007, or just days after classes began. The vote was sold to students as a means "to take Roadrunner Athletics to the next level of NCAA competition." UTSA, a fledgling school established in 1969, competed in Division I in basketball and other sports, but this was Texas, where football is king.[60]

The current fee had been capped at a maximum of $120 per semester; the referendum authorized this to rise to $240 per semester, though the boost would be phased in over at least five years. The prime beneficiary of the hike would be football: UTSA had recently conducted a feasibility study that determined that big-time football, with its manifold blessings, could be up and running within three years of getting the OK. Although a new stadium was unnecessary—UTSA could play in San Antonio's Alamodome—weight rooms, locker rooms, training rooms, and coaches' offices must be built, and the various travel, recruiting, and administrative expenses of a football program must be borne. Alumni contributions and corporate support alone would not be sufficient, even under the most optimistic estimates. After all, the school was less than 40 years old.

What would the students get out of this? "Free" admission to games, which would "provide fun, affordable entertainment . . . [and] build pride and tradition in UTSA and increase equity in a UTSA degree," even for those who loathe football or were wholly indifferent to the fortunes of the Roadrunners.

The referendum, scheduled nice and early per Dr. Bronzan, won in a two-to-one landslide. The wheels, having been set in motion, propelled the UTSA Roadrunners into Division 1 football, with FCS/FBS transition years in 2011–12 and membership in the mid-level Conference USA beginning in 2013. UTSA hired Larry Coker, who had won a national championship with the ethically challenged University of Miami, paying him $200,000 annually to launch the ship. He bailed after three years, the last a disappointing 3–9 season in which a student government poll found that students opposed any further increase in the athletic fee. As Ileana Gonzalez, student body president, said, "People were like, we are not even winning. Why is our money going to athletics when we are here in college to get an education?"[61]

At this writing, full-time UTSA students are paying $240 per semester to support the athletic program; the more than $12 million thereby raised is second among all public Texas universities, trailing only Texas State, whose $300 per semester fee pulls in over $17 million. (Of the eight public Texas universities playing FBS football, only Texas A&M and the University of Texas at Austin forego student athletic fees, though the Texas A&M Board of Regents actually approved a $72 per student fee in 2013 that has not yet gone into effect. "We have not needed to impose it at this time, but that doesn't mean we won't need to impose it down the road," said an A&M spokeswoman in 2015.) Texas State is the only Texas FBS school with a higher student fee—$300—than that of UTSA.[62]

Miami-based Florida International University was established in 1965 and opened its doors in 1972. It didn't field a football team until 2002, and it took but three years for the Panthers to join what was then called Division I-A, and is now the FBS. To keep up with the Joneses, or at least with rival Florida Atlantic, FIU undertook a $31 million renovation of its stadium in 2007, which was largely funded by a hike in student fees.

FIU was acting very much in the tradition of state schools in the Sunshine State. An Associated Press study in December 2014 found that eight "public universities in Florida with NCAA-sanctioned teams get between 36 percent and 75 percent of their athletic funding from student athletic fees," and that those fees had risen by 31 percent over the previous five years. The exceptions were the two most successful football factories in the state: the University of Florida, whose athletic department budget was $110.3 million, extracted only $2.5 million, or 2.2 percent of the budget, from student fees, while Florida State funded 14.5 percent of its athletic budget ($7.8 million of $54 million) from mandatory student levies.

The fees at the other schools, which ranged from $350–$480 per student per academic year, funded a substantial portion of the athletic budgets:

West Florida Athletic Budget: $7 million; Student Fee revenue: $5.3 million (75.9 percent)
North Florida $9.5 million; $6.6 million; 69.4 percent
Florida International $28.3 million; $19.5 million; 68.8 percent
Central Florida $41 million; $20.1 million; 49 percent
Florida Atlantic $24.5 million; $11.2 million; 46 percent
Florida Gulf Coast $12.1 million; $5.4 million; 45 percent
Florida A&M $12.5 million; $4.9 million; 39 percent
South Florida $45 million; $16 million; 36 percent[63]

Florida Atlantic, which began Division I play in 2005, loses about $4 million a year on football; its $70 million stadium was "financed with a bank loan" at what its athletic director later called "the worst moment in banking history."[64] But hope springs eternal in the nether regions of the FBS: in December 2016, FAU hired as its head football coach the notorious Lane Kiffin, whose previous stints as head coach of the Oakland Raiders, University of Tennessee Volunteers, and USC Trojans, and offensive coordinator under Nick Saban at the University of Alabama, had gone up in flames of controversy. His salary? About $950,000 annually, which puts him in the high-rent district of the mid-level Sun Belt Conference.[65] In Kiffin's first year, Florida Atlantic surprised the pundits with a 10–3 record, though Kiffin's recruitment of players with questionable backgrounds surprised no one.

Admittedly, a successful football program, or at least a football program that plays and loses to successful teams, is valued by a significant portion of any college community. Utah State University students approved by a slim 2,415–2,159 (53–47 percent) margin a $130 per year fee increase (from $113 to $243) in March 2009. This will give "our coaches and student-athletes" a "fighting chance," said USU Director of Athletics Scott Barnes.[66] It seemed to work: new football coach Gary Anderson took the Aggies from the dregs to prominence, peaking with an

11–2 record and a national ranking in 2012. But what goes up, must come down, especially for mid-major teams. The University of Wisconsin lured Anderson away, and by 2016 the Aggies had sunk to 3–9, rebounding slightly to 6–6 in 2017. The purse strings were also tightening: the Utah State University Fee Board rejected, by a vote of 13–10, a proposal to boost the student athletics fee by a modest $10 in the 2016–17 season.[67]

Disgruntlement over fees is almost always most evident where the records of the football and/or basketball teams are stuck in a sub-.500 rut. At the University of New Mexico, whose football team may as well call its home stadium The Mire, so long has it been stuck therein, students, or at least those conscious of the situation, revolted against a 2013 doubling (over two years) of the athletic fee to $165.20, which enriched the coffers of the athletic department by $900,000 annually. The UNM Board of Regents approved the hike over the bootless objections of the Student Fee Review Board, whose reviewing powers were proved to be without effect. "People who are constantly struggling because they're underemployed or unsupported . . . The feeling is, overwhelmingly, we can't shoulder additional fees," said Marisa Silva, president of the Graduate and Professional Student Association. Silva went on to say that financial pressures are the major reason for the high dropout rate at UNM, which graduates only 15 percent of its students within four years and 44 percent within six years.

Administrators protested that New Mexico's reliance on fees and university subsidies, which accounted for 41.2 percent of athletic department revenue, were in line with the other public schools in the Mountain West Conference. For instance, Boise State University collected $3.2 million from students and the sum of its subsidies totaled 28 percent of its athletic revenue, while the comparable figures for the University of Nevada at Las Vegas ($2.8 million; 54.2 percent) and San Diego State University ($9.7 million; 40.1 percent) were more or less in line with UNM's numbers, and those of other mid-major conferences such as the MAC and the Sun Belt.[68]

In 2010, fellow Mountain West cellar dweller, the University of Hawaii, facing an athletics department debt of $10 million and rising, prevailed on the state board of regents to institute a first-ever athletics fee of $50 per semester. Students kicked up a fuss, but the associate athletics director assured them that "a strong, successful athletic program is very important to the connection with alumni, donors and leaders in the state, and it magnifies the university not only in Hawaii but beyond the state."[69]

At Colorado State University, another Mountain West Conference bottom feeder, President Tony Frank did something unusual for a college president: he attempted to defend athletic department spending. And he did so based not so much on such nebulous benefits as character building and school spirit, but rather on the alleged boosts to institutional reputation and fiscal health. In the former case, President Frank argued that there are schools—and by implication CSU may be among them—whose public reputation is less than it ought to be because "a sense of excellence is missing from the athletic programs that are so often the most visible side of the university to the public"—the Front Porch Theory.[70] (This lends credence to "beer and circuses" critic Murray Sperber's theory that universities, which often emphasize graduate and research programs, appease the undergraduates with the bread and circuses of intercollegiate sports, keeping them "happy and distracted" while "the tuition dollars roll in.")[71]

President Frank pointed out that Colorado State is one of 17 universities "never to have had a major NCAA violation," and that student–athletes graduate at a higher rate than do non-student-athletes. (A not uncommon occurrence, especially if basketball and football players are removed from the pool.) Writing in 2011, President Frank noted that of CSU's $25 million athletic budget, $14.4 million, or 57.6 percent, comes from student fees and direct university support. This was third highest in the Mountain West Conference, but the athletic budget was sixth, and fully 30 percent below the conference mean. Although spending, he admitted, does not guarantee victories on the field, CSU needs at least to approach "a national norm" if it is to achieve a reputation as a *have*, and not a *have-not*, in the sporting world. This increased spending, combined with a scandal-free environment, will lift the school's national reputation and enhance the value of a CSU degree. "[D]ream big, work hard, and settle for nothing less than excellence," exhorted Dr. Frank, who deserved credit for at least defending what many consider the indefensible: mid-major sports spending.[72]

But whence the windfall that will make this possible? President Frank speculates, or dreams, of "non-public funds"—a Boone Pickens or Phil Knight with a CSU degree!—to underwrite new and better facilities. Seven years later, this benevolent billionaire has yet to materialize. But President Frank pointed to the stinginess of the Colorado legislature, and not runaway sports spending, as the culprit in tuition increases.

Steven Shulman, CSU professor of economics, disputed the president's assertion that state budget reductions are driving increases in CSU tuition. Writing in November 2016, Professor Shulman noted that the fiscal year (FY) 2017 budget was enriched by $18.8 million due to tuition increases, while state budget cuts shaved only $100,000 from revenues. So who or what is benefiting from the influx of tuition monies? Athletics, of course. Spending thereon "has risen from $26.0 million to $38.8 million since Tony Frank was appointed president in 2009," writes Professor Shulman, while revenue from athletics—ticket sales, donations, merchandise—has, over the same period, edged up from $14.2 million to $18.0 million. "Driving up costs faster than revenues would be a losing strategy in any industry aside from higher education," avers Shulman. "CSU is forced to make up the difference by subsidizing athletics with increased tuition and fees."[73] In 2015, CSU athletics were subsidized to the tune of $20.4 million; adding insult to injury, the football coach, Mike Bobo, pulled down the highest salary ($1.45 million) in the Mountain West—not bad for a coach who was finishing his second consecutive 7–6 season at Colorado State.

And in 2017, the Rams got a new place to play: Colorado State Stadium, a $220 million football palace with a capacity of 41,000, or 9,000 higher than the stadium it replaced, which rarely sold out.[74] Private donations for the stadium were well behind projections, though in 2016 an anonymous donor pledged $20 million—over 30 years—to transfer the name "Sonny Lubick Field," honoring a former old coach, from the old stadium to the new.[75]

You can never have too much

Even powerhouses whose budgets dwarf those of lower-level strivers like New Mexico and Colorado State are not loath to tap the student body for revenue. Clemson University, which sits atop the football hill these days, as 2015 National Championship runner-up and 2016 and 2018 National Champion, is unusual within the Atlantic Coast Conference in that, unlike other public schools in the conference (Florida State, Georgia Tech, Louisville, North Carolina, NC State, South Carolina, Virginia, Virginia Tech), it has avoided taxing students to pay for its mammoth sports program. Clemson's IPTAY—I Pay Ten a Year—begun in 1934 as a way for supporters to finance athletics at Clemson. Its founder, radiologist Dr. Rupert H. Fike, declared that its purpose "shall be to provide financial support to the athletic department at Clemson and to assist in every other way possible to regain for Clemson the high athletic standing which rightfully belongs to her."[76]

In its wild and woolly early years, Clemson head coach Frank Howard would drive the byroads of rural South Carolina, stopping at service stations and country stores to collect donations for the Tigers.[77] The Clemson boosters put the federal government to shame when it came to acronyms: besides IPTAY, they communicated with such terms as GOCAMS (Giving Our Clemson All My Support) and WDWE (When Do We Eat?). Coach Howard was known as the Exalted IRYAAS (I Received Yours and Acknowledge Same).[78] In the years since, IPTAY, which funds all athletic scholarships, has become the envy of the college athletic fundraising world. In 2016, IPTAY brought in revenue of $56.8 million, which surpasses the annual athletic budgets of most D-I schools.

Clemson sits at or near the apex of the FBS today. Its gladiators, to borrow a locution favored by the purple-prosed sportswriters of yesteryear, train at a $55 million facility that includes, in addition to the usual offices and accoutrements, "a miniature golf course, a movie theater, bowling lanes," laser tag, and other amenities not enjoyed by your typical Clemson undergrad or in any way, shape, or form related to the purported academic mission of Clemson University. Yet the backlog of deferred maintenance projects at Clemson, according to the *Washington Post*, exceeds $550 million, and the library floor is stippled with buckets to catch raindrops until money is found for $900,000 in waterproofing repairs.[79] Priorities, priorities, priorities.

This is only one of the spectacular instances of an explosion in athletic facilities spending, which, adjusted for inflation, increased by 89 percent ($408 million to $772 million) from 2004 to 2014. "This is all about pandering to the fantasies of 18-year-olds," Gerald Gurney, president of the reformist Drake Group, told the *Washington Post*. "It has nothing whatsoever to do with the mission of a university." Indoor training facilities replete with amphitheaters, sporting museums, hydrotherapy rooms, barbershops, and every electronic gadget known to man are routine at football factories. As Will Hobson and Steven Rich of the *Washington Post* point out, many of these Lucullan facilities have been built over the last decade at schools which extract considerable mandatory fees from the non-football and basketball-playing student body: the Universities of Virginia and Maryland, Rutgers, Georgia Tech, and others. "While the football team is getting something new and nice," said University of Maryland student government president Patrick Ronk, "there's a sentiment among students that they have to pay more and more every year, but they're not necessarily getting anything more for their spending."[80] The current mandatory student athletic fee at UM is $406 per academic year, and no one even pretends it is going to disappear in the foreseeable future.[81]

Clemson students have yet to see this line item on their due bills, though in 2014, athletics director Dan Radakovich floated the idea of a $350 fee, which would bring in $6 million annually to what was already a $72 million budget. Faculty and students balked, even though Radakovich had wisely proposed to delay implementing the fee until then-current students were out of school. As Senator Russell Long used to poetize, "Don't tax you, don't tax me, tax that fellow behind the tree!" Student government president Maddy Thompson was incredulous. "Do we really want all students paying so that they can recruit better athletes?" she asked. Well, yes, though the athletics department wouldn't exactly put it that way.[82] "It's about putting something into effect that will allow Clemson athletics to be strong for the next decade and beyond," said Radakovich. "It is currently a revenue source that is not tapped."[83]

It still isn't. But Clemson administrators know that there's more than one way to skin a cat. In early 2016, Radakovich proposed to charge students $225 for seating in their traditional seating section. Theretofore such tickets had been distributed free of charge. The howls of protest could be heard from Aiken to Charleston, and by June, Radakovich had backed off. Free tickets survived. But notice had been served; a fee or seat license or some levy is coming, sooner or later.[84]

When in April 2017 the Arizona Board of Regents approved a new $100 athletic fee for incoming University of Arizona undergraduates, that left the University of Washington as the only Pac-12 school without such a fee. The Regents meeting was not without its comic side; obeying instructions to avoid any talk of tuition or fees, dissenting students spoke instead in opposition to *fruition* and *bees*. The $100 fee was lower than the $300 that had been requested by the athletic department, but it was still too high for Alexandra Cordell, a senior majoring in philosophy, politics, and economics, who said, "I valued athletics while I was here, but it's unfair to make all students pay when they don't all share these values." Ms. Cordell was unusual in that as a senior, she would soon be gone from UA and not subject to the fee, yet she spoke up as a matter of principle.[85]

North of UA, Arizona State had earlier jumped aboard the athletic fee bandwagon. It instituted a $75 per semester athletic fee in 2015, bringing in an additional $9.9 million into the school's sports coffers. ASU president Michael Crow said wistfully that someday, eventually, in time, down the road a piece, athletics at Arizona State will be self-supporting. But not quite yet.[86] Going in the other direction, Kansas State announced in 2015 that thanks to escalating Big 12 revenues and corporate and alumni donations, it would phase out its athletic fee— euphemistically termed a "privilege fee"—by fiscal year 2020.[87]

Even smaller schools, far from the D-I limelight, squeeze fees from their students. SUNY College at Oswego, for instance, assesses a $17.83 per credit hour athletic fee, which the college justifies with the dubious claim that "everyone benefits from the success of our teams and their contribution to the college's reputation and recognition." If you don't know that Oswego's teams are called the Lakers, you have the company of 99.99 percent of your fellow Americans. The Oswego fee adds up to over $200 per semester for a full-time student, and does not include the $55 cost for a fitness center membership. It is, in effect, a "season pass to hockey games," as the student newspaper put it, and actually exceeds the student health fee by $3 per credit hour. The student editorialist concludes:

> When Oswego State students receive their diploma they will spend years paying off, it is highly unlikely that many will look at that framed piece of paper and think, "Oh man, I am so glad I paid more for the baseball program than my flu shot."[88]

Nor are community colleges safe havens from the fee collectors. Erie Community College in Buffalo levies a $140 yearly activity fee on full-time students. This covers activities unrelated to sports, among them childcare and commencement. Community college teams have paltry gate receipts, though in the case of ECC, athletics took in almost $700,000 annually in revenues, almost all of it (about $650,000) in the form of double tuition rates charged to out-of-state students. Nevertheless, when college trustees rejected a $40 student activity fee hike in May 2017, administrators threatened to cut men's ice hockey and baseball as a way of saving $134,000. (The salary of the college president, an ex-congressman and politician named Jack Quinn, was $192,000, along with a generous travel and expense budget.)[89] ECC Director of Athletics Peter Jerebko said that men's sports, and not new or on-the-drawing-board women's sports such as swimming, diving, and cross country, would have to take the hit, as the U.S. Department of Education had pressed ECC to provide more opportunities for females, consistent with Title IX.[90]

Parents, who often foot the bill for their progeny's education, are reduced to sputtering helplessly. Back in 2010, *USA Today* interviewed the mother of a student at Radford University, a non-football Division I school that was charging its young scholars nearly $1,000 a year to prop up its never very distinguished athletic program. The Highlanders, a member of the subsidy-laden Big South Conference, have made the NCAA men's basketball tournament twice: in 1998, as a 16 seed, they lost to Duke, 99–63, and in 2009, as a 16 seed, they lost to North Carolina, 101–53. So the most the school's only "glamour" D-I team can hope for is to be blown out in the opening round of March Madness. By whose calculation is that a good deal? It might better be called sheer madness. Yet parents like Linda Randall are paying the price. "We're looking at five years because [our daughter] changed majors," she told *USA Today*. "That's $5,000. That's one of her loans. That would have paid rent off-campus for a year. It's kind of disheartening."[91] In the years since, the burden has only increased. The Radford student athletic fee for the 2017–18 school year was $590 per term, or $1,180 per year. In-state tuition was $7,407 per year.[92]

Showing 'em who's boss

Despite assertions of autonomy, state-subsidized schools must ultimately answer to the state. One cannot take the King's shilling without becoming the King's man. The subsidized are indebted to the subsidizers; if not quite at their mercy, they are nevertheless at the end of a tether, however long, that may be jerked at any time, on any pretense.

Consider Utah. In July 2015, the Utah State Auditor released a report, "NCAA Athletics Revenue Subsidization for Utah's Public Colleges and Universities,"[93] which examined the extent of public subsidization of Utah's eight state-supported colleges and universities. The auditor itemized the components of the athletic subsidy as student fees, tuition waivers, direct institutional support, and support from the state of Utah. Total athletic subsidies for FY 2014 ranged from a high of $14.18 million for Utah State University to $1.29 million for the mostly two-year Snow College (which ought to, but does not, have a ski team, though it does support a rodeo squad). Athletic subsidies for all eight Utah public schools totaled $56.24 million.

The most heavily subsidized athletic departments, in percentage terms, were attached to the most obscure schools, whose revenues were minimal. While the University of Utah, which competes at the highest level of FBS and Division I basketball, had by far the highest athletic budget ($56.47 million), it brought in $46.61 million in revenue, so that its total athletics subsidy of $9.87 million represented an effective 17.5 percent subsidy. Utah State, despite "boasting" the highest subsidy in dollar amount, pulled in $10.97 million in revenue, lessening the portion of its athletics budget that is subsidized to 56.4 percent. The remaining sextet relied primarily, in some cases almost exclusively, on subsidies: Dixie State University (66.1 percent), Weber State University (66.4 percent), Southern Utah University (72.9 percent), Snow College (77.6 percent), Utah Valley University (85.8 percent), and Salt Lake Community College (88.0 percent).[94] Utah Valley's 85.8 percent subsidy was higher than all but 11 of the nation's 230 Division I public schools.[95] The athletics subsidy per full-time equivalent student reached its acme, or perhaps nadir is the more accurate term, at Southern Utah University ($1,164.90), with Utah State second at $708.62; the lowest subsidies per FTE student belonged to the University of Utah ($334.33) and Salt Lake Community College ($98.97.)[96]

The state of Utah auditor disclaimed any partisan motive to this study; his goal, rather, was to encourage policy makers to consider two questions: (1) To what extent should NCAA athletics be subsidized? and, (2) To what extent should students be required to subsidize NCAA athletics?[97] State auditor John Dougall told the press:

> The key purpose from our perspective is to provide more transparency to the public and policymakers. The key thing, I think, is for the public to understand where the money goes . . . so they can express their will to what extent they agree or disagree with various decisions.[98]

He added, "I would say there is no right number"[99]—but in merely raising the issue he prodded a debate in which school administrators would rather not partake. Perhaps, the *Salt Lake Tribune* editorialized, state leaders should ask whether "some of the money that goes to keep all those balls in the air might be better spent on labs, teachers and computers. Or left in the pockets of already struggling and indebted students."[100]

This is not the first time that Utah has taken the lead in raising prescient or provocative questions, or even acting on them. In 1870 its territorial legislature granted women the vote, well in advance of Utah's less enlightened eastern confederates, and in the mid-1960s Salt Lake City became the largest American city to reject the disastrous and destructive federal urban renewal program. Might Utah lead the way in curbing—or even abolishing—state and student subsidization of intercollegiate athletics? The auditor's report opened some eyes and started a discussion, if not exactly a debate. But seven months later, Utah's legislature provided an object lesson in the ways that public subsidy enables the politicization of college sport.

Larry Krystkowiak, basketball coach of the Utah Utes (salary: $2,575,000), and the school's athletic director announced the cancellation of the next season's game with archival (and private) Brigham Young University after a game-ending fight marred the latest iteration of this rivalry, which dates back to a 32–9 victory by BYU in 1909 in the initial game of what is known locally as the "Holy War." Utah, which joined the Pac-12 for the 2011–12 season, had in recent years been dropping in-state opponents like a social-climbing parvenu shedding old but unfashionable friends, and many in the Beehive State saw Krystkowiak's seemingly impulsive cancellation of the BYU game as another step away from regional rivalries and toward a national focus. But Brigham Young enjoys as large an in-state following as does the flagship public school, and on February 1, 2016, the state legislature's Legislative Audit Subcommittee voted unanimously to subject the University of Utah's athletics department to an "efficiency and effectiveness" audit.[101]

Refreshingly refusing to dissemble, Senate President Wayne Niederhauser—a graduate of Utah State, not BYU—admitted that the rupture in the rivalry prompted this act. "[T]he purpose of auditing the athletic department of the

University of Utah was brought to my attention by the controversy that was around playing BYU," he said. "I'm not necessarily as a Legislature wanting to get involved in deciding what teams play what, but we would encourage our universities to play each other."

Utah House Rep. Daniel McCay told the president of the University of Utah that "the antic of your athletic director, as well as your basketball coach," were indicators of deeper problems within the university, specifically that "athletics takes a superior position to academics."[102] McCay also raised the red flag of student fees, and the extent to which they subsidize Krystkowiak's program. McCay issued a pointed warning: "If you ever, athletic department, feel like you have taken over [the university], we'll get rid of you."[103] (McCay, like Niederhauser, is a Utah State grad; the Utes had dropped Utah State—which they had played since 1892— and Weber State from their schedule in 2010 and 2011.) "They're all funded by taxpayer money," added Senate President Niederhauser.[104] Even the governor of Utah, BYU grad Gary R. Herbert, got in on the action, tweeting "Play the game" after the Utes cancelled the next BYU tilt.[105]

The audit was conducted. State investigators discovered only minor flaws.[106] But by then tempers had cooled, for back in May 2016, the Utes announced that they would, in fact, resume the series with BYU in 2017. Moreover, athletics director Chris Hill said that "We are also looking at future match-ups with other in-state schools." The Utah State grad politicians had gotten their way.[107] Utah's arrogant coach and athletic administration had been taught just who is boss.

Revolt—or submission?

Cattle, having been fleeced with grim regularity, may grow restive. But revolts remain few and far between. In 2009, University of New Orleans students rejected by a vote of 1,418–1,251 a proposed doubling of the athletic fee to almost $400 a year, prompting the UNO administrators to threaten to drop the entire athletic program. The commissioner of the Sun Belt Conference, of which UNO was a member, played a sympathetic tune: "They're like a guy sitting at the blackjack table all night who hasn't seen a face card yet. How many more cards can they be dealt?" But UNO student government president Eric Gallatin, in no mood for forlorn gambler sob stories, was defiant: "Why contribute to athletics when they can seek out other revenue such as sponsors, which they haven't seemed to do?" he asked. Good question. And no sooner had it been asked than a group of local businesspeople, led by George Shinn, owner of the NBA's New Orleans Hornets, came to the rescue of this Hurricane Katrina-beleaguered public school with a successful fund-raising campaign that saved sports at UNO.

The battle of New Orleans came on the heels of fee increase rejections by students at a trio of California state universities—Fullerton, Long Beach, and Sacramento—and a failed effort to limit such fees at Fresno State. Roberto Torres, president-elect of the Sacramento State student government, explained to Jere Longman of the *New York Times*, "I couldn't afford the increases they were asking for." Moreover, "I just don't think students care too much about it, because they're not winning the big games."[108] (Almost a decade later, the Hornets are still mired near the bottom of the Big Sky Conference.)

A year later, students at the University of Montana voted 2–1 to reject a hike in the annual athletics fee from a relatively modest $92 to $144. But not to worry, Grizzlies' fans: the administration kept pushing, and the fee now stands at $142.

As is the case with the University of New Orleans, Fullerton, Long Beach, and Sacramento do not field FBS football teams. "Midmajors like us, Division I without football, we're really struggling," lamented Long Beach athletic director Vic Cegles. "Student fees make a huge difference." At Fresno State, which does compete at the highest level in football, students rejected a septupling of the athletics fee from $7 to $50 per semester, though the president nullified this vote and imposed a "compromise" hike to $32. His excuse was Title IX; uttering the magic words "gender equity," Fresno president John D. Welty explained that like it or not, students had to pony up $1.4 million more in fees to add women's lacrosse and women's swimming to FSU's athletic roster.[109]

The disparity between flagship state schools and lesser-known or satellite schools is much the same from Pacific to Atlantic and everywhere in-between. For instance, a 2014 *Chicago Tribune* investigation into the athletic departments of the state colleges of Illinois found that whereas the annual student fee of $34 accounted for just 4 percent of athletic department revenue at the University of Illinois over the five-year period 2009–13, student fees as a percentage of total revenue were considerably higher at Chicago State (27 percent), Eastern Illinois (27 percent), Western Illinois (31 percent), Northern Illinois (36 percent), Southern Illinois University at Carbondale (43 percent), University of Illinois at Chicago (47 percent), Illinois State (49 percent), and Southern Illinois University at Edwardsville (59 percent). If student fees are combined with direct support from the schools, what we might call the dependence rate jumps to a low of 55 percent at Northern Illinois and to a high of 84 percent at SIU Edwardsville.[110]

The University of Illinois, with its flea-bite fees, plays FBS football (if not very well; it is a perennial cellar dweller) in the Big Ten, where it is one of only two schools that charge an athletic fee. Northern Illinois, which resides in the notoriously fee-heavy MAC, is also an FBS school. The other seven schools under consideration lack FBS programs but do play Division I basketball, all of them in minor conferences where the summit of achievement is an invitation to the March Madness NCAA men's basketball tournament. A victory therein is out of the question; a blowout is the expectation, and a competitive loss is a moral victory. But the invite alone, and the playing of a single tournament game, earns the team's conference just over $1.7 million.[111] Yet D-I basketball lightens the wallets of the students at those schools; as the *Chicago Tribune* noted, the student athletic fee at SIU Edwardsville was $113 annually in 2005, when the school competed at the Division II level. A decade later, in D-I, it had more than trebled, to $352.80. Still, this was less than the fee at SIU Carbondale, which extracted just over $600 from each student for the benefit of its sports teams.

In defense of fees, Northern Illinois spokesman Brad Hoey explained that "Intercollegiate athletics is really part of the DNA" at NIU. "All of our students get into every single athletic event for free—basketball, football, soccer. That's one of the benefits."[112] But as the previously described studies at Ohio University and the University of Toledo reveal, few students at MAC schools place a premium on attendance at sporting events.

Fighting back against the athletic machine is not without consequences. The *Washington Post* reported the saga of David Catt, a golfer on the Kansas University team. KU charged a modest fee of just $50 per year in 2014. But it was the principle of the thing. The Jayhawks had paid out $9 million in two years for severance deals with Mark Mangino and Turner Gill, football coaches who had been given their walking papers. Athletics revenue exceeded $90 million. Did the school really need the $1.16 million it sucked out of students every year?[113] Golfer Catt prepared a 35-page paper arguing against the student fee. He presented it to the student senate. The senate voted to kill the fee, though the athletics department was able to restore it at a greatly reduced rate of $12, since increased to $14.

In retaliation, wrote Will Hobson and Steven Rich in the *Washington Post*, the administration "eliminated one of the best student sections at men's games—120 seats right behind the Jayhawks' bench—and gave the seats to donors who contributed at least $25,000 per year." That'll teach those insolent kids! Or as an athletics department spokesman explained, sneeringly, "When the student government [tried to eliminate the fee] . . . it made it very clear that it wanted the athletic department to find other ways to raise revenue. That's what we did." The experience taught Catt a lesson in just who has the upper hand at big-time sports colleges. "You think you're paying for a degree and you wind up as a piggy bank for a semi-professional sports team," he said.[114]

So where does this all lead? David Ridpath sees dark days ahead for the mid-majors. "These costs are not slowing down," he says, "and I think the pushback is going to grow. Eventually, it is going to affect people's ability to go to school."[115] Ridpath adds:

> It's frustrating to see universities, especially public ones, pleading poverty . . . and it is morally wrong for schools bringing in millions extra on athletics to continue to charge students and academics to support programs that, with a little bit of fiscal sense, could turn profits or at least break even.[116]

Richard Vedder and Matthew Denhart concede that universities are not about to unilaterally disarm in the athletics arms race. (As Wally Renfro, an NCAA vice president, has said, "The concept of a level playing field is aspirational, but I'm not sure it's ever completely achievable."[117] It was nice of Mr. Renfro to use the world *aspirational* rather than *delusional*, but we get his point.) Vedder and Denhart look with disfavor on any solution coming from the federal government, and fear the politicization of what ought to be an apolitical matter. But they do see a role for state governments, which after all subsidize the vast majority of FBS schools. They would like to see states cap subsidies and student fees at perhaps 5 percent of tuition revenues, or 2 percent of core expenditures, for any school receiving state funds.[118] Or, they suggest, the presidents of those conferences taking the worst beating in the arms race—not to mention on the football field—could "meet and agree on a conference rule on expenditures or institutional subsides." Alas, expecting college presidents to take meaningful action to limit the scope of intercollegiate athletics would try the patience of those waiting for Godot.[119] Academicians who have studied the issue seem more riled up than are the transient students. "I don't care to subsidize soccer teams and swim teams," says Jeff Smith, the South Carolina Upstate professor. "That's not doing any benefit to my kids' education."[120]

In the meantime, sporadic revolts against fees are probably the most opponents can hope for. "We're definitely seeing in recent times students refusing to pay a lot of these fees," said Bill Shiebler, national field director of the United States Student Association, back in 2009.

> There is a spectrum of reasons, ranging from "I think it costs too much to go to school here" to "I don't want to support any new fees" to "I just don't want to have my dollars go to athletics because I don't use it."

These are most common at commuter schools and at schools without FBS programs.[121] But students graduate or transfer or drop out, while athletic departments are, it seems, eternal.

Back in 1990, Murray Sperber, professor of English and American Studies at Indiana University, quoted an athletic director's speculation that students might stage "the tea party on campus" if they ever found out about the extent to which their activity fees were subsidizing big-time sports. "Perhaps if American college students understood how College Sports Inc. extracts money from them, they would be less passive about it and, as a result, would consider throwing some athletic programs overboard," wrote Sperber.[122] Alas, the tea was never dumped, nor were the athletic programs. The students, it seems, just keep getting steeped.

Notes

1 Matthew Denhart and David Ridpath, "Funding the Arms Race: A Case Study of Student Athletic Fees," Center for College Affordability and Productivity, January 2011, p. 3.
2 Katherine Ott, "Students' Awareness and Perceptions of the Activity Fee at the University of Toledo: A Descriptive Research Study," University of Toledo Digital Repository, 2009, pp. 4, 19.
3 B. David Ridpath, Jeff Smith, Daniel Garrett, and Jonathan Robe, "Shaping Policy and Practice in Intercollegiate Athletics: A Study of Student Perceptions of Resource Allocation for Athletics and its Effect on Affordability of Higher Education," *Journal of Sport* 4, Issue 1 (2015): 23.
4 "College Finances," *USA Today*, www.usatoday.com/sports/college/schools/finances//, accessed August 2, 2017. Steve Berkowitz, "Pair of Texas Schools Dominate Revenue List, Exceeding $210 Million Each," *USA Today*, June 29, 2018.

5   Will Hobson and Steven Rich, "Why Students Foot the Bill for College Sports, and How Some Are Fighting Back," *Washington Post*, November 30, 2015.

6   "College Finances," *USA Today*.

7   Denhart, Villwock, and Vedder, "The Academics–Athletics Trade-Off," p. 18.

8   Steve Berkowitz, "Two States Require Fee Disclosure, But Athletics Charges Can Be Buried," *USA Today*, September 22, 2010.

9   Ridpath, Smith, Garrett, and Robe, "Shaping Policy and Practice in Intercollegiate Athletics: A Study of Student Perceptions of Resource Allocation for Athletics and its Effect on Affordability of Higher Education," p. 39.

10 Steve Berkowitz, "Two States Require Fee Disclosure, But Athletics Charges Can Be Buried."

11 Harry Minium, "McAuliffe Signs Bills That Limits Athletic Student Fees," Norfolk *Virginian-Pilot*, March 31, 2015, www.espn.com/college-sports/news/story?id=3040343.

12 Vedder, "Introduction" to Denhart and Ridpath, "Funding the Arms Race: A Case Study of Student Athletic Fees," p. 1.

13 Jared S. Hopkins, "Illinois College Athletic Programs Heavily Funded by Students," *Chicago Tribune*, August 18, 2014.

14 David Ridpath, "Who Actually Funds Intercollegiate Athletic Programs?" *Forbes.com*, December 12, 2014.

15 Berkowitz, "Two States Require Fee Disclosure, but Athletics Charges Can Be Buried," *USA Today*.

16 "Florida State Tuition Rates, Main Campus," http://controller.vpfa.fsu.edu/sites/defa ult/files/media/doc/Student_Business/2016Tuition_Main.pdf, accessed August 4, 2017.

17 Berkowitz, "Two States Require Fee Disclosure, but Athletics Charges Can Be Buried," *USA Today*.

18 Kyle Hightower, "Some Students Pay Big Share of Colleges' Athletic Costs," *Florida Today*, December 10, 2014, www.floridatoday.com/story/news/local/2014/12/10/students-pay-big-share-colleges-athletic-costs/20219399.

19 Matthew Denhart and Richard Vedder, "Intercollegiate Athletics Subsidies: A Regressive Tax," Center for College Affordability and Productivity, April 2010, p. 4; See also David Moltz, "The Athletics Tax," *Inside Higher Ed*, June 1, 2010.

20 Katie Thomas, "Call to Curb Athletic Spending Strikes Some as Unrealistic," *Chronicle of Higher Education*, October 27, 2009.

21 Jonathan Orszag and Mark Israel, "The Empirical Effects of Collegiate Athletics: An Update Based on 2004–2007 Data," National Collegiate Athletic Association, February 2009, p. 9.

22 Denhart and Vedder, "Intercollegiate Athletics Subsidies: A Regressive Tax," p. 4.

23 Ibid., pp. 6–8.

24 Ibid., pp. 9–10.

25 Ibid., p. 12.

26 Ibid., p. 4.

27 Hobson and Rich, "Why Students Foot the Bill for College Sports, and How Some Are Fighting Back," *Washington Post*.

28 Richard Vedder, "How Poor Students Subsidize Unworthy College Sports," *Bloomberg.net*, June 17, 2013.

29 Ridpath, Smith, Garrett, and Robe, "Shaping Policy and Practice in Intercollegiate Athletics: A Study of Student Perceptions of Resource Allocation for Athletics and its Effect on Affordability of Higher Education," p. 25.

30 Ibid., p. 27.

31 Ibid.

32 David Moltz, "Seething Over Sports Subsidies," *Inside Higher Ed*, May 20, 2010.

33 Denhart and Ridpath, "Funding the Arms Race: A Case Study of Student Athletic Fees," pp. 5, 8.

34 Ibid., pp. 6, 8–9.
35 Ibid., pp. 11–12.
36 Ridpath, Smith, Garrett, and Robe, "Shaping Policy and Practice in Intercollegiate Athletics: A Study of Student Perceptions of Resource Allocation for Athletics and its Effect on Affordability of Higher Education," p. 29.
37 Ibid., p. 35.
38 Ibid., p. 36.
39 Ibid., p. 38.
40 Ott, "Students' Awareness and Perceptions of the Activity Fee at the University of Toledo: A Descriptive Research Study," p. 1.
41 Ibid., pp. 31, 33.
42 Ibid., pp. 54, 56–7.
43 Ibid., pp. 60–1.
44 Ibid., p. 66.
45 Staff, "Robin Hood in Reverse," *CityBeat*, May 6, 2015, www.citybeat.com/home/a rticle/13002610/robin-hood-in-reverse.
46 Ibid.
47 Jodi Upton, Steve Berkowitz, and Jack Gillum, "Big-Time College Athletics: Are They Worth the Cost?" *USA Today*, January 15, 2010.
48 "Robin Hood in Reverse," *CityBeat*.
49 Alex Graham, "Georgia State Students Pay Some of the Highest Athletic Fees in the Country," *The Signal*, November 1, 2016.
50 "Undergraduate Tuition/Fees: Fall 2017 & Spring 2018," Georgia State University, http://sfs.gsu.edu/files/2017/06/FY18-Undergrad.pdf, accessed July 5, 2017.
51 Brad Wolverton, Ben Hallman, Shane Shifflett, and Sandhya Kambhampati, "Sports at Any Cost," *Huffington Post*, November 15, 2015.
52 Graham, "Georgia State Students Pay Some of the Highest Athletic Fees in the Country," *The Signal*.
53 Wolverton, Hallman, Shifflett, and Kambhampati, "Sports at Any Cost," *Huffington Post;* Mike Tierney, "Georgia State Hoping Football Builds Community in a Football Town," *New York Times*, April 19, 2009.
54 Tierney, "Georgia State Hoping Football Builds Community in a Football Town," *New York Times*.
55 "Stadium Project," http://stadium.gsu.edu/, accessed July 20, 2017.
56 Wolverton, Hallman, Shifflett, and Kambhampati, "Sports at Any Cost," *Huffington Post*.
57 Robert T. Bronzan, "Student Fees: A New Source for Funding Facilities," *Athletic Business* 8, Issue 3 (March 1984): 4, 18.
58 Ibid.: 19.
59 Ibid.: 22.
60 Brad Parrott, "Q&A: UTSA Athletics Fee Student Referendum," *UTSA Today*, September 10, 2007.
61 Matthew Watkins, "Students Pitching in More as Texas Universities' Athletics Costs Climb," *Texas Tribune*, March 18, 2016, www.texastribune.org/2016/03/18/texa s-universities-are-hiking-student-fees-support/.
62 Hobson and Rich, "Why Students Foot the Bill for College Sports, and How Some Are Fighting Back," *Washington Post;* Watkins, "Students Pitching In More as Texas Universities' Athletics Costs Climb," *Texas Tribune*.
63 Hightower, "Some Students Pay Big Share of Colleges' Athletic Costs," *Florida Today*.
64 Gilbert M. Gaul, *Billion-Dollar Ball: A Journey through the Big-Money Culture of College Football* (New York: Viking, 2015), p. xviii.
65 Nick Cole, "Lane Kiffin: Details Released on New Contract at FAU," www.sec country.com/alabama/lane-kiffin-details-released-new-contract-fau, accessed February 22, 2017.

66   "Utah State University Students Vote to Support Athletic Fee Increase," *Utah State Today*, March 25, 2009.

67   "USU Student Fee Board Votes to Not Increase Athletics Fee," USU Student Media, undated, www.usu.edu/studentmedia/index.php/2016/02/04/usu-student-fee-board-votes-to-not-increase-athletics-fee/, accessed July 5, 2017.

68   Allie Grasgreen, "New Mexico Students Protest Continual Athletic Fee Increase," *Inside Higher Ed*, May 1, 2013.

69   Berkowitz, "Two States Require Fee Disclosure, but Athletics Charges Can Be Buried," *USA Today*.

70   Dr. Tony Frank, "Athletics—Why and At What Cost?" Colorado State University, December 2011, http://president.colostate.edu/athletics-why-and-at-what-cost.

71   George Leef, "Murray Sperber Blames College Sports for Poor Undergraduate Education," John William Pope Center for Higher Education Policy, March 29, 2004.

72   Frank, "Athletics—Why and at What Cost?" Colorado State University.

73   Steven Shulman, "Athletic Spending Drives up Tuition and Fees," *Rocky Mountain Collegian*, November 16, 2016.

74   Kelly Lyell, "Average Attendance for CSU Football Likely to Fall," *The Coloradoan*, November 12, 2015.

75   "$20 Million Gift Ensures Winning Tradition of 'Sonny Lubick Field' Continues at CSU's New On-Campus Stadium," Colorado State Rams, www.csurams.com/news/2016/3/25/_20_million_gift_ensures_winning_tradition_of_Sonny_Lubick_Field_continues_at_CSU_s_new_on_campus_stadium.aspx, March 25, 2016.

76   Sam Blackman, "History of IPTAY," September 5, 2000, www.clemsontigers.com/ViewArticle.dbml?ATCLID=205524148.

77   Arthur Padilla and Janice L. Boucher, "On the Economics of Intercollegiate Athletic Programs," *Journal of Sport & Social Issues* 11, Issue 1–2 (1987): 68.

78   Curry Kirkpatrick, "PAWS!" *Sports Illustrated*, October 23, 1989, www.si.com/vault.

79   Will Hobson, "At Thriving Clemson, Orange is the New Green," *Washington Post*, September 22, 2016.

80   Will Hobson and Steven Rich, "Colleges Spend Fortunes on Lavish Athletic Facilities," *Washington Post*, December 22, 2015.

81   "Schedule of Tuition and Mandatory Fees," University of Maryland, Fiscal 2017, Otcads.umd.edu.

82   Hobson and Rich, "Why Students Foot the Bill for College Sports, and How Some Are Fighting Back," *Washington Post*.

83   Ed McGranahan, "Clemson Ponders Athletics Fee for Students," *The State*, November 11, 2014.

84   Aaron Brenner, "Clemson Decides Against Charging Students for Football Tickets in 2016," (Charleston, SC) *Post & Courier*, June 28, 2016. The University of Michigan's Crisler Arena (now Crisler Center), home of the school's basketball teams, was built in 1967 with bonds financed by student fees, according to former UM president James J. Duderstadt. He criticizes the strategy of using special student fees to finance athletic facilities that the students would later have to purchase tickets to attend as a time-honored practice and example of the sleight of hand used to disguise the institutional subsidy of varsity sports. James J. Duderstadt, *Intercollegiate Athletics and the American University: A University President's Perspective* (Ann Arbor: University of Michigan Press, 2003), p. 327.

85   Marissa Heffernan, "Incoming Students Face New $100 Mandatory Athletics Fee," *The Daily Wildcat*, April 12, 2017, www.wildcat.arizona.edu/article/2017/04/incoming-students-face-new-100-mandatory-athletics-fee.

86   Jeff Metcalfe and Anne Ryman, "Student Fee Boosts ASU Athletic Revenue to Record $84 Million in 2014–15," *Arizona Republic*, March 3, 2016.

87   "K-State to Phase Out Annual Student Privilege Fees," October 17, 2015, www.kstatesports.com/news/k-state-to-phase-out-annual-student-privilege-fees-10-16-2015.

88   "Mandatory Fee Deemed Unfair for Students Who Dislike Sports," *The Oswegonian*, December 1, 2016.

89   Dan Miner, "ECC Board Chair Still Has 'Full Confidence' in Quinn as College President after State Audit," *Buffalo Business First*, January 19, 2016, www.bizjournals.com/buffalo/news/2016/01/14/ecc-board-chair-still-has-full-confidence-in-quinn.html.

90   Jay Tokasz, "Future of Hockey, Baseball in Question at ECC," *Buffalo News*, May 26, 2017.

91   Steve Berkowitz, Jodi Upton, Michael McCarthy, and Jack Gillum, "How Student Fees Boost College Sports amid Rising Budgets," *USA Today*, September 21, 2010.

92   "2017–18 Comprehensive Fee Components," Office of the Bursar, Radford University, www.radford.edu/content/bursar/home/accounts/tuition/CompFeeDist1718.html#par_text, accessed August 3, 2017.

93   Office of the Utah State Auditor, "NCAA Athletics Revenue Subsidization for Utah's Public Colleges and Universities," Analysis Report No. AR 15–02, July 7, 2015, p. 2.

94   Ibid.

95   Matthew Piper, "Report Shows State's NCAA Athletic Programs Received $56M Subsidy in 2014," *Salt Lake Tribune*, July 7, 2015.

96   Office of the Utah State Auditor, "NCAA Athletics Revenue Subsidization for Utah's Public Colleges and Universities," p. 2.

97   Ibid., p. 3.

98   Morgan Jacobsen, "State Audit Shows Costs to Students for NCAA Sports," *Deseret News*, July 7, 2015.

99   Piper, "Report Shows State's NCAA Athletic Programs Received $56M Subsidy in 2014," *Salt Lake Tribune*.

100 "Keep Your Eye on Utah College Athletic Program Costs," *Salt Lake Tribune*, editorial, July 8, 2015.

101 Morgan Jacobsen, "A Look at What's Behind Audit of University of Utah Athletics," *Deseret News*, February 28, 2016.

102 Ibid.

103 Annie Know and Kyle Goon, "Legislature Will Audit University of Utah Athletics in Wake of BYU Rivalry Suspension," *Salt Lake Tribune*, February 20, 2016.

104 Jacobsen, "A Look at What's Behind Audit of University of Utah Athletics," *Deseret News*.

105 Know and Goon, "Legislature Will Audit University of Utah Athletics in Wake of BYU Rivalry Suspension," *Salt Lake Tribune*.

106 Kyle Goon, "State Audit Dings University of Utah Athletic Department over Hiring, Travel and Equipment; Probe Finds Pac-12 Positives," *Salt Lake Tribune*, November 15, 2016.

107 Ibid.; Mark Green, "BYU vs. Utah Basketball Rivalry to Resume in 2017," http://fox13now.com/2016/05/26/byu-vs-utah-basketball-rivalry-to-resume-in-2017/, May 26, 2016.

108 Jere Longman, "As Costs of Sports Rise, Students Balk at Fees," *New York Times*, May 29, 2009.

109 Ibid.

110 Hopkins, "Illinois College Athletic Programs Heavily Funded by Students," *Chicago Tribune*.

111 Colt Kesselring, "How Much Money Each NCAA Tournament Team Earned for their Conference," *HEROSports*, March 26, 2017, http://herosports.com/ncaa-tournament/how-much-money-ncaa-tournament-earned-conference-2017-basketball-fund-a7a7.

112 Hopkins, "Illinois College Athletic Programs Heavily Funded by Students," *Chicago Tribune*.

113 Mike Vernon, "Student Senate Fights to Eliminate KU Athletics Title IX and Non-Revenue Sports Fee," *Daily Kansan*, February 18, 2014.

114   Hobson and Rich, "Why Students Foot the Bill for College Sports, and How Some are Fighting Back," *Washington Post*.

115   Grasgreen, "New Mexico Students Protest Continual Athletic Fee Increase," *Inside Higher Ed*.

116   Will Hobson and Steven Rich, "In NCAA, Big Revenue Means Bigger Spending," *Washington Post*, November 24, 2015.

117   Thomas, "Call to Curb Athletic Spending Strikes Some as Unrealistic," *Chronicle of Higher Education*.

118   Kentucky State Representative Joni Jenkins introduced legislation to ban public universities from levying mandatory athletics fees on commuters, but the bill went nowhere. Berkowitz, "Two States Require Fee Disclosure, but Athletics Charges Can Be Buried," *USA Today*.

119   Denhart and Vedder, "Intercollegiate Athletics Subsidies: A Regressive Tax," p. 16.

120   Hopkins, "Illinois College Athletic Programs Heavily Funded by Students," *Chicago Tribune*.

121   Longman, "As Costs of Sports Rise, Students Balk at Fees," *New York Times*.

122   Murray Sperber, *College Sports, Inc.: The Athletic Department vs. the University* (New York: Henry Holt, 1990), p. 83.

5

MONEY CHANGES EVERYTHING

David Riesman and Reuel Denney, coauthors of the sociological classic *The Lonely Crowd*, turned their focus to football in a 1951 essay for *The American Quarterly*. They observed how the sport at the college level had come to "resemble other industries or mechanized farms," in that entry required a large initial outlay: "The production of a team involves the heavy overhead and staff personnel characteristic of high-capital, functionally rationalized industries." The "entry fee" had become formidable enough to deter schools from taking up the sport; they instanced Milligan College of Tennessee, which in 1950 dropped football because it was consuming $17,000, or two-thirds of its athletic budget, and was not recouping this expenditure at the box office.[1] The school had learned a lesson about big-time college sports later pungently phrased by Indiana University basketball coach Bobby Knight: "If it isn't a business, then General Motors is a charity."[2]

But the business of sports has overgrown its customary courts and fields of play. At some state schools, it overshadows, or even overwhelms, academic pursuits. Richard Vedder warns that intercollegiate athletic spending "threatens to crowd out other higher education activities, including the core mission of teaching and research."[3] Salaries are, typically, the single most expensive line item in an athletic department budget. So we turn there next.

Is Nick Saban worth 50 full professors?

USA Today has done invaluable service for several years by compiling salaries of Division I men's basketball and FBS football coaches. It is, annually, an eye-opener, and one wonders why those who protest income inequality seem not to have noticed the glaring discrepancies between the pay of head football coaches at public—that is, taxpayer-supported—universities and those employed by those same universities in capacities that are educational rather than bone-shattering. The

18 most lavishly compensated college football coaches all ply their trade at public universities. It's not until #19 that we meet a private school coach: David Shaw of Stanford, whose $4,067,219 salary would merit barely a raised eyebrow in surrounding Silicon Valley.[4]

Is it worth it? Are those multimillion dollar coaches really all that much better than the fellow at the directional-state university who is making about as much as the University of Kentucky's rifle team coach? William Tsitsos and Howard L. Nixon II, writing in the *Journal of Sport & Social Issues*, tested the proposition that "paying top salaries to coaches assures or improves success on the field and in the rankings."[5] It does not. Using data from the 2003–4 through 2010–11 seasons, the researchers found that luring a big-money coach to your football or men's basketball team does not result in "sustained big-time success" in either the long or short terms.[6] And Jonathan Orszag and Mark Israel, in a 2009 study commissioned by the NCAA, found no significant relationship between coaching salaries and a team's record.[7] But don't tell that to coaches, their agents, and the athletic directors.

Excluding bonuses, contract-buyout provisions, expense accounts, and other perks, the ten most highly paid college football coaches in 2016 were: Jim Harbaugh, Michigan, $9,004,000; Nick Saban, Alabama $6,939,395; Urban Meyer, Ohio State, $6,003,000; Bob Stoops, Oklahoma, $5,550,000; Jimbo Fisher, Florida State, $5,250,000; Charlie Strong, Texas, $5,200,000; Kevin Sumlin, Texas A&M, $5,000,000; Gus Malzahn, Auburn, $4,725,000; Hugh Freeze, Mississippi, $4,700,000; James Franklin, Penn State and Kirk Ferentz, Iowa, $4,500,000.[8]

Charlie Strong, number six on our hit parade, was unceremoniously fired after a disappointing season at Texas, but shed no tears for Coach Strong: his buyout package was estimated at $11 million.[9] At least 36 coaches made $3 million or more, and at least 72 coaches had salaries of $1 million or more (figures were not available for nine of the 128 FBS teams), with Scottie Montgomery of East Carolina bringing up the rear of this millionaire list. Montgomery earned a cool mill for piloting the Pirates to a 3–9 record. The lowest paid coaches of the 128 FBS teams still made salaries high enough to put them in the top 1, or in some cases 2, percent of Americans in income. At bottom was New Mexico State's Doug Martin, whose income of $376,044 was almost ten times the average income of the bottom 99 percent of earners in the Land of Enchantment.[10] Aggies fans were disenchanted with the 3–9 record Martin's Sun Belt Conference team posted in 2016.

Coaches also make substantial money on the side through radio and television shows, speaking engagements, sports camps for children, and, for the real coaching royalty, cars and houses and lavish expense accounts. In addition, most coaches have performance bonuses built into their contracts. These bonuses are rather more elaborate than a gold watch or even a week's trip to Hawaii. They ran as high as $3.823 million for Arizona State's Todd Graham. Others who stood to rake in multiple millions if their teams did well included Iowa's Kirk Ferentz ($2.875 million), Kentucky's Mark Stoops ($2.8 million), Virginia's Bronco Mendenhall

($2.445 million), and Arizona's Rich Rodriguez ($2.025 million). What is it about Arizona's public universities that make them dangle such fat and luscious carrots before their football coaches? In any event, the carrots went uneaten in 2016, as Arizona State posted a 5–7 record and the University of Arizona stumbled to 3–9. Even New Mexico State's Doug Martin, lowest man on the totem pole, has the potential to earn a bonus of $135,000. Not much had changed when, shortly before publication, *USA Today* released the latest salary numbers. Alabama's Nick Saban ($8.307 million) had overtaken Michigan's Jim Harbaugh ($7.504 million), who had fallen to third, behind Ohio State's Urban Meyer, who pulled down $7.6 million in what proved to be his final year, as his failure to take more decisive steps against an assistant coach accused of sexual abuse led to Meyer's resignation.[11]

But save an ounce of pity for these fabulously paid motivators and drawers-up of Xs and Os. Myles Brand, former NCAA president, notes that "faculty members have the protection of tenure while coaches are employed at will and can be dismissed for lackluster win-loss records or the inappropriate behavior of 18- to 22-year olds."[12] On the other hand, rare is the D-I coach who would trade his salary, insecure as his future may be, for the security of tenure and an assistant professor's salary.

Between 1985–6 and 2009–10, according to Charles Clotfelter, while the average full professor's salary at the 44 public universities with football teams in the largest conferences increased by 32 percent (adjusted for inflation), the average compensation of the college presidents at those schools rose by 90 percent, and the average compensation for the football coaches rocketed by 750 percent.[13]

No one has ever accused college presidents of being underpaid, but their salaries are dwarfed by those of the football coaches whose putative bosses they are. According to the *Chronicle of Higher Education*, median take-home pay for college presidents was $431,000 in 2015, the most recent year for which figures were available. Leading the list was Renu Khator, president of the University of Houston, whose total compensation came to what *Forbes* called "a stunning $1.3 million."[14] That's a nice haul, to be sure, though Tom Herman, coach of President Khator's football team, had a salary of $3 million. (President Khator's fondest dream, it seems, is for Houston to leave the second-tier American Athletic Conference for a Power Five school.)

Five public university presidents had compensation above $1 million. Besides Khator, they were: Michael R. Gottfredson, University of Oregon, $1,215,142; Michael K. Young, Texas A&M, $1,133,333; William H. McRaven, University of Texas system, $1,090,909; and Mark P. Becker, Georgia State, $1,051,204. President Becker is that rara avis: a college president who makes more than the football coach! Tyson Summer, coach of Georgia State, pulled down just $500,000, or less than half of the president's munificent salary, but then the Panthers fared poorly (3–9) in 2016. Let them make a run at the Sun Belt title and Coach Summer may lap President Becker.

A 2014 study by Andrew Erwin and Marjorie Wood for the Institute for Policy Studies (IPS) concluded that "the student debt crisis is worse at state schools with the highest-paid presidents." They found that the 25 highest-paid public university presidents earned an average of $974,006 in 2012, or "nearly double the [$544,554] national average for public research university presidents." The highest paid public university president was Ohio State's Gordon Gee, with a total compensation of $8.9 million between FY 2008 and FY 2012.[15] Not bad, though current Ohio State coach Urban Meyer makes that much in less than a year and a half.

The IPS scholars awarded Ohio State top billing in its "Top 5 Most Unequal Public Universities," with Penn State a close second. Penn State's outgoing president, Graham Spanier, left campus in FY 2012 with a whopping $2.9 million in salary and severance after he was canned for mishandling the Jerry Sandusky pedophilia scandal.[16] (Severance pay for coaches is no less generous. In recent years, fired University of Illinois football coach Ron Zook pocketed $1.3 million, terminated University of California coach Jeff Tedford left Berkeley for a year's vacation in New Zealand with a $1.8 million deal, and the University of Maryland's erstwhile coach Ralph Friedgen cashed out at $2 million to spend a year playing golf and sailing. Will Hobson and Steven Rich of the *Washington Post* point out that Maryland's $406 per student athletics fee funds about 15 percent of the athletic budget, or about $300,000 toward the Friedgen buyout. The administrations awarding such generous packages are apparently unacquainted with scholarly research that shows little connection between the firing of a coach and a team's improvement over the next five years.[17])

Rubbing salt in faculty wounds, the percentage of adjunct faculty at the 25 public universities with the highest paid presidents rose at a rate 22 percent faster than the national average during the years 2005–11. All but two of those 25 college presidents served at FBS schools, the exceptions being the University of Delaware (#3) and George Mason University (#7). The weakest football program of the remaining 23 schools belongs to the aforementioned Georgia State (#20) of the ever-aspiring Sun Belt Conference.[18]

The greybeards among us, on hearing the words "assistant coach," may think of auto mechanics, insurance salesmen, and bartending yesterday's heroes who drop by practice after work (or drinking) and hold tackling dummies as a favor to their friend, the head coach. *Anachronism* doesn't do this image justice. For the 2016 season, *USA Today* found a dozen assistant football coaches whose salaries were $1 million or higher. Just one (Brian VanGorder, Notre Dame's defensive coordinator: $1,106,156) was employed by a private school, and he was fired partway through Notre Dame's disappointing season. (While *USA Today* had access to the salaries of public university employees, it had only partial access to private school payrolls, so it is possible that an assistant coach at, for instance, the University of Southern California may also have cracked the million dollar mark.)[19]

The highest paid assistant coach in 2016 was John Chavis, defensive coordinator of Texas A&M, who pulled down $1,558,000. Not bad for an 8–5 season. Chavis's boss, Kevin Sumlin, made $5 million, or five times the wage paid the university's president, Michael K. Young. The median salary of Texas A&M's 8,701 employees was $60,000.[20] The professors of agriculture and mechanics who built Texas A&M

would be astonished. The football-mad South dominates assistant coaches' pay (as well as results, most years). The Top Ten for 2016 were Texas A&M, Clemson, Alabama, LSU, Louisville, LSU, Baylor, Tennessee, Notre Dame, and Auburn. Putting aside Notre Dame, we don't find a school north of the Mason-Dixon line until #17 Michigan, which paid Don Brown $880,000 for his labors as a defensive coordinator.

These Brobdingnagian salaries for assistant coaches extend well into the nether reaches of the football world. Sitting at #132 is Drew Mehringer of perennial doormat Rutgers, who was paid a cool $450,000 as offensive coordinator of one of the worst offenses in America. As Ryan Dunleavy of NJ.com noted, Rutgers finished the season "ranked last out of 128 FBS teams with 283.2 yards per game of total offense, No. 122 in FBS in passing offense, No. 104 in rushing offense and No. 125 in first downs."[21] Was the nonmiracle worker Mehringer fired for this pathetic performance? Was his pay docked? Of course not—he jumped ship to serve as "pass game coordinator" for his friend Tom Herman, who left his $3 million job as head coach at the University of Houston to take the same position at the University of Texas, where his 2017 compensation was $5.25 million.[22] (Houston, like Texas, is a public university.)

Assistant coaches from the mid-majors start showing up well down the USA Today list, though their salaries still dwarf those of full professors at their universities. For instance, Boise State's Andy Avalos checks in at #290 with a salary of $309,500, San Diego State's Jeff Horton is at #296 ($300,012), and tied at #298 are Conference USA assistant coaches Tyrone Nix of Middle Tennessee and Nick Holt of Western Kentucky at an even $300,000. The lowest salaries on the USA Today list belonged to folks like linebackers coach Pat Bastien of the Sun Belt Conference's Georgia Southern and offensive line coach Johnson Richardson of Conference USA's Charlotte (tied at #957 with $50,000), and defensive line coach Colin Ferrell of the Mid-American Conference's Kent State at $42,840 (#962). (Johnson Richardson is the grandson of then-Carolina Panthers owner Jerry Richardson, so he could probably scrape by on the $50K.)[23]

Even strength coaches at the public university powerhouses pull down salaries beside which the average professor of biochemistry's paycheck looks downright puny. (USA Today was unable to determine the salaries of private school strength coaches, though again, since those are not funded by tax dollars they are outside our realm of concern.) The highest-paid strength coach in the survey was Iowa's Chris Doyle, whose pay was $625,000 in 2016. The rest of the top ten consisted of Alabama's Scott Cochran ($525,000), Ohio State's Mickey Marotti ($520,500), UCLA's Sal Alosi ($410,000), South Carolina's Jeff Dillman ($400,000), Oklahoma State's Rob Glass ($395,000), Ole Miss's Paul Jackson ($375,000), Clemson's Joey Batson ($368,833), Florida State's Vic Viloria ($362,000), and Missouri's Rohrk Cutchlow ($360,000). In all, 41 strength coaches earned salaries of $200,000 or above, and these included the Air Force Academy's Matt McGettigan, whose $204,000 income was covered almost entirely (the AFA does accept private gifts, mostly from alums) by the American taxpayer.[24]

Division I basketball coaches aren't eating ramen for dinner, either. The *USA Today* survey did not cover all 300-plus D-I coaches; rather, it was limited to the 68 coaches whose teams made the 2017 NCAA men's basketball tournament. Of the 63 coaches whose salaries were discoverable, 41 made at least $1 million annually. Topping the list was Louisville's controversial (and later fired) Rick Pitino, whose pay of $7,769,200 would have put him second, behind Michigan's Jim Harbaugh, among football coaches. Second on the list was the University of Kentucky's John Calipari, famed for his "one and done" players—exceptional athletes who attend UK for one year and don't even bother with the pretense of being students; they are there to audition for the NBA. Calipari's pay at this tax-payer-supported school was $7,453,376.

Duke's legendary Mike Krzyzewski was third at $5,550,475. Duke is a private university; all but one (Baylor's Scott Drew, at #9) of the remainder of the ten highest-paid men's basketball coaches toiled at public universities. They were Kansas's Bill Self ($4,932,626), Michigan State's Tom Izzo ($4,251,751), West Virginia's Bob Huggins ($3,590,000), Michigan's John Beilein ($3,370,000), Wichita State's Gregg Marshall ($3,035,500), and Virginia Tech's Buzz Williams ($2,655,000).

The lowest-paid coaches on this rather lucrative totem pole earned perhaps one-third as much as the lowest-paid FBS football head coaches. They were Jacksonville State's Ray Harper ($175,000), Mark Slessinger of the University of New Orleans ($120,000), and, bringing up the rear, the University of North Dakota's Brian Jones ($109,273).[25] The previous year's last-place finisher in the men's basketball coaching derby was University of North Carolina Asheville's Nick McDevitt, whose $124,000 salary still exceeded the average pay for a full professor at every school within the University of North Carolina system with the exception of the flagship UNC Chapel Hill, where the average salary for a full professor with a nine-month workload was $143,532.

The most recent figures show salaries trending—of course!— upward. Mike Krzyzewski of Duke sits atop the heap with an annual salary of $9 million, while in second place at $8 million is John Calipari of the University of Kentucky, still the king of the "one and done" basketball player who makes a mockery of the "student athlete" model. The disgraced Rick Pitino is out, at least until some desperate program gives him another chance. Rounding out the top five were Chris Holtmann of Ohio State ($7.1 million), Bill Self of Kansas ($5 million), and Tom Izzo of Michigan State ($4.4 million).[26]

The head coach of the University of North Carolina basketball team, Roy Williams, was the highest paid public official in the Tar Heel State, with an annual salary of $2,088,557, and a maximum potential bonus of another million. Margaret Spellings, president of the UNC system, had a base salary of $775,000 and received a bonus of $90,000 in 2017.[27] When in 2007 reporters for *The Daily Tar Heel*, the UNC student paper, pressed athletic director Dick Baddour on the matter of coaching salaries, he wrapped himself in the red, white, and blue:

I look at it in terms of, "What does it take for the University of North Carolina to be competitive and to attract and then maintain the high level of coaches?" We live in a great country, and a great country doesn't have those kind of restrictions. So I just have to live in that real world.[28]

Depicting a publicly subsidized university, whose existence is due not to the marketplace but rather the state, as the real world, in contrast to the dream world of those who worry about excessive public spending, was a nimble, almost gymnastic act by athletic director Baddour.

Women's basketball coaches make less, though their programs also bring in far less money for their schools. Geno Auriemma, who has piloted the University of Connecticut Huskies to a record 11 NCAA Division I championships, signed a five-year, $13 million contract in late 2016.[29] In recent years, UConn has been the only D-I women's basketball program to occasionally show a profit. Yet the salaries of women's coaches—most of whom are men—can consume an inordinate share of the revenue. Economist Andrew Zimbalist says, "It's insane. You show me a Fortune 500 company that would be profitable if the CEO got 75 percent of the revenue." At some schools, salaries alone actually outweigh total revenue from women's basketball programs.

When in 2011 the *New York Times* noted that the 53 public-school women's teams in the six major conferences lost $109.7 million, while their male counterparts claimed operating profits of $240 million, Atlantic 10 Conference commissioner Bernadette McGlade said:

> There is intrinsic value in being able to carry your own weight. For the amount of resources going into intercollegiate women's basketball, there's going to be a time where there has to be a rational decision of, is it worth it?[30]

That time hasn't come yet. Asked by *USA Today* whether escalating salaries for women's coaches were justified given the relatively modest earnings from television and ticket sales, Beth Bass, CEO of the Women's Basketball Coaches Association, pointed to the inspiration provided by outstanding female athletes and the fact that graduation rates are higher for women basketball players than for men.[31]

Even salaries for non-coaches have skyrocketed in recent years. A *Washington Post* investigation found that the non-coaching payrolls of 48 public schools in the Power Five conferences zoomed 69 percent (from $454 million to $767 million) between 2004 and 2014. Athletic directors scaled new heights in lucrativeness: over that same decade, UCLA athletic director Dan Guerrero's salary went from $299,000 to $900,000. Alabama's football support staff payroll climbed from $630,000 to $2.6 million in those ten years, which were marked by a serious recession that affected most of those outside the world of taxpayer-supported university athletic departments.[32]

The commissioners of the major conferences are no pikers in the salary department, either. The most recent available figures revealed commissioner salaries of

$4.3 million for the SEC's top dog, $4.05 million in the Pac-12, $2.7 million in the Big 12, $2.7 million in the ACC, and $2.4 million in the Big Ten. But don't cry for Big Ten commissioner Jim Delany in last place: he has $20 million bonus payments due over the next several years. In 2004, Delany's salary was $549,000, but the almost fourfold increase was worth it, said University of Minnesota president Eric Kaler, because Delany had "successfully balanced the missions of academic achievement, student-athlete development and athletic success." Notwithstanding, one supposes, the football scandals at Ohio State and the pedophilia scandal at Penn State. Delany's real value was in helping to boost the conference's annual revenue well above $500 million per year, with 2017 disbursals of $34.8 million to eleven of the anachronistically named Big Ten's 14 member schools. The three new-bies—Nebraska, poached from the Big 12, Rutgers, ex of the Big East, and Maryland, formerly of the ACC—received lesser amounts, for not all schools are created equal.[33]

The money comes, the money goes

Football, especially, is a very expensive sport: there are capital costs that include construction or maintenance of a stadium seating tens of thousands of people; sal-aries of myriad coaches and support personnel; player scholarships, travel, equip-ment, medical care, game-day employees, public relations—even in the case of FBS football and Division I basketball, these almost always outpace revenue derived from ticket sales, television, concessions, gifts, merchandise sales, royalties, corporate sponsors, parking, media payments (radio and television), student fees, university subsidies, and bowl or tournament or conference payouts. The single largest item in the average athletic department expenditure sheet is salaries and benefits, which eat up 32 percent of the budget. This is followed by tuition and scholarships (16 percent), facilities maintenance and rental (14 percent), travel, recruiting, and equipment (12 percent), and a combination of fundraising costs, game-day expenses, guaranteed payments to opponents, medical expenses, and miscellaneous (12 percent).[34]

Scholarship costs are particularly high for public schools that recruit primarily out of state: for instance, at the University of Oregon, where 80 percent of scholarship athletes are non-Oregonians.[35] This raises the question, which coaches never bother to answer, of whether a state university, propped up by the tax dollars of state residents, ought to give preference to in-state over out-of-state athletes.

Ticket sales for the glamour FBS programs can account for as much as 30 per-cent of revenue; the bottom feeders struggle to meet a 10 percent level.[36] And while school officials may fill the air with clichés about equality and closing the gap between rich and poor, limiting salaries, putting a cap on expenditures, or other-wise leveling the economic playing field is off the table for discussion. As Big Ten commissioner Jim Delany replied when asked about such proposals, "When I look at Harvard or Yale and their endowments, I do not see money moving to Haver-ford or Hofstra."[37]

Desperate circumstances call for desperate means. For instance, doormats that run chronic deficits take appearance guarantee fees from powerhouses looking to wipe their feet. Yes, there's something unseemly about being paid to take one on the nose, but you do what you have to do. As an example, Mississippi Valley State, an historically black and underfunded college, picked up $800,000 by getting whipped by basketball powers Indiana, Butler, Kentucky, and Marquette in 2012, thereby enabling the school to put in a badly needed new floor on the hoops court. The school's entire athletics budget that year was $4 million.[38]

At bigger-budget schools, belt-tightening is for the English and physics departments. D-I schools routinely engage in ridiculously wasteful practices such as lodging football and basketball teams in local hotels the night before home games, or bringing a caravansary of hundreds of hangers-on to bowl games, all on the athletic department's dime. Schools typically spend most or all of their bowl game payout on bowl-related costs. Washington State University economist Rodney D. Fort noted that when his school's team went to the Copper Bowl in Tucson in 1992, its athletic department spent the entire $650,000 Copper Bowl purse, with the bulk of it ($345,000) going to air transportation, lodging, and food for "approximately 200 players, coaches, administrators, faculty, staff, and their families," and much of the rest on the purchase of 10,000 tickets, of which about half were sold.[39]

The athletic director, if he or she oversees a powerful enough department, sometimes reports directly to the school's president. FBS and Division I athletic departments are, compared to academic departments, semiautonomous, often with hundreds of employees. Faculty and trustees have little say in matters of athletics. The professor of classics may despair all she wants to over the corrosive influence of football or D-I basketball, but its operations are almost entirely beyond her reach. As Peter N. Stearns, University Professor and Provost Emeritus at George Mason University, notes, due to the often pathetically lax academic standards for D-I athletes, "in many athletic hotbeds, provosts and other academic officials are warned to keep a distance" lest their interference compromise a star athlete's eligibility.[40] For all the hypocritical cant about "student-athletes," most coaches and athletic directors have a firm fix on which of those hyphenated terms is firmly in the noun's place, and which is merely a weak adjective.

The claim is often made that the bounties brought in by football and basketball are worth it, despite the occasional embarrassments, because this money enriches other departments which don't have television contracts and 80,000 people buying tickets to watch them function on fall Saturdays. In fact, as the *Chronicle of Higher Education* discovered, "less than $1 of every $100 generated by major college athletic departments at public colleges is directed to academic programs." As Brad Wolverton and Sandhya Kambhampati reported in 2016, while 40 of the 205 athletic programs in the study claimed to have transferred money to academic activities in their parent school, in most cases these transfers amounted to less than the institutional subsidies and student athletic fees they received. Only ten athletic departments—those of the University of Texas at Austin, Ohio State, University of Alabama, University of Florida, LSU, University of Oklahoma, University of

Nebraska, University of Kentucky, University of Michigan, and Purdue—can truthfully claim to have transferred money back to the school. In four cases (Texas: $37.147 million; Ohio State: $36.283 million; LSU: $19.037 million; and Oklahoma: $11.114 million), the transfer exceeded $10 million over the four-year period. In the case of Texas, its television network, which partners with ESPN, will bring in $10–$15 million each year through 2031, with half dedicated to academics. (Calculating net profit or loss can be tricky, since some athletic departments include expenses for the general student population—physical education, facilities maintenance—or exclude depreciation on the cost of facilities.)

Gene Smith of Ohio State, a school whose spokesmen have never been reluctant to mix pious public pronouncements with football-factory ethics, said of giving back, "When you're at our level, we should be doing that . . . It is a behavioral thing that I think some places need to shift."[41]

DeLoss Dodds, Texas athletic director from 1981–2013, under whose guidance the athletic budget at UT skyrocketed from $4.5 million to almost $170 million, explained to Gilbert Gaul, author of *Billion-Dollar Ball: A Journey Through the Big-Money Culture of College Football* (2015): "Football is the train that drives everything and pays for everything. It just is. Everything begins and ends with football." Over that same period Dodds's salary rose from $65,000 to $1.1 million. The university, as Gaul wrote, spends $261,728 on each of its football players annually but less than one-tenth of that, $20,903, on each student.[42] Its unusually profitable football team is the centerpiece of an essentially autonomous athletic department. Sure, its panjandrums pull down salaries of five or even 20 times that of UT's professors, but when's the last time 100,119 people packed Darrell K Royal-Texas Memorial Stadium to watch a Physics 101 lesson?

The University of Texas's chief financial officer said, "We eat what we kill," and its meaning was broken down by Dodds:

> Texas athletics pays its own way. We don't get anything from the university. The university used to fund women's athletics, but over time we took that over. We cover all of that fully, and the way we do it is with the money we make off of football.[43]

This is only possible at the largest and most productive football manufactories, with their expensive seat licenses, their sold-out 100,000-capacity stadia, their lucrative television deals, their bowl revenue, their deep-pocketed and fanatical alumni. By contrast, Weber State, Charlotte, and UL-Monroe are sticking their students with the bills.

The economic model of a school like Texas raises thorny ethical questions about the purpose of a university, but no one in the athletic department is losing sleep over *those*. Gilbert Gaul notes that the athletic department does owe $243 million on its "stadiums, arenas, and practice facilities," with an annual mortgage payment of $18 million, but this is easily affordable—as long as the well never runs dry.[44] And for all the bluster of their officials, the Longhorns, wrote Gaul, with their $170 million budget, were sponsoring only 20 varsity teams with 549 athletes. Just 2 percent of Texas undergrads played a varsity sport, the same as at Auburn, Georgia, Florida, Oregon, and LSU. Michigan and Alabama were at 3 percent. Private schools were much higher: Harvard (15 percent), Princeton (19 percent), Williams (37 percent), Haverford (34 percent), Amherst (31 percent), and even MIT (17 percent), for goodness sake, eternally mocked as geek central, had wider athletic participation than is found at the major state universities.[45] (Not that we need to swallow whole the self-advertisements of the Ivies and little Ivies. No one really believes that Ivy League football and basketball players have the same academic qualifications as other students, and occasionally a serious scandal, such as that engulfing Harvard basketball in 2012, reveals the blemishes. How far Harvard had come from the days when President Eliot could say, with an easily lampooned priggishness:

> Well, this year I'm told the team did well because one pitcher had a fine curve ball. I understand that a curve ball is thrown with a deliberate attempt to deceive. Surely this is not an ability we should want to foster at Harvard.)[46]

Dave Brandon, CEO of Domino's Pizza for 11 years before taking over as Michigan's athletic director, told Jeff Benedict and Armen Keteyian, authors of *The System: The Glory and Scandal of Big-Time College Football* (2013):

> If anybody looked at the business model of big-time college athletics, they would say this is the dumbest business in the history of the world. You just don't have the revenue to support the costs. And the costs continue to go up.[47]

Brandon oversaw a $250 million sports facilities renovation project before resigning under pressure in October 2014. Students and alumni demanded his scalp for various offenses, ranging from his proposal to enliven games with fireworks—seen as an offense against tradition—to his hiring of Brady Hoke, who failed to field top-flight football teams, to his imposition of personal seat license fees. Brandon even junked the pregame marching band for the same rock-pop-rap pap they play in every other sports venue in America. It was the Domino's–ization of Michigan.[48] But you can't say Brandon didn't deliver for his department: by the time he left his post, Michigan's spending per athlete was up by 36 percent over the previous six years, while its academic spending per student was down by 3 percent.[49]

Seat licenses, à la Brandon, may offend fans' sense of fairness, but they have become as fixed a part of the college football scene as the goalposts. And to soften the blow, they carry tax advantages. According to the IRS, 80 percent of the "donation" one makes to obtain a seat license for a college football season is deductible. (Donation? Try *not* donating and see if you still get your seat.) These donations can range from a couple hundred dollars to tens of thousands of dollars per seat depending on the program and the seat location. For instance, Preferred

Seat Donations at the University of Michigan for the 2016–17 season at Michigan Stadium ranged from $78 for an end zone seat to $630 for a seat on the 50-yard line to $4,000 for an indoor club level seat to between $40,000–$90,000 for a 16-seat suite. At the UM's Crisler Center basketball arena, Preferred Seat Donations ranged from $100 annually for the worst seats in the house—no, actually, the worst seats in this house and most others are reserved for students—to $2,500–$6,000 for courtside seats to $12,500–$15,000 for six-seat "Championship Boxes."[50] It's a dog eat dog world out there, and Wolverines coach Jim Harbaugh's is not the face one usually associates with charities. During the 2016 football season, Virginia Tech and Notre Dame were the only schools in the top 30 in attendance that did not charge seat licenses, though in 2017 Virginia Tech began charging Hokies fans between $50–$800 for the privilege of being able to buy a season ticket.[51] But hey, it's deductible.

As Gilbert Gaul details in his fine book, the Internal Revenue Service issued a ruling in 1984 that college football seat donations were *not* a charitable contribution and should not be deductible, but after years of wrangling, in 1988 Congress enacted legislation codifying the 80 percent tax deduction. Russell Long (D-LA) of the Senate Finance Committee and Rep. Jake Pickle (D-TX) of the House Ways and Means Committee served as blocking backs, sweeping what little opposition there was off its feet.[52] It's no coincidence that Long and Pickle represented states with major college football and basketball programs. Professor John D. Colombo of the University of Illinois College of Law has estimated that the federal tax deduction for donations to athletic booster clubs and for seat preferences amounts to at least a $200 million subsidy. He says that the feds are "essentially subsidizing seat licenses for wealthy football fans. As a tax theorist, I find that offensive. But that's the way it is."[53]

Division III sports programs all run at a deficit, but then that is expected. No one believes that the English or astronomy department at good old State U. is going to operate at a profit; assuming, as Andrew Zimbalist writes, that:

> [T]he athletic programs at these schools are an integral part of the educational curriculum, as opposed to a commercial appendage to the university, then there is presumably nothing wrong with an athletic department deficit as long as it is within manageable proportions.[54]

But are athletics really "an integral part" of a meaningful educational curriculum?

Sugar daddies: private and public

There is one shortcut to athletic riches, though it comes with a catch: the megabucks sugar daddy. Phil Knight, Nike founder and University of Oregon grad, Class of 1959, financed a $60 million renovation of UO's Autzen Stadium, and, in late 2016, announced a $500 million gift, to be paid in ten yearly installments of $50 million, to build the school a science complex.[55] Michael Schill, the university's president, told *The Oregonian* that this was "the largest donation to a public flagship university in the nation's history."[56] The Knight surname also graces the school's library and law school. He is that rare sports booster whose alms also go academic.

Knight, whose net worth is estimated at $26 billion, has built a fortune on running shoes, and it is the running sports with which his name is most strongly linked. The Oregon Ducks basketball team's home is the Matthew Knight Arena, its eponym Knight's late son, and toward which the Nike mogul is believed to have contributed $100 million, or about a third of the total sum he has given to Oregon athletics over the years.[57] Among Knight-subsidized projects is Oregon's $41.7 million academic support building for athletes, which features "a three-story atrium, a 113-seat auditorium," and a "room of bronze athlete-award statues commissioned by a Spanish artist whose sculptures are featured at the Olympic Museum in Lausanne, Switzerland." And just in case a member of the women's soccer or swim team might forget who is footing the bill for all this, a "larger-than-life mirror etching of Knight" decorates the second and third-floor women's restrooms. Nike designs Oregon's uniforms and accessories—its football team never repeats a color combination—and its ubiquitous swoosh logo might as well decorate (or deface) the university's entry gates.

In return for his generosity, Knight has privileges not enjoyed in the dreams of even the most ardent booster. He can listen to the Ducks' football coaches call plays over a special headset. He receives private tutorials from offensive and defensive coaches.[58] When Oregon's men's basketball team won a big March Madness game against Kansas in 2017, 79-year-old Phil Knight was on the ladder under the backboard, cutting down the net in celebration.

And yet, for all this alms-giving showered on the school in Eugene, University of Oregon students are *still* paying an athletics tax. Among the mandatory UO fees is an "incidental fee," $71 of which is funneled to the athletics department in return for a chance to enter a lottery to win tickets to football and basketball games. There are 23,634 students but only 3,948 available student tickets for home football games against Pac-12 opponents, 1,849 tickets for home football games against nonconference foes, and 1,854 tickets for men's home basketball games. Most students come up lottery losers. If they want to attend a game, they'll need to spend hundreds of dollars for season tickets. In 2017, UO's Nike-bloated athletic department raised $2.3 million from these student ticket plans.[59]

Despite Oregon's boast that its athletic department is self-sufficient, *Oregonian* reporter Rachel Bachman revealed in 2010 that the school had drawn on the general fund to the tune of about $8.5 million over the previous nine years for tutoring and other academic support for its athletes. Oregon State had similarly drawn on the university for academic support for athletes ($636,000 annually at the time of Bachman's report), but then OSU, the poor sister in this relationship, never claimed to be self-sufficient. Among the comments on Bachman's article was this from an instructor at UO who called himself or herself "duckteacher":

Unlike most of the posters here I have direct knowledge how UO athletes use far more than their share of academic resources. I teach these student-athletes on a day to day basis. Many, though not all, do not have the academic skills to be in college. It is no wonder that they need all of that extra funding from Support for Student Athletes, which provides one on one tutoring and plenty of other hand holding support that other students would love access to, to maintain a barely passing GPA to keep their eligibility. On top of that, because some of these students are often not prepared and not interested in academics they are a drain on the classroom space for other students and student athletes that want to learn.

The real tragedy is that many of these stars are not getting any kind of real education. When they blow out their knee next season and can barely read at a 5th grade level where are those donors that will keep them going? If you want to do a service to these young people then make sure they get an education and not just a ride to passing grades on a cloud of money. If you want big time sports then get some more pro teams, Oregon, and stop exploiting these young people in our educational institutions.[60]

T. Boone Pickens, oilman and hedge fund chairman and, critically, a 1951 alumnus of a different OSU, Oklahoma State University (which was then called Oklahoma A&M), has made a series of donations earmarked for athletics totaling at least $265 million to his alma mater. The single biggest piece of that philanthropic mega-gift was $165 million—paid in full—to help build facilities for the football, soccer, track, and tennis teams. The resurgent Cowboys football program now plays in Boone Pickens Stadium. Pickens has not ignored non-pigskin-related pursuits, either, as the name of the Boone Pickens School of Geology at OSU indicates. (The previous record for the largest single gift to a college athletics program was held by Ralph Engelstad, who parlayed a $100 million fraction of his Las Vegas casino-derived fortune into the Ralph Engelstad Arena at his alma mater, the University of North Dakota.)[61]

At some point, the chronic loser must face reality—unless, that is, one can count on a steady stream of student fees. But if you've tapped out your students, fleeced them with fees, and you haven't enough (or any) billionaire graduates who want their names plastered to stadia or training facilities, where do you turn? To the state legislature, of course.

The invaluable data set compiled by USA Today reveals that in the most recent period for which figures are available (2015–16), 34 of the 230 Division I public schools (15 percent) received direct state or other government support for athletics. Leading the pack, predictably, was Army, whose athletics programs were enriched by $13.1 million in taxpayer monies. (Navy and Air Force, whose athletic departments have nonprofit status, were not required to file this information with the NCAA.) Other sports programs receiving more than $2 million in direct taxpayer subsidies—from state governments, in contrast to federal government-dependent Army—were the University of Nevada at Las Vegas ($7.3 million), the University of Nevada ($5.2 million), the University of Wyoming ($4.9 million), Idaho State ($3.6 million), New Mexico State ($3.4 million), Northern Arizona ($3.2 million), and New Mexico, North Dakota State, and Boise State (each at $2.8 million).

Setting the special case of Army aside, these dependents are almost all Western and Rocky Mountain schools with FBS programs in non-elite conferences. Five are members of the Mountain West. (Northern Arizona and North Dakota State are D-I in basketball but FCS in football.) Boise State is a regular in the purlieus of the Top 25, but the other FBS programs are often in the doldrums, at best, though on occasion Nevada and Wyoming produce pleasant surprises.

In the case of Wyoming, as Steve Berkowitz and Paul Myerberg document in *USA Today*, the university received $20 million in state matching funds toward a $44 million athletic training facility, and $15 million in matching funds toward a $30 million basketball arena renovation. Tom Burman, UW athletics director, defended the subsidy:

> It's easy to say no right now when there are important projects in the state that are being cut. Some could say, "This really isn't important." I say it's an economic engine. I also say it's important for the institution, the university, and we only have one.[62]

Priorities, priorities. If the classic choice in federal fisc is between guns and butter, among the decisions university administrators must make is one between academics and athletics. Or, in shorthand, books or balls.

In 2012, John V. Lombardi, professor of history at Louisiana State University, compared the recent spending on libraries and athletic subsidies of the 64 Division I schools that are also members of the Association of Research Libraries. Spending on sports, writes Lombardi, "represents an institutional investment that the institution could have allocated to academic enterprises but instead uses to pay part of the cost of the intercollegiate athletic program, a nonacademic enterprise." He found that eight schools—the University of Delaware, Ohio University (which shows up everywhere subsidies are discussed, doesn't it?), the University of Massachusetts at Amherst, Kent State, SUNY Stony Brook, the University of California at Davis, the University of Houston, and SUNY Albany—spent more on athletic subsidies—not athletic *budgets*, merely athletic *subsidies*—than they did on total library expenditures. Four of these—Delaware, Davis, Albany, and Stony Brook— had Division I basketball programs and played FCS football, while OHIO and Kent State play in the fee-heavy MAC. The sports subsidy to library expenditure ratio ranged from 1.52 for Delaware ($28.54 million/$18.74 million) to zero for barely more than a handful of schools where athletics pays its own way (LSU, Ohio State, Penn State, Purdue, University of Nebraska at Lincoln, University of Oklahoma, and the University of Texas at Austin).[63]

Lombardi's home base of Louisiana State University literally had to choose between books and balls three-quarters of a century ago. When LSU, squeezed by the exigencies of World War II, was faced with a choice between continuing to subsidize the *Southern Review*, its acclaimed literary magazine, or keeping its tiger mascot fed with fresh meat, it was bye-bye, litterateurs. Poets can starve, but carnivores must be fed.[64]

The other guys aren't doing so badly, either

While fully 78 percent of athletic operating expenses for men's sports at D-I FBS schools are directed toward football and basketball, minor sports at major athletic universities are hardly holding bake sales to buy equipment.[65] At the University of Kentucky, for instance, even the coaches of minor or Olympic sports are cashing in. Between 2006 and 2016, salaries zoomed for coaches in track and field ($108,000 to $429,000), men's tennis ($122,000 to $230,000), and gymnastics ($112,000 to $252,000)—this despite the fact that the 20 varsity sports other than football and men's basketball, whose ticket sales totaled $16.4 million and $19.5 million, respectively, in 2016, accounted for just $1.3 million in ticket sales.

Tennis, lacrosse, swimming: the vast majority of intercollegiate sports have no hope of "paying for themselves," which is not in and of itself a problem, if the budgets, especially for travel and coaching, are kept reasonable. But as Will Hobson noted in the *Washington Post*, every varsity coach at the University of Kentucky makes more than the average salary of a full professor at UK. Even the rifle coach—*the rifle coach*—made $133,000, or $12,000 more than the average for a full professor. Kentucky is no anomaly. The *Post*'s investigation also revealed big 2006–16 boosts in the salaries of such non-glamour positions as University of Kansas men's golf coach ($84,000 to $201,000) and University of Virginia women's volleyball coach ($94,000 to $221,000). Not even the most creative athletic department accountant would claim that ticket sales and TV revenue are funding these jobs. And these huge raises were made during a major recession that held the rise in median pay for the average American worker to just 0.7 percent over the decade.[66]

Softball, soccer, track and field, and even lacrosse coaches at public D-I schools, especially in the major conferences, routinely pull in salaries in the hundreds of thousands of dollars. Median expenses for a sport like track and field typically exceed revenue by a factor of ten, 20, even 30—but what does it matter?[67] As University of Florida president J. Bernard Machen told the *New York Times*, when asked about a raft of athletic expenses, including a $15 million lacrosse complex:

> If we are going to compete in something, we want to win at it—whether it is in pediatrics or women's gymnastics. It is important to our supporters, both financial and among our community. It is part of our culture. We want people to know that Florida is a place for winners.

Putting aside the curious notion of "winning" at pediatrics, the university had, over the three previous years, laid off 139 faculty and staff due to state budget cuts, but the athletic budget kept rising.[68]

The exceptions to the boom in minor sports are those men's sports that have been cut for a combination of reasons, among them reduced high school participation and pressures from Title IX. For instance, NCAA men's gymnastics, which had more than 200 programs half a century ago, is down to 16 teams. They represent a mixture of schools, both high-profile (Ohio State, Stanford, Illinois, Oklahoma) and at the margins of the average sports fan's consciousness (Springfield College, William and Mary).

UC Berkeley is one of the sweet 16, though as the only public Pac-12 school to field a men's gymnastics team, it competes in the makeshift Mountain Pacific Sports Federation. When the university announced in September 2010 that it was giving men's gymnastics and four other sports—women's gymnastics, baseball, rugby, and women's lacrosse—the quietus, supporters of those venerable if non-revenue producing teams went to work raising money. The other four raised the necessary funds without overly much fuss, but it took more time for men's gymnastics to hit its $4 million target. With an annual budget of over half a million dollars and a squad of between 15 and 20, it lacked the fundraising base of higher-profile "minor" sports like baseball and women's gymnastics. As the Berkeley story played out, supporters of gymnastics expressed their frustration. "Do we need 110 kids playing football at every major university, even though 60 of them will never see the light of day in four years?" asked Bob Wuornos of the Men's Intercollegiate Gymnastics Support Program.[69]

These nonrevenue sports haven't even the justification that they provide entertainment or foster community. Few attend their games or meets, and the likelihood of an ordinary student walking on to the team is minimal. Their existence can only be justified if fielding athletic teams is a core, or at least significant peripheral, function of the university.

Movin' on up

The paucity of athletic programs that can plausibly be called profitable is no secret, yet the lure of the D-I siren song seems too powerful to resist. At the author's home perch, George Mason University, we are best known, sports-wise, for our men's basketball team, which as a member of the mid-major Colonial Athletic Conference shocked the basketball world by donning Cinderella's slipper and making the NCAA Final Four in 2006. The Patriots moved into the more athletically prestigious Atlantic 10 Conference in 2013. GMU's Provost Emeritus Stearns notes that despite the success of the basketball team, when "a new president came on the scene, football issues constituted far and away the number one topic of conversation" on campus.[70] In the eyes of the sports-mad, if you don't have a Division I football team you're just not an elite university. (Tell that to the University of Chicago, Case Western, MIT, Caltech . . .)

Yet even schools that not even the most delusional booster would call elite are adding football teams at a rate belying the common view that due to concussion-related injuries and the expense of maintaining a team, football is, or soon will be, on the wane.[71] The number of colleges fielding NCAA teams (FBS, FCS, Division II, and Division III) increased from 484 in 1978 to 668 in 2016, and if you add in the NAIA and independent teams that climbs to a record 777 college football teams in the 2017 season.[72]

In recent years, "commuter schools"—Georgia State, UNC Charlotte, the University of Texas at San Antonio—have been the most common newcomers to the FBS party. While these launches are justified by scenarios that would make Pollyanna seem a sourpuss skeptic, they are not impulsive but rather part of strategic plans, or visions, or whatever the academic business-speak term of the day may be. The hope is that the presence of a football team, with all the hype and color and excitement that may bring, will enhance the ordinary student's experience and make for a "better college product."[73] Tailgating, homecoming, banners proclaiming BEAT THE UNIVERSITY OF SOUTH ALABAMA: football and festivity go together like a cold beer and its koozie. (Binge drinking, assaults, and special treatment for academically unprepared athletes are also part of that package, alas.)

Less facetiously, advocates of a move to FBS status invariably hope that big-time football, or at least football played against big-time schools, will bring (preferably deep-pocketed) alumni back to campus and residents of the surrounding area to campus on high-spirited Saturday game days. The heightened visibility as a result of a higher-profile football team may also, it is hoped, encourage applications for enrollment, though whether these additional applicants are likelier to be talented scholars or jock-worshiping mediocre students is not a settled question. One might assume that a high school senior who applies to, say, Ohio State because its football team is a national titlist is more fanboy or fangirl than brainiac, but it is certainly possible that in a general way, the wider name recognition generated by big-time athletic schools draws in serious students, too, functioning much as "a national advertising campaign."[74]

In their inspection of football feasibility studies from those schools exploring the possibility of adding the sport, Darren Kelly and Marlene A. Dixon found such wishful-thinking sentences as "The representatives envisioned the football program as the tool that would bring the student body together for a common cause and help cultivate the culture of GSU [Georgia State University] into a 'real university'" and "Consistently it was expressed that football would help increase the public perception that UNC Charlotte is a great institution." (The latter was a perception previously unperceived.) The UTSA report asked if the San Antonio school would "ever be considered a leading university without sponsoring a successful and visible football program."[75]

Fostering a sense of community was the most frequent benefit cited in the feasibility studies, followed by student recruitment, financial gain, prestige, and media exposure. Amusingly—or depressingly:

> [T]he feasibility studies were . . . completely lacking in discussion or even mention of the educational benefits of football programs. In fact, if one did

not know that these were feasibility studies for universities, one would have no indication that they were dealing with matters related to education at all.[76]

Football was seen as a passkey to the big time by the administrators at the University of North Carolina at Charlotte, which since its creation in 1946 had only sponsored a gridiron team, and a rather desultorily scheduled team at that, from 1946–8. Fast forward six decades. In 2007, Chancellor Philip Dubois appointed a committee charged with studying the feasibility of bringing football back to the campus. The UNC Charlotte Football Feasibility Committee operated under six assumptions, covering such areas as Title IX compliance, the need for conference membership, and the permanency of any decision, but with nary a word about academics. More important, it seems, was that "Any decision on football must protect and, if possible, strengthen the national positioning of men's basketball for post-season play and contribute to the further strengthening of women's basketball and all other athletic programs."[77] That's setting priorities!

The committee examined two scenarios: the impact of adding a football team, and the impact of not doing so. The latter, it concluded, was a bad bargain. UNC Charlotte's football-less condition, and its resultant less than desirable athletic conference, made scheduling quality competition difficult for the men's and women's basketball teams. Alumni had exiguous ties to the school because it lacked a football team. Their monetary contributions reflected that enthusiasm deficit. The surrounding community of Charlotte felt no strong bond with the school. And, in a rare mention of readin', writin', and 'rithemetic, "The projected growth of the University demands continued academic excellence as UNC Charlotte establishes a national reputation. Without the addition of football, the athletic program will be unable to reach its potential to match the academic reputation of excellence."[78] Whence this reputation for academic excellence came is a bit of a mystery, but no matter: adding a football program would solve all problems. The committee asserted that it would make scheduling easier for the basketball teams; it would aid the recruitment of student and faculty; it would strengthen ties between the school and both alumni and the community, thus encouraging donations; it would build school spirit; it would "brand" the university; and "football would help increase the public perception that UNC Charlotte is a great institution."[79]

The committee unanimously recommended that UNC Charlotte add football—or "men's football," as it gratuitously termed the sport.[80] Skeptics came out of the woodwork, or the ivy, as it were. C.D. "Dick" Spangler, former president of the University of North Carolina system, told UNC Charlotte faculty that "I fear that football will damage the university's academic position." Football would suck up more and more money, and students can only be beggared so much through the imposition of fees. Academic departments would pay the price. "As university people," said former president Spangler, "what we must guard against above all is the integrity of the institutions where we teach and serve."[81] Given the scandal brewing at the University of North Carolina at Chapel Hill (which is discussed in Chapter 6), a travesty that dwarfs anything that has happened in Charlotte, such cautions seem punchless, even querulous. And two years later, without fuss, the University of North Carolina Board of Governors approved the additional fees necessary to install football as the newest 49ers sport. Student Body President Joey Lemons expressed the hope that UNC Charlotte's days as a "suitcase campus" were over.[82]

Because adding football would double the UNC Charlotte athletic budget, the committee had urged the university to implement a student fee. It estimated that such a fee would provide two-thirds of football revenues; in fact, the figure has been closer to three-fourths. What was already a substantial annual athletics fee of $1,160 per student in 2003–4 reached $1,648 in 2017–18.[83]

The committee also recommended that the 49ers be built a new stadium in which to play. They were: the $40 million Jerry Richardson Stadium, its construction funded by the sale of state bonds, opened in time for the inaugural 2013 season. Questioned about the financial burden, UNC Charlotte athletic director Judy Rose said, "People always talk about the cost of football. They ought to look at the cost of not having football." She added, "If we're going to be the university we want to be, if we're going to be perceived as the university we want to be perceived as, football is the way to get there."[84] As for the burdensome student fee, Ms. Rose told Libby Sander of the *Chronicle of Higher Education*, "I certainly wish we wouldn't have to tax the students as much, but at the same time, this is their desire (underline in original)."[85]

Schools like UNC Charlotte rushed into football despite the 2008 recession and despite straitened budgets at state-sponsored schools. Philip Dubois, the UNC Charlotte chancellor, said, "Your academic opportunities open up when you're perceived as an institution of significance and quality, and if you do football right you'll be able to help achieve that."[86] But why should anyone assume that UNC Charlotte had even a remote chance of doing football right? Murray Sperber said at the time of the feasibility study,

> Charlotte, in a basketball region, would have trouble getting blue chippers. Since Duke, Chapel Hill, and NC State all lose in football, how will Charlotte do it from the bottom of a rather thin food chain? How will it get players from football-rich states like Georgia and Florida? It will hire a coach who will go into those states and recruit guys who can play but are so marginal socially and academically that the ACC and Big East won't touch them. How will the resulting scandals help Charlotte?[87]

The early returns from Charlotte are not promising. The 2013 and 2014 teams played an independent schedule in the FCS, posting sub-.500 records. Since joining the big boys in Conference USA of the FBS in 2015, UNC Charlotte has posted records of 2–10, 4–8, and 1–11. The only ranked team they played in 2016 or 2017, the University of Louisville, crushed the 49ers by a score of 70–14. As for the envisioned leap in the academic reputation of the school, in the admittedly dubious, but popular, *U.S. News & World Report* rankings of "Best Colleges" for

2017, UNC Charlotte tied for #202 out of 310 schools in the national universities category.[88] It does rank highly, however, in the category of percentage (74 percent) of the athletic budget that is supplied by subsidies.[89]

No doubt it's a brief thrill to see your school featured on ESPN, or your stadium packed with cheering fans, the parking lot abuzz with tailgaters, but these images obscure the reality that UNCC is going to lose millions of dollars on football, suffer with a losing team for years, perhaps unto football eternity, unless lightning strikes and somehow UNCC is elevated to the Atlantic Coast Conference, and even if by some stroke of luck or providence UNCC does "succeed" in football, it will be at a cost to its academic integrity, as players who have no business sitting in a college classroom take phony courses, have papers written for them by others, and in general make a mockery of UNCC's academic mission. Is it worth it just to see a three-second crawl along the bottom of the ESPN screen reading "Charlotte 24 Old Dominion 7"?

Or perhaps it will be "Old Dominion 24 Charlotte 7." For Old Dominion, the public school in Norfolk, Virginia, was one of that flurry of mostly Southern public universities that joined the FBS in the fevered years of 2009–14. To finance the Monarchs football program and three women's teams the school had to add to remain compliant with Title IX, ODU instituted a $450 per student annual fee in 2007 "on top of existing athletic fees." President John R. Broderick said that everyone understood that "if we decide to go this route, it is going to cost the students more."[90] And ODU has a $55 million stadium redevelopment on the drawing board, though the method of financing remains uncertain.[91]

The Old Dominion football team has had some success. As the 2017 season ended, it had posted 60 consecutive home sell-outs (its stadium seats 20,118) and went an impressive 9–3 in the 2016 season, playing in the mid-level Conference USA, before falling to 5–7 in 2017 and 4–8 in 2018. But still, the student body is paying well for the privilege of having a so-so mid-major team. The athletic fee for a full-time student was $1,710.15 in 2017–18.[92] Administrators understand that they must further reduce it to meet (by 2025) the 55 percent cap imposed by the 2015 Virginia law which limited student fees and school subsidies at state schools.

Not every school administration responds to the Division I siren song. James Madison University, a public institution in Harrisonburg, Virginia, has in recent years dominated the football competition in the FCS Colonial Athletic Association (CAA). Though playing at the Division III level until 1980, the Dukes won the FCS (previously Division I-AA) national title in 2004 and 2016, and since the 2010–11 academic year, JMU has won more conference titles in all sports than any other school in the CAA. Its squads have had banner seasons in women's lacrosse, field hockey, baseball, men's and women's soccer, and other sports. So the question arises: why not move up to FBS, which is thought to be the desideratum of all colleges everywhere? Well, JMU's leaders have thought about it. In October 2013, they released an Athletics Feasibility Study the school had commissioned from CarrSports Consulting. The CAA had been hit by defections—Old Dominion was going FBS and joining Conference USA, Georgia State was jumping to the Sun

Belt Conference, while George Mason and Virginia Commonwealth, having achieved basketball prominence, jumped to the Atlantic 10.

The real reason most schools commission studies of this sort is to provide justification for athletic department aspirations. But in this case, JMU did not use the CarrSports Consulting report as a catapult into the FBS. It's not that the consultants recommended against such a move—no consultant with an eye on the next job would ever do such a thing—but they did detail the "significant financial ramifications" of such a move.[93] These include:

—An increase in football scholarships from 63 to 85 and a presumed increase in the total number of players, scholarship and non-scholarship, from the then-current 102 to the national FBS average of 120.[94]

—Average minimum attendance requirement of 15,000 every two years. (JMU has exceeded that average while playing in the FCS; its stadium has a capacity of 24,877.)

—Rising travel costs, given the inevitable increase in air travel in a more geographically dispersed league. (The closest Sun Belt school, Appalachian State, is 300 miles distant.)[95]

—Salary boosts and a passel of new positions, since FBS teams have need of well-compensated persons to fill such jobs as Assistant Director of Compliance, Video Coordinator, Associate Director of Strength and Conditioning, and Assistant Equipment Room Manager.[96]

—Expanded Title IX compliance costs due to increased football expenditures.

—And the least of a school's worries: the $5,000 fee for applying for a reclassification from FCS to FBS.

Elevation to the FBS would require the Dukes to move to an FBS conference, presumably a lower-tier group such as Conference USA or the Sun Belt Conference, dragging along its other men's and women's programs. The steeper level of competition would be daunting; those conference championships would not come quite so easily anymore.

The consultants held out one savory if speculative carrot to the students: the projected boost in athletics-generated revenue to between 25.2 percent and 27.3 percent of athletics expenses (compared to 19 percent if JMU remained in the CAA) "has the potential to decrease the university's reliance on athletic fees," which are, in Virginia's public schools, not inconsiderable.[97] In the 2017–18 school year, the student athletic fee was $1,366 for full-time JMU students.[98] And yet the claim by the consultants is misleading. While the percentage of the athletics department budget that would be funded by student fees was projected to fall from 81 percent to somewhere between 72.7 percent and 74.8 percent, the added expenses of moving to an FBS conference meant that total university allocated revenue from student fees would rise from $37.98 million to somewhere between $38.74 million and $39.56 million.[99] Additional revenue might be gleaned, according to the consultants, from seat licenses, alumni donations, conference revenue sharing, and sacrificial-lamb games against Power Five conference teams looking for 63–3 type tune-up games against FBS weaklings.

In the end, the consultants optimistically stated that JMU is "well-positioned for a potential transition to FBS."[100] But unlike UNC Charlotte, Georgia State, Old Dominion, and the other schools that used consultant reports as launching pads into the stratosphere of big-time football, James Madison remains, contentedly, in the FCS. Jeff Bourne, JMU's director of athletics, told the student newspaper in May 2017 that "if an FBS opportunity were presented to us, it would be something we would look at very closely," but no such opportunity is on the table. Football coach Mike Houston, while admitting the increased costs of such a move, was gung-ho: "Do I think that our program is ready for that? Absolutely. I think if the right opportunity were to present itself for James Madison University, not just for football [but] for all sports, I would enthusiastically support it."[101] So stay tuned: in the near future, depending on this elusive opportunity that may or may not come knocking in Harrisonburg, you just might see *James Madison* on your ESPN crawl—presumably on the hind end of some pretty lopsided scores.

Money is not the only thing a school can lose when making the jump to the big time. The tale of SUNY Binghamton stands as a caution. Binghamton, a well-thought-of cornerstone of the state university system of New York, had played basketball at the Division III level until school president Lois B. DeFleur and athletic director Joel Thirer determined that what Binghamton really needed was a Division I basketball team. They got their wish in 2001, and within a short period of time the Binghamton Bearcats were playing in a new $33.1 million events center and contending in the lower-level D-I America East Conference.

But there were more red flags than at a Stalin-era Moscow May Day march. In 2007 the team hired Kevin Broadus, formerly with Georgetown, who was "known for recruiting good players with questionable backgrounds," as Pete Thamel put it in the *New York Times*. Coach Broadus brought in, as he had done at previous stops, players from notorious high-school-diploma mills. The faculty athletic representative to the athletic department, Professor Dennis Lasser of the school of management, charged that "minimum qualifications as specified by the NCAA are the only academic criteria currently needed for the men's basketball team to be admitted to Binghamton University." Sally Dear, a lecturer in human development, told the *Times* that the three men's basketball players in her class were disruptive, disrespectful, and chronically late. When she docked their grades, the associate athletic director for student services harassed her, pressuring Ms. Dear to cut the players special breaks not available to non-ball players. Another player, a native Serbian, thrashed a fellow student into a coma in a bar fight; he fled the country.

Representatives of opposing teams went on record in criticism of Binghamton, an exceedingly unusual act. Tom Brennan, former coach of the University of Vermont Catamounts, told the *Times*, "It certainly appears to me that Binghamton has decided they're going to take a lot of risks, and it also appears that it hasn't worked out. Even if they win an America East championship, what is it worth?"

Somewhat more circumspectly, SUNY Stony Brook athletic director Jim Fiore said, "It certainly causes you to pause when you think that on a different level in the league, someone has a different philosophy than we do."[102] But the team won. In 2009, the year things started blowing up and his mini-fiefdom started falling down, Broadus led Binghamton to its first and only NCAA tournament appearance, an 86–62 loss to Duke. But the unflattering newspaper stories piled up. The star point guard was arrested for selling crack. Six players were dropped from the team. Kevin Carey, a Binghamton alumnus who was then policy director at an education think tank, told *USA Today*:

> This is now what Binghamton is known for—a corrupt basketball program. Why wasn't it good enough to be a very well-respected public university? So we could be national TV for 45 minutes getting blown out by Duke? Our graduates go on to do important things. That should be enough.[103]

Bad PR was the least of Binghamton's worries. In February 2010, a SUNY-ordered investigation led by Judith S. Kaye, former Chief Judge of the New York State Court of Appeals, revealed a basketball program "out of control," with an appalling "lack of oversight" from school president De Fleur and athletic director Thirer. Players were being paid by assistant coaches and having papers written for them; they were stealing debit cards and condoms; they were steered toward lax, jock-coddling professors, joke independent studies classes, and given transfer credit for such courses as Bowling I and Theories of Softball. When an admissions official had the temerity to question the credentials of dribbling and dunking applicants, an athletic official replied "Why do you care if we take six players who don't attend classes?"[104]

President De Fleur was encouraged to retire. Athletic director Thirer resigned, though as a tenured professor he made $195,447 in 2010, and in 2011 he was installed in the SUNY Binghamton athletic hall of fame. Coach Kevin Broadus, ringmaster of this circus, was placed on paid administrative leave for several months before receiving a $1.2 million settlement in return for withdrawing a discrimination lawsuit. (Broadus is African American.) "This is why people don't blow the whistle," said Sally Dear, the lecturer who had refused to change grades for basketball players. "My life has been a living hell since all this took place." Yet Coach Broadus walked off with over a million dollars, to the astonishment of much of the Binghamton community. "Everyone that did something has been rewarded," concluded Dear.

The Human Development department in which Dear taught was singled out by investigators as the epicenter of academic corruption. One former secretary told the *New York Times* that Chairman Leo Wilton, whom the investigators criticized for providing favorable treatment to basketball players, created an atmosphere of "harassment and bullying." In response, Wilton wrote:

> This is the first time an African-American professor has served as chairperson of human development, and this racialized attack on my leadership is a libelous

misrepresentation of my character, integrity and professionalism. These attacks are grounded in the continuous racialized attitudes about black men in this country.[105]

In 2012, Professor Wilton received the Chancellor's Award for Excellence in Teaching.

For the basketball team, though, it all fell apart. By 2012, the Bearcats were posting an incredible 1–28 record. The program has yet to recover, as it is now a perennial cellar dweller in the America East. And as Pete Thamel, who covered the saga for the *New York Times*, concluded, what makes the "program's flurry of arrests, lowered standards and lust for winning stand out" in the often shady world of big-time intercollegiate athletics is that "Binghamton had thrived for years without nationally relevant sports programs."[106] It had sold its soul for a mess of pottage.

Utica College, another small school in Upstate New York, made a splash into the Division I basketball pool in 1981, hiring former Milwaukee Bucks NBA championship-winning coach Larry Costello.[107] All it got for its trouble were lopsided defeats and mounting costs. As the Utica athletic director admitted, "The travel was crazy, and it wasn't fair to the kids to play teams they didn't have a chance against. It felt like we were selling our souls." So Utica returned to Division III in 1988, and the Pioneers have played there ever since, contentedly.

Seattle University, a Jesuit school, also dropped its D-I basketball program. The Chieftains, as they were known, had an impressive pedigree, producing NBA Hall of Famer Elgin Baylor as well as pros like John Tresvant and Tom Workman. But in 1980, SU de-emphasized basketball, dropping from D-I to an independent NAIA schedule. Father William Sullivan, Seattle University president, when asked, "Why did Seattle U drop sports?" answered: "We didn't. We dropped the semipro program. We decided not to pay people to play for us."[108] He phrased the question this way: "Should an institution like Seattle be placing such large amounts of money into subsidizing a program for a handful of students—one that in many ways contaminates the educational ideals of a university?"

In the first five years of its post-Division I life, Seattle's enrollment rose by 15 percent, the number of club sports rose from four to twelve, intramural funding greatly increased, and while "there are fewer blacks on the basketball court," as Frank Deford wrote, "there are more black students in the classrooms."[109] The operation was a success. But something about an American university cannot stand to be out of the sports limelight. Father Sullivan stepped down from the presidency in 1996 but served as chancellor until 2009; Seattle U, now nicknamed the Redhawks, rejoined D-I that same year.[110]

As the late Frank Deford noted in a typically felicitous article in *Sports Illustrated*, Catholic colleges—Marquette, University of Detroit, University of San Francisco—dropped football en masse in the mid-twentieth century. Only Notre Dame and Boston College remain in the FBS. And they aren't going anywhere.

Notes

1 David Riesman and Reuel Denney, "Football in America: A Study in Culture Diffusion," *American Quarterly* 3, No. 4 (Winter 1951): 309.

2 Rodney D. Fort, *Sports Economics*, second edition (Upper Saddle River, NJ: Pearson Prentice Hall, 2006), p. 458.

3 Vedder, "Introduction" to Denhart and Ridpath, "Funding the Arms Race," p. 1.

4 All salaries, unless otherwise noted, are from "NCAA Salaries," http://sports.usatoday.com/ncaa/salaries, accessed January 20, 2017.

5 William Tsitsos and Howard L. Nixon II, "The Star War Arms Race in College Athletics: Coaches' Pay and Athletic Program Success," *Journal of Sport & Social Issues* 36, No. 1 (2012): 68.

6 Ibid.: 80.

7 Orszag and Israel, "The Empirical Effects of Collegiate Athletics: An Update Based on 2004–2007 Data," p. 8.

8 "NCAA Salaries," http://sports.usatoday.com/ncaa/salaries.

9 *USA Today* Sports, "Texas Fires Coach Charlie Strong after Three Losing Seasons," November 26, 2016.

10 Suman Bhattacharyya, "How Much Money It Takes to Be in the Top 1% in Every State," *The Fiscal Times*, June 17, 2016, www.thefiscaltimes.com/2016/06/17/How-Much-Money-It-Takes-Be-Top-1-Every-State.

11 Some public schools attempt a fiscal sleight-of-hand by claiming that their coaches are paid in part or full by voluntary contributions—for instance, Florida State's head coach's salary comes, putatively, from booster club funds—but such monies are fungible. Erik Brady, Jodi Upton, and Steve Berkowitz, "Salaries for College Football Coaches Back on Rise," *USA Today*, November 17, 2011;"NCAAF Salaries," *USA Today*, http://sports.usatoday.com/ncaa/salaries/, accessed February 18, 2019.

12 Yost, *Varsity Green: A Behind the Scenes Look at Culture and Corruption in College Athletics*, p. 119.

13 Charles T. Clotfelter, *Big-Time Sports in American Universities* (New York: Cambridge University Press, 2011), p. 106.

14 Monica Wang, "The 10 Public University Presidents with the Highest Pay," *Forbes*, July 17, 2016, www.forbes.com/sites/monicawang/2016/07/17/the-10-public-university-presidents-with-the-highest-pay/#68fd5f6c3b61.

15 Andrew Erwin and Marjorie Wood, "The One Percent at State U: How Public University Presidents Profit from Rising Student Debt and Low-Wage Faculty Labor," Institute for Policy Studies, May 21, 2014, pp. 3–5.

16 Ibid., p. 11.

17 Will Hobson and Steven Rich, "In Major College Sports, a System of Pay as They Go," *Washington Post*, December 12, 2015.

18 Erwin and Wood, "The One Percent at State U: How Public University Presidents Profit from Rising Student Debt and Low-Wage Faculty Labor," p. 14.

19 These and subsequent football assistant salaries are from "NCAA Salaries," *USA Today*, http://sports.usatoday.com/ncaa/salaries/football/assistant, accessed January 19, 2017.

20 "Government Salaries Explorer," *The Texas Tribune*, https://salaries.texastribune.org/texas-am-university/, accessed January 19, 2017.

21 Ryan Dunleavy, "Rutgers Search for Coordinator to Replace Drew Mehringer Has Begun," *NJ.com*, December 11, 2016.

22 Steve Berkowitz, "Tom Herman Cashes In; Texas Releases Terms of Contract," *USA Today*, December 3, 2016.

23 "Johnson Richardson," www.charlotte49ers.com/coaches.aspx?rc=63&path=football.

24 "NCAA Salaries: NCAAF Strength Coaches," *USA Today*, http://sports.usatoday.com/ncaa/salaries/football/strength, accessed January 31, 2017.

25 "NCAA Salaries: NCAAB Coaches," *USA Today*, http://sports.usatoday.com/ncaa/salaries/mens-basketball/coach/, accessed August 17, 2017.

26 "Faculty Salaries," http://faculty-salaries.startclass.com/, accessed January 31, 2017; NCAA Salaries: NCAAB Coaches, *USA Today*, http://sports.usatoday.com/ncaa/salaries/mens-basketball/coach, accessed January 31, 2017. Erik Brady, Steve Berkowitz, and Christopher Schnaars, "Capitalism Meets Amateurism," *USA Today*, March 1, 2018.

27 Jane Stancill, "Spellings Will Receive $90,000 Performance Bonus after First Year," *Charlotte Observer*, March 3, 2017.

28 Lindsay Michel, Brian Sopp, and Michaele Stafford, "Athletics Costs Outpace Returns," *The Daily Tar Heel*, April 26, 2007.

29 Steve Berkowitz, "Geno Auriemma's Latest Contract Could Keep Him at UConn Through 2020–2021," *USA Today*, February 16, 2017.

30 Curtis Eichelberger, "Women Basketball Loses Money as Salaries Break College Budgets," *New York Times*, April 1, 2011.

31 Steve Berkowitz and Jodi Upton, "Salaries Dramatically Rise for Top Women's Basketball Coaches," *USA Today*, July 18, 2011.

32 Will Hobson and Steven Rich, "College Athletic Departments Spending Heavily on Staff Pay," *Washington Post*, December 30, 2015.

33 Will Hobson and Steven Rich, "Good to Be Commish: Salaries for Power Five Conference Bosses Soar," *Washington Post*, January 8, 2016; Steve Berkowitz, "Jim Delany, Big Ten Commissioner, Earns $20 Million Bonus," *USA Today*, May 12, 2017.

34 "College Sports 101," Knight Commission on Intercollegiate Athletics, p. 10.

35 Michael Smith, "Athletic Budgets Continue to Climb," *Sports Business Journal*, August 22–8, 2011, www.sportsbusinessdaily.com/journal.

36 "College Sports 101," Knight Commission on Intercollegiate Athletics, p. 13.

37 Thomas, "Call to Curb Athletic Spending Strikes Some as Unrealistic," *Chronicle of Higher Education*.

38 Erin Durkin, "Small Budgets Present Division I Challenges," *USA Today*, May 15, 2012.

39 Fort, *Sports Economics*, p. 481.

40 Peter N. Stearns, *Guiding the American University: Contemporary Challenges and Choices* (New York: Routledge, 2016), p. 78.

41 Brad Wolverton and Sandhya Kambhampati, "As Sports Programs Get Richer, Few Give Much to Academics," *Chronicle of Higher Education*, January 24, 2016.

42 Gaul, *Billion-Dollar Ball: A Journey through the Big-Money Culture of College Football*, pp. x, 13, 15, 6.

43 Ibid., pp. 29–30.

44 Ibid., p. 32.

45 Ibid., p. 37.

46 Skip McAfee, "Quoting Baseball: The Intellectual Take on Our National Pastime," *NINE: A Journal of Baseball History and Culture* 13, No. 2 (2005): 82. Just what Eliot really said is in doubt; the quote may be apocryphal. But it's too good to ignore.

47 Benedict and Keteyian, *The System: The Glory and Scandal of Big-Time College Football*, p. 2.

48 David Jesse and Mark Snyder, "Dave Brandon out at U-M," *Detroit Free Press*, October 31, 2014.

49 Kirk Carapezza, "How Much Is Too Much When It Comes to Spending on College Sports?" *PBS NewsHour*, March 30, 2015, www.pbs.org/newshour.

50 "Preferred Seat Donation" brochure, http://support.mgoblue.com/wp-content/uploads/2017/01/um_athletics_2016_psd_brochure_06-1.pdf, accessed February 22, 2017.

51 Norm Wood, "Virginia Tech Unveils Per-Seat Donation Requirements for Football, Men's Hoops Season-Ticket Holders," [Hampton Roads, VA] *Daily Press*, May 2, 2016, www.dailypress.com/sports/virginia-tech/dp-spt-virginia-tech-hokie-club-per-seat-fees-0503-20160502-story.html.

52 Gaul, *Billion-Dollar Ball: A Journey Through the Big-Money Culture of College Football*, pp. 63–4.

53 Upton, Berkowitz, and Gillum, "Big-Time College Athletics: Are They Worth the Cost?" *USA Today*.

54 Andrew Zimbalist, *Unpaid Professionals: Commercialism and Conflict in Big-Time College Sports* (Princeton, NJ: Princeton University Press, 2001/1999), p. 150.

55 Mark J. Burns, "Nike Co-Founder Phil Knight Gives $500 Million to Oregon for Science Complex," *Sports Illustrated*, October 20, 2016, www.si.com/tech-media/2016/10/20/nike-co-founder-phil-knight-gives-500-million-oregon-science-complex.

56 Andrew Theen, "Phil and Penny Knight Will Give $500 Million to University of Oregon for Science Complex," *The Oregonian*, October 17, 2016.

57 Sean Cunningham, "The Oregon Ducks' Special Relationship with Nike and Billionaire Phil Knight," *Real Clear Life.com*, March 17, 2017.

58 Michael Rosenberg, "Nike's Phil Knight Has Branded Oregon into National Power," *Sports Illustrated*, January 7, 2011, www.si.com/more-sports/2011/01/07/oregon-knight.

59 Kenny Jacoby, "ASUO Pays Athletic Department $10,000 in Effort to Save Student Football and Basketball Tickets," *Daily Emerald*, June 14, 2017, www.dailyemerald.com/2017/06/14/asuo-pays-athletic-department-10000-in-effort-to-save-student-football-tickets/.

60 Rachel Bachman, "Oregon Athletic Department Uses State Money for Academic Needs Despite Claims of Self-Sufficiency," *The Oregonian*, October 7, 2010, http://blog.oregonlive.com/behindducksbeat/2010/10/oregon_athletic_department_use.html.

61 Erin Strout, "Oklahoma State U. Receives a Record $165-Million Donation for Athletics," *Chronicle of Higher Education*, January 11, 2006.

62 Steve Berkowitz and Paul Myerberg, "State of Wyoming Answers Call for Cowboys Athletics," *USA Today*, July 6, 2017.

63 John V. Lombardi, "Comparing Universities' Sports Subsidies to Library Spending," *Inside Higher Ed*, June 1, 2012.

64 Allan Guttmann, "The Anomaly of Intercollegiate Athletics," in *Rethinking College Athletics*, edited by Judith Andre and David N. James (Philadelphia: Temple University Press, 1991), p. 17.

65 "Position Statement: Establishment of a Presidential Commission on Intercollegiate Athletics Reform," The Drake Group, March 31, 2015, p. 7.

66 Will Hobson, "As NCAA Money Trickles Down, All Coaches Cash In," *Washington Post*, March 13, 2017.

67 Eric Kelderman, "Colleges Foot a Large Share of Athletics Expenses, New NCAA Data Show," *Chronicle of Higher Education*, May 15, 2008.

68 Joe Drape and Katie Thomas, "As Colleges Compete, Major Money Flows to Minor Sports," *New York Times*, September 2, 2010.

69 Libby Sander, "As Men's Gymnastics Programs Dwindle, Backers Try to Save Them," *Chronicle of Higher Education*, May 1, 2011.

70 Stearns, *Guiding the American University: Contemporary Challenges and Choices*, p. 30.

71 For data on sports-related concussions, of which football produces the most annually, see "Study Looks at Concussion Rates Among NCAA Sports," www.apta.org/PTinMotion/News/2015/10/7/ConcussionNCAA/, October 7, 2015.

72 "All-Time High 777 Colleges and Universities Now Offering Football," National Football Foundation, August 1, 2017, www.footballfoundation.org, accessed September 11, 2017.

73 Darren Kelly and Marlene A. Dixon, "Becoming a 'Real University': The Strategic Benefits of Adding Football for NCAA Division I Institutions," *Journal of Intercollegiate Sport* 4 (2011): 286.

74 Robert H. Frank, "Challenging the Myth: A Review of the Links Among College Athletic Success, Student Quality, and Donations," Knight Commission on Intercollegiate Athletics, May 2004, p. 15. For an optimistic view of the effects of a move

to Division I-A, or the FBS, see Donald P. Roy, Timothy R. Graeff, and Susan K. Harmon, "Repositioning a University Through NCAA Division I-A Football Membership," *Journal of Sport Management* 22 (2008): 11–29.

75 Kelly and Dixon, "Becoming a 'Real University': The Strategic Benefits of Adding Football for NCAA Division I Institutions," *Journal of Intercollegiate Sport*: 292–3.

76 Ibid.: 297.

77 "Recommendation to the Chancellor, UNC Charlotte Football Feasibility Committee," February 15, 2008, p. 2.

78 Ibid., p. 3.

79 Ibid., pp. 3–4.

80 Ibid., p. 2.

81 David Scott, "UNCC Football Deflated," *Charlotte Observer*, February 23, 2008.

82 Mark Johnson and Meghan Cooke, "Board Approves UNCC Football," *Charlotte Observer*, February 13, 2010.

83 "Tuition Billing Statement," UNC Charlotte, http://finance.uncc.edu/student-a ccounts/tuition-billing-statement, accessed August 15, 2017.

84 Libby Sander, "Charlotte Makes Way for Football," *Chronicle of Higher Education*, August 10, 2010.

85 Libby Sander, "At What Price Football?" *Chronicle of Higher Education*, February 14, 2010.

86 Howard L. Nixon II, *The Athletic Trap: How College Sports Corrupted the Academy* (Baltimore: Johns Hopkins University Press, 2014), p. 12.

87 George Leef, "Should UNC-Charlotte Students Pay Exorbitant Fees to Fund a Football Team?" John William Pope Center for Higher Education Policy, March 5, 2008.

88 National Universities Rankings, *U.S. News & World Report*, www.usnews.com/best-colleges/rankings/national-universities, accessed April 3, 2017.

89 George Leef, "College Sports: Isn't It Time to De-Escalate the Arms Race?" John William Pope Center for Higher Education Policy, September 7, 2016.

90 Sander, "At What Price Football?" *Chronicle of Higher Education*.

91 Harry Minium, "ODU Proposes 22,130-Seat Football Stadium to Be Built without New Student Fees," *The Virginian-Pilot*, June 9, 2016.

92 "2017–18 Tuition Rates," Old Dominion University, www.odu.edu/tuition-aid/cost s-tuition/tuition/tuition-rates, accessed August 15, 2017.

93 "James Madison University: FBS Athletics Feasibility Study," CarrSports Consulting, October 4, 2013, p. V–25.

94 Ibid., p. IV–12.

95 T.K. Maxwell, "Why the Hell Did James Madison University Not Join the FBS?" *Underdog Dynasty*, June 18, 2016, www.underdogdynasty.com/2016/6/18/11857710/james-madison-university-jmu-dukes-harrisonburg-shenandoah-fbs.

96 "James Madison University: FBS Athletics Feasibility Study," p. VII–48.

97 Ibid., p. 2.

98 "Undergraduate Rates," James Madison University, www.jmu.edu/ubo/rates-under graduate.shtml, accessed August 11, 2017.

99 "James Madison University: FBS Athletics Feasibility Study," p. VII–50.

100 Ibid., p. IX–52.

101 Matt Weyrich, "JMU Would Be Prepared to Consider Move to an FBS Conference," *The Breeze*, May 29, 2017.

102 Pete Thamel, "At Binghamton, Division I Move Brings Recognition and Regret," *New York Times*, February 22, 2009.

103 Erik Brady and Steve Wieberg, "Binghamton Mess a Recurring Tale for Schools' D-I Dreams," *USA Today*, October 12, 2009.

104 Pete Thamel, "Report Faults Binghamton's Leaders in Scandal," *New York Times*, February 11, 2010.

105 Pete Thamel, "Binghamton Coach Gets $1.2 Million to Resign," *New York Times*, October 29, 2010.
106 Pete Thamel, "After a Costly Scandal, Binghamton Begins Rebuilding," *New York Times*, March 1, 2012.
107 "Sports People; Change of Emphasis," *New York Times*, February 25, 1987.
108 Sperber, *College Sports, Inc.: The Athletic Department vs. the University*, p. 141.
109 Frank Deford, "A Heavenly Game?" *Sports Illustrated*, March 3, 1986, www.si.com/vault.
110 Miguel Otarola, "The Rev. William Sullivan, Seattle U.'s Longest-Serving President, Dies at 84," *Seattle Times*, June 17, 2015.

6

ATHLETICS

The best boost academics ever had?

For decades, the unexamined assumption had it that a winning athletic team, especially in football, and secondarily in basketball, "charms alumni to give money," in the words of Bowdoin director of admissions Richard Moll.[1] (Who was not the 6-foot-8-inch tall, shaved-head actor Richard Moll, and just why anyone would be charmed into giving money by the decidedly low-key Bowdoin athletics program is another question altogether.) Research over the past four decades has debunked that myth. As early as 1985, the "overwhelming conclusion" of the dozen then-extant studies was that was that there "is no relation between athletic success and any measure of voluntary financial contributions," wrote University of Nevada, Las Vegas, sociology professor James H. Frey.[2] Frey had earlier punctured the fantasy that alumni were rabid sports boosters who subordinated academic and social life at the old alma mater to the fortunes of its athletic teams. In a study published in the *Review of Sport & Leisure*, Frey related the results of a mail survey of alumni and the Alumni Board of Directors of Washington State University, a member of what was then known as the Pac-8.

Frey received completed questionnaires from an exceptionally high 90 percent of his random sample of 886 WSU alums, as well as the 32 members of the Alumni Association's Board of Directors.[3] Each was asked to choose his or her three highest priorities from a list of 12 items. Both the general alumni and the directors ranked "Maintain traditional academic programs" first, and though in different order, selected "Salary increases—faculty" and "Build and maintain classroom facilities" second and third. But whereas the directors ranked "Build and maintain athletic facilities & programs" fourth and "Recruitment of athletes" fifth, the general alumni ranked those in ninth and eighth place, respectively—near the bottom, and just ahead of "Special activities such as music and drama."[4] (Sorry, thespians.)

This "large and surprising discrepancy" between alumni leaders and the broader alumni base "contradicts the ever-present myth and usual justification of athletics," which is that the alumni will go into paroxysmal spasms and close their checkbooks should the school ever de-emphasize big-time sports. The alumni directors, who are more favorably disposed to institutional spending on sports, are wined and dined and given free tickets to athletic events, notes Frey. And since they are also much closer to the administration, they understand and sometimes share a belief in the perceived necessity of advertising the school through sporting events.[5] Interestingly, when asked about their "most remembered" experience at Washington State, only 2.9 percent of alumni respondents mentioned athletics—placing that category dead last, and well behind character development, fraternities and sororities, parties, dorm life, lectures, faculty relations . . . and even studying for exams![6] Memories of that Washington-Washington State Apple Cup tilt just don't rate.

In sum, concludes Frey on an almost hortatory note, "If college and university presidents were to act to curtail and even eliminate athletic programs the reaction would not be as severe as anticipated."[7] Perhaps—but there is no realistic prospect of us finding out the accuracy of that prophecy any time soon.

Allen L. Sack and Charles Watkins tested the relationship between alumni giving and changes in won-loss record for 166 Division I football schools between 1969–78. They found "no relationship between winning and giving," even when a team's record sharply improved from one year to the next. But they do not discount the possibility that the mere presence of a football team may stimulate giving for some alumni; as the authors speculated, "an attempt to eliminate college sport at a school with a strong athletic tradition might well lead to financial disaster."[8]

This is not to say that always and everywhere a great success—a national championship, say—has no effect on donations. It may—but only with regard to the athletic department. In a 1983 study of 57 big-time sports programs in the academic year 1980–1, Lee Sigelman and Samuel Bookheimer found a nonsignificant relationship between a football team's success and alumni donations to the annual fund, but a positive correlation between football success and donations expressly directed to the athletic department. Whatever benefits a good football season may bring, they do not accrue to the primary—or putatively primary—mission of the university.[9] In 1996, Robert A. Baade and Jeffrey O. Sundberg found that while the winning percentages of the football and basketball teams in doctorate-granting institutions from 1973–90 were not significantly linked to alumni giving, football bowl appearances were, as were NCAA basketball tournament appearances, but only in the case of public, and not private, universities.[10] (This was before the proliferation of bowl games, which are so numerous today that sub-.500 teams get postseason invites to these ESPN productions.)

In 2004, Robert Frank, reviewing a sextet of studies on the relations between winning games and attracting applicants and alumni donations, reported that the preponderance of evidence suggests no significant link, though there are outlier cases such as that of Boston College and what is called the Flutie Effect. The results of these studies are mixed, said Frank, but even if winning teams do generate indirect benefits, "the effects almost surely are very small."[11] Apart from the two or three year jumps in applications and donations that are sometimes seen in the case of schools that win football and basketball national championships, the much-touted indirect benefits of big-time sports are minimal, though Frank conceded that athletic programs can provide a rallying point for students and alumni and teach athletes important skills in teamwork, discipline, and the setting of goals.[12]

Maurice Mitchell, who served as chancellor of the football-less University of Denver from 1967–77, remarked with acerbity in 1982:

> We are told that alumni contributions are important. Well, I have watched alumni, and my observation is that alumni are all talk and no money. The largest hot-air balloon that floats over the average university is the myth about alumni giving. If you need a new stadium, the alumni run around foaming at the mouth, promising you the sky if you build it, but giving you nothing. Alumni are good at threatening you with reprisals, but they don't even give you a chance to watch their checks bounce. Pleasing the alumni is the big excuse for having intercollegiate football, but it is not legitimate.[13]

The real determinants of alumni donation levels, as Robert A. Baade and Jeffrey O. Sundberg write, are "[h]igher student wealth, better institutional quality (as measured by student ability, admissions selectivity and instructional expenditures per student), and greater development efforts." These reasons account in part for higher donation levels to private than public schools, though as Baade and Sundberg note, the relative affluence of private versus public school graduates and the attitude that public schools are already being subsidized by taxpayer dollars are also likely causes.[14]

Not all givers are impervious to the effect of a winning team. Jonathan Meer of Stanford and Harvey S. Rosen of Princeton isolated the relationship between an alumni-athlete's donations and the fortunes of the team he used to play on. In other words, while the success or lack thereof of the football team may have a negligible influence on the donations of a former rower, perhaps the record of the *crew team* does make a difference. In fact it does, in the case of the selective research university that served as Meer and Rosen's data source. Their examination of giving patterns for 7,228 former male athletes and 3,542 former female athletes revealed that donations by the men to both the university's general fund and the athletic program increased by about 7 percent when their former team won a conference championship, while the success of her former team has no statistically significant impact on women's donations. The success or lack thereof of the football and basketball teams had no statistically significant effect on the giving by either male or female ex-athletes.[15] The authors suggest that universities with an eye on the bottom line—which is to say all universities—might consider a greater investment in minor sports as a way to encourage future donations.[16]

Yet scattered through the literature is also evidence that winning teams may actually *depress* alumni donations to the general fund. Most donors take pride in their alma mater; to see it dragged through the mud of athletic scandal, or to earn a reputation as a school for "dumb jocks" or the criminally inclined, embarrasses them. A degree from a football or basketball factory can seem tainted, as if it had been awarded for courses in basket weaving and Bowling 101.

"University fund-raising staff have known for many years that the most valuable support of a university generally comes from alumni and friends who identify with the *academic* programs of the university, not its athletic prowess," writes former Michigan president James Duderstadt. "In fact, many of the university's most generous donors care little about its athletic success and are sometimes alienated by the attention given to winning athletics programs."[17]

A 2007 study in the *Journal of Sport Management* suggested that while donations to the 119 largest athletic programs had greatly increased in the five-year period under consideration, it may have been at the expense of donations to the general fund. The percentage of total donations to universities that are earmarked for the athletic department is rising. The fear, said coauthor Dennis R. Howard of the University of Oregon, is that "the more the athletic program gets, the less there is to support the academic program." Jeffrey L. Stinson, a North Dakota State assistant professor of marketing, told the *Chronicle of Higher Education* that expensive seat licenses had also caused some donors to reduce their academic-destined donations.[18]

At some schools, donations now "account for one-quarter or more of the athletic department revenue." In 2015, the last year for which figures were available, 25 university athletic departments received at least $20 million in contributions. This marked a fivefold increase since 2005. Leading the pack was Texas A&M ($66.99 million), followed by the Nike-fed University of Oregon ($53.70 million), the University of Michigan ($51.72 million), and the University of Texas at Austin ($42.23 million.) Of the top ten beneficiaries of private donations to the athletic department, only two schools (Texas Christian University and Notre Dame) were private.[19]

Football boosters like to claim that high profile teams forge bonds between the school and those non-alumni who pay taxes for its support. "If you're a state university," explained one University of Nebraska fundraiser, "they're something that people who don't give a damn about higher education can take pride in. It gives them a link to the university that otherwise wouldn't be there at all." Yet that link does not convey donations. Athletic supporters do *not* become academic supporters.[20]

The ever-quotable former press relations maven of Notre Dame, Richard Conklin, stressed:

> We at Notre Dame have had extensive experience trying to turn athletic interests of "subway alumni" to development purposes—and we have had no success . . . There is no evidence that the typical nonalumnus athletic fan of Notre Dame has much interest in its educational mission.[21]

Conklin, who served Notre Dame in various capacities from 1967–2001, also said: "There isn't any correlation between giving at Notre Dame and athletic success. We raised more money during the [subpar] Gerry Faust era than during any other period in the university's history. What does that tell you?"[22] Conklin attributed the persistence of this myth to "anecdotal evidence from sports reporters who apparently spend more time in bars than in development offices."[23]

If winning games doesn't necessarily induce alumni to add zeroes at the end of their fundraising-drive checks, it does seem to have a laxative effect on those who write checks with other people's money: politicians. Brad R. Humphreys of the University of Maryland, Baltimore County examined the effect of a football team—and then a *winning* football team—on state appropriations to the 120 public universities that fielded Division I football teams for at least two years between 1974 and 2000. Over that period, disbursements from the state constituted 32 percent of the revenue of these schools, as compared to 19 percent from tuition and fees.[24] In Humphreys's study, state schools that fielded a Division I-A football team received approximately 8 percent more in annual appropriations than did state schools without a Division I-A team, other things being equal. Perhaps surprisingly, this heightened appropriation did not vary depending on the team's success the previous year. In an earlier working paper, Humphreys had found that a win in a traditional in-state rivalry game—say, Michigan vs. Michigan State, or Oklahoma vs. Oklahoma State—was also associated with a higher government appropriation, which would suggest that the best thing the University of Alabama at Birmingham can do would be to roll the Crimson Tide of the University of Alabama.[25] But that is easier said than done. (So improbable is the event that it isn't even easy to *write*.)

Humphreys speculated that one reason for this relationship is that "[m]any taxpayers in states and state legislators are alumni of a state's public institutions of higher education."[26] Many more citizens of the state follow these teams avidly, even if they have no personal connection to the school. When the old alma mater, or state flagship school, is doing well, and making the homefolk proud, it may help to loosen the public purse strings. He concluded, "Simply operating a Division 1-A athletic program at a public university appears to have a positive impact on a university's finances"—in this case the size of a state appropriation—but the win-loss record matters not so much, "in contrast to the conventional wisdom that only successful intercollegiate athletic programs generate financial gains."[27]

Winning games makes students smarter! (or something like that . . .)

But what of the effect that a strong emphasis on athletics has on a university's academic mission? Is it corrosive? Pernicious? Benign? Might it actually be supportive? Irvin B. Tucker III, examining the graduation rates in the six largest extant conferences between 1984 and 1989, found no connection between the existence of a big-time basketball program and graduation rates, but a negative relation in the case of big-time football. He explains that "the nature of a football game"—with its tailgating, its pep rallies, its weekend-long parties—"invites sacrificing more weekend and weekday study time than basketball," which is a contained, two-hour affair.[28] Researchers also detected an inverse relationship between the grades of male students and the football team's success at the University of Oregon—one thing that Phil Knight's money apparently cannot fix.[29]

Could the same inverse relationship exist between a team's success and the output of the faculty? Drawing on data from the economics departments of 126 U.S. colleges and universities, William F. Shughart II, Robert D. Tollison, and Brian L. Goff of the Center for Study of Public Choice at George Mason University calculated that other things being equal, a "school whose football team goes 11–0 will have about 1.05 fewer journal pages published per faculty member than will a school whose team goes 6–5." They inferred that when the home town is doing well, the professoriate is likelier to attend or watch games on television, tailgate, and otherwise engage in football-related communal gatherings, and as result devote less time to the pursuit of academic research.[30] Thankfully, the trio was based at George Mason, which has no football team, so the study got written!

Successful football or basketball teams may draw more attention to the university, especially schools without high profiles (Gonzaga and the University of Northern Iowa in basketball, Boise State in football), but do they really lead to a spike in applications? If so, is the spike attributable to jock-sniffing fanboys—not necessarily the studious or the engaged? Does a 12–0 team really bring in a bevy of students the next fall? In his annual report of 1900–1, Harvard president Eliot wrote, "there is no relation between athletic victory or defeat for Harvard, and the increase or decrease of preliminary candidates in the following year."[31] But if Eliot's shade could turn its gaze toward Chestnut Hill in Boston, he might reconsider.

When on November 23, 1984, Boston College quarterback Doug Flutie launched a Hail Mary pass that Gerard Phelan caught in the end zone, securing a last-second 47–45 victory over the defending national champion and glamorous bad boys of the University of Miami, he likely won the Heisman Trophy in that instant but he also put his name to a college admissions phenomenon: the Flutie Effect. This effect, which is real but temporary, describes the sudden uptick in applications when a high-profile sports team commands unexpected national attention. The Flutie Effect supposedly boosts national name recognition so much that the applications for the following school year pour in. Schools receive millions of dollars worth of free publicity from the televised, online, and print media. "We're 227 years old and until we had a team in the Top 25, nobody had heard of us," marveled Alex Sanders, president of the College of Charleston (SC), when his school's team briefly became Cinderellas in the 1997 March Madness tournament. Online inquiries to the College of Charleston's admissions office zoomed from 80 per week to 380 per day as the team caught the nation's fancy, according to Mike Dodd in *USA Today*. School officials estimated the value of the airtime and advertising space received as a result of the NCAA tournament at $3.27 million. In the subsequent fall of that same tournament year, St. Joseph's University of Philadelphia, which made the Sweet 16, saw a 22 percent hike in its admissions.[32]

My school, George Mason University, had its own experience with the Flutie Effect. In 2006, the Patriots basketball team made a magical run through March

Madness, knocking off such perennial powers as the University of North Carolina, Michigan State, and the University of Connecticut, en route to a berth in the Final Four. Two years later, school officials reported a 22 percent increase in freshman applications, a 40 percent increase in out-of-state applications, and a 350-percent boost in admissions inquiries, which they ascribed, in part, to the basketball team's meteoric streak. Professor Robert E. Baker, director of the Center for Sport Management at GMU, estimated that George Mason (which made it considerably farther than had the College of Charleston) had received over $677 million in free advertising due to the March Madness tournament.[33] Professor Baker cautioned that "there's no statistical proof" linking the upsurge to the basketball team, and he noted that George Mason applications and exposure were already trending upwards. But some level of causation seems likely.[34]

Sustained excellence in sport can also raise a school's national profile. Boise State University in Idaho, which competed at the junior college level until 1968, made a concerted effort to crash football's top tier in the early twenty-first century. Incredibly, the Broncos succeeded, recording undefeated seasons as a member of the Western Athletic Conference in 2006 and 2009 and defeating traditional powerhouses along the way, including a thrilling 43–42 victory over Oklahoma in the 2007 Fiesta Bowl. Boise State—*Boise State!*—became a fixture in the Top 25, even the Top 10, for a while, under Coach Chris Peterson, who finally succumbed to the lure of coaching megabucks when he left Boise for the University of Washington at the end of 2013. Boise State, as Stu Woo noted in a faintly mocking article in the *Wall Street Journal*, was long an obscure state school, a distinct second fiddle to the University of Idaho (actually, more like a third fiddle, behind Idaho State, too) in the Gem State.[35] It fails even to crack the top 50 in ratings of Western regional universities, and only 14 percent of its almost 20,000 students live on campus.[36] But its greatly heightened profile due to its outstanding football teams has clearly attracted out-of-staters: whereas in 2003, just 7 percent of the incoming class consisted of non-Idahoans, almost 43 percent of the entering class in 2016 were not Idaho residents.[37] (On a parallel track, the percentage of Idahoans on the football team rarely exceeds 20 percent. Only 20 of the 107 members of the Broncos' 2017 roster were from Idaho; a plurality were from California.)[38]

Professors George A. Chressanthis and Paul W. Grimes sought to measure the effect of football and basketball success on applications to their school, Mississippi State University, in a 1993 paper in the *Sociology of Sport Journal*. Mississippi State is a founding member of the Southeastern Conference, which is the ground zero, or maybe even Bethlehem, of American college football. Parsing data covering the 21-year period between the fall of 1971 and the fall of 1991, Chressanthis and Grimes found that an increase in the percentage of wins by first the football, and then the combined football and men's basketball teams, translated into an increase in the subsequent first-year student enrollment numbers.[39] Whether the revenue from this boost in enrollment was sufficient to cover the additional "costs associated with developing and maintaining a winning sports program is an open question," they concede.[40] It should also be pointed out, as Robert Frank has, that because "tuition payments typically fall well short of the cost of educating each student," an increase in enrollment may actually *harm* a university's financial condition.[41]

Flutie Effect to the side, the evidence that gridiron or on-court success leads to a larger or more talented student body is mixed. Studying schools within the six major conferences between 1978 and 1987, economists Robert G. Murphy of the putatively Flutie-fattened Boston College and Gregory A. Trandel of the University of Georgia found that an increase of .250 in a football team's winning percentage is positively related to a 1.3 percent boost in the number of applicants the next year.[42] In 1992, a team of researchers reported a link between an increased basketball winning percentage and higher enrollment at Western Kentucky University over a 30-year period.[43]

Similarly, Michael L. Anderson of the Department of Agricultural and Resource Economics of the University of California, Berkeley, using a data set of bookmaker spreads on FBS games, found that a winning football team boosts donations to the athletic department and, in the case of "large increases in team performance," is associated with significant increases in applications, in-state enrollment, and incoming Scholastic Aptitude Test (SAT) scores, and a drop in the acceptance rate.[44] Much less conclusively, Irvin B. Tucker and L. Ted Amato of the University of North Carolina at Charlotte, examining a pool of schools that had been ranked by the Associated Press or victorious in NCAA tournament games, detected a brief bump in the average SAT scores for successful schools, but the relationship between SAT scores and NCAA tournament success fades and then disappears beyond two years.[45] Like athletic glory, the March Madness bump is fleeting.

A stronger link between success on the field and a more impressive applicant pool was discerned by Devin G. Pope and Jaren C. Pope in a 2009 study for the *Southern Economic Journal*. Proceeding from a data set of SAT scores, applications, and indicators of athletic success for 332 Division 1 schools from 1983–2002, the Popes found that applications to schools that finished in the Top 20 in college football or the Sweet 16 in the NCAA men's basketball tournament rose by between 2–8 percent the following year.[46] The academic quality of these additional applicants varied: "lower SAT scoring students (less than 900) respond to sports success about twice as much as the higher SAT scoring students," noted the Popes, but whereas the benefits to football powers appear to be exclusively quantitative rather than qualitative, there is some evidence that schools doing well during March Madness experience incoming classes the next year with a 1–4 percent increase in the number of students scoring above 500 on both portions of the SAT and above 600 on both portions of the SAT.[47]

It seems implausible on its face, but can a good football team actually lift a school's reputation, as measured by the most popular such gimmick, the annual *US News & World Report* college and university rankings? One piece of anecdotal evidence has it that when Northwestern, after decades as a Big Ten doormat, made the 1995 Rose Bowl, it crept up from 13th to ninth in the *USNWR* rankings the next year—no easy thing to do. Brian Fisher explored just this question in a 2009 article in *New Directions for Higher Education.* Since the *US News & World Report* (*USNWR*) rankings are a function of a school's reputation among its peers, selectivity, alumni donations, and graduation and retention rates, and because it is sometimes argued that donations and applications vary depending on the fortunes of a school's high-profile athletic teams, the connection may not be as tenuous as it at first seems.[48] Fisher, however, found "very little connection between year-to-year changes in winning and the ranking *USNWR* assigns an institution the following year." There is no Flutie Effect when it comes to school rankings.[49] In sum, the Flutie effect seems short-lived and exaggerated.

There actually may be a kind of reverse Flutie Effect for academic reputation in the case of scofflaw athletic departments. "The worst fear of any academic department would be what one might call the 'UNLV Syndrome,'" said Stephen Greyser, professor of consumer marketing and sports management at Harvard Business School.[50] The UNLV Runnin' Rebels basketball team, coached by the rule-bending Jerry Tarkanian, was constantly in hot NCAA water for rules violations throughout the 1970s and 1980s, making the school's acronym shorthand for a sports-corrupted university.

The attitude of the general public is another matter. Two scholars from Louisiana State University measured the extent to which athletic success and academic reputation are connected in the public mind. Their assumption was that because "[m]uch of the public is poorly informed about the quality of state colleges and universities," they are likely to overestimate a school's quality as a result of favorable media coverage of its athletic teams. Surveying Louisiana residents in the aftermath first of the LSU football team's national championship team of the 2003 season, and next after its disappointing 9–3 finish the following year, Robert Kirby Goidel and John Maxwell Hamilton found little difference in the portion of respondents (about 64 percent) who said that success in football makes for a better university academically. The less-well-educated were likelier to make this connection than were those with a greater amount of education.[51] The authors found "very limited support," however, for the hypothesis that those who see a connection between athletic and academic success therefore favor higher spending on public education.[52] Sure, they may feel a swelling of pride when LSU takes on, and beats, the world, but that doesn't mean they want to be taxed as a result.

Ah, and there are costs of FBS football that go beyond the mere monetary, or the embarrassment of watching the crawl on ESPN read OHIO STATE 62 YOUR SCHOOL 3. For instance, crime. Not that committed by various gridiron scofflaws—though these are real enough, as the recent cases of Baylor, Florida State, Florida Atlantic, and numerous other schools indicate. No, this is crime as a fallout, a byproduct, of game day. Writing in the *Journal of Sports Economics*, Daniel I. Rees and Kevin T. Schnepel collated figures from the National Incident-Based Reporting System with the home playing dates of 26 Division I-A football teams between 2000 and 2005. The schools were located in the Midwest (11), the South (10), and the West (5). The results? The "host community registers sharp increases [9 percent] in assaults on game days." Also up are vandalism (18 percent), disorderly conduct (41 percent), and alcohol-related arrests (13 percent for DUI, 76 percent for liquor law violations).[53] These numbers especially spike during upsets, which is why the police departments in Birmingham, Atlanta, and Charlotte had better prepare themselves for that day—that distant day—when UAB, Georgia State, and UNC Charlotte knock off the Universities of Alabama, Georgia, and North Carolina, respectively. But only at home: away games see no such crime waves.

The authors do not estimate the additional costs imposed by these crimes, but other studies find no evidence that college football is in any way a boon to host cities. Robert A. Baade, Robert Baumann, and Victor A. Matheson analyzed 63 cities that were home to Bowl Championship Series (BCS) conference teams between 1970 and 2004, as well as Notre Dame, Air Force, and Brigham Young, prominent programs lying outside that cohort. They found that "neither the number of home games played, the winning percentage of the local team, nor winning a national championship has a discernible impact on either employment or personal income in the cities where the teams play." Fame, perhaps—or even, in some cases, infamy—but fortune, no.[54]

Nor is college football a windfall for the local governments in the form of sales tax revenue. Dennis Coates and Craig A. Depken II studied 1984–2008 sales tax data from Austin, College Station, Lubbock, and Waco, Texas—the homes, respectively, of the University of Texas, Texas A&M, Texas Tech, and Baylor. They discerned no statistically significant difference in revenues when the local teams played at home. Yes, each game brought visitors to the area, and some of those visitors patronized restaurants and hotels and other service industries, but any sales tax revenue therefrom seemed to be offset by lower spending by the locals, a portion of whom presumably "hunker down" at home or "skedaddle" to avoid the crowds.[55]

"Student-athlete" and other useful myths

Big-time college sports are about entertainment, first and foremost. Any academic benefits the athletes receive are purely incidental, and even resented. Murray Sperber, the muckraking Indiana University professor and author of several valuable books on college sports, says:

> If colleges searched for and awarded scholarships to upcoming rock stars so that they could entertain the university community and earn money for their schools through concerts and tours, educational authorities would call this "a perversion of academic values" and would not stand for it.[56]

Yet they stand at attention for the star quarterback or point guard. Sperber is no egghead killjoy, no spoilsport still bitter that the jocks dated the cheerleaders back in high school. He played semi-pro basketball in France and was a newspaper sports reporter before his academic career. But he has the gift of clear-sightedness in a field so often distorted by fantasy and wishful thinking.

As early as 1905, reformers were asking, "Can a football man attend the arduous daily practice, earn his way through college, and still be a student?"[57] The answer then, as now, is *rarely*—even though scholarship athletes no longer have to earn their way by cleaning dishes in the mess hall or reshelving books in the library. The scholarship athlete today receives four years of tuition, room, and board—as well as tutoring services unavailable to other students and, in the money sports, aliment of a rather higher class than the usual college-student victuals—valued at, conservatively, $200,000. (In 2016, the average price of a private college was $43,921, and for in-state public universities about $20,000.)[58] If the athlete achieves a degree, which at least for appearance purposes the athletic department dearly hopes he or she does, his or her future earnings potential is significantly boosted. Except at Division III programs, where athletes really do play for love the game, and the fellow returning a kickoff for a touchdown or draining a three-pointer is sitting next to you in Bio 201 the next school day, intercollegiate athletes have little contact with ordinary students. Once in a while the quarterback might be witnessed walking across campus, and this is accounted a celebrity sighting, but even at top-ranked institutions such as Stanford or Notre Dame no one pretends that these athletes are part of the general student population. They are on campus in order to play sports: period.

Athletes at many sports factories are wholly disconnected from the student body. They attend class seldom, if at all, and are only in the technical sense of the word *students*. Yes, they matriculated, but of academic life they know nil. A distressing number of athletes read at grade-school levels and have trouble with addition and subtraction, never mind algebra or calculus. Special care is lavished on their education, or at least their eligibility. Nathan Tublitz, a biology professor at the University of Oregon who spearheaded the reformist Coalition on Intercollegiate Athletics, says:

> Every athlete has individual tutors for every class. They have mandatory study halls, people who look at their homework every day. They get free computers. And then the administration trumpets the fact that student athletes are graduating at the rate of the student body. I say to them, the rest of the student body doesn't get all of these perks. It's a sham. The athletes are living in a different parallel universe.

That is not to say that the Stanfords and Notre Dames of the football world recruit in the same sordid manner as do Florida State or the Miami Hurricanes. Stanford, annually ranked one of the top five undergraduate institutions in the country, has also become a habitual member of major college football's Top 25. While no one pretends that its players have academic records on a par with those of the rest of the non-athletic student body, it has avoided scandals of the sort that embarrassed the Harvard basketball team or the Vanderbilt football team. David Shaw, the head football coach since 2011, explains that his staff does not even watch film of potential recruits until their academic transcripts have been reviewed. "We can't afford to waste time," he explained to Bruce Feldman of CBS Sports. "I need to look at kids who are great players and great students."

But Stanford is hardly sitting back and waiting for smart teenagers with prodigious football talents to fall into its lap. The school has also sent letters to top recruits touting the material advantages of coming to the Palo Alto school instead of, say, the University of Oklahoma. And that advantage is calculated in cold hard cash. A sample Stanford letter to a recruit, obtained by ESPN, is blunt:

> While the complete college experience sets Stanford apart, there is no question that a Stanford degree will later provide you earning power which can forever change your life. The average Stanford graduate pulls down more than $42,000 per year above the grads of the rest of the Top 25 college football programs in the country. Compounded over a career, this represents an advantage of millions of dollars. That's just the salary advantage for the average Stanford grad, and there has been nothing average to this point in your life. Stanford Varsity Athlete alumni are the most sought-after employees across all sectors of the economy in every corner of the country.

The letter goes on to compare the average Stanford graduate's annual income 15 years after graduation ($126,400 in 2014) with those of the other 24 schools in the Associated Press Top 25. Its closest competitor was Notre Dame ($108,400), with USC, Texas A&M, UCLA, and Brigham Young next in line; bringing up the rear was East Carolina, whose graduates made less than half of what a Stanford grad was pulling down 15 years after obtaining his or her degree.[59]

In the most recent year for which full statistics were available (2014), the median Football Spending per Football Scholarship Player for all FBS schools was $155,200, or almost ten times higher than the median Academic Spending per Full Time Equivalent Student ($15,615). At the most profligate end of the spectrum, the median Spending per Football Scholarship Player soared to $301,878 (versus a median of $15,632 for the Full Time Equivalent Student) in the football-crazed Southeastern Conference. Just behind the SEC in the imbalance sweepstakes were the Big Ten ($272,982–$20,455), the Pac-12 ($234,448–$17,539), and the Atlantic Coast Conference ($231,737–$17,229). These were followed, in order, by the Big 12 ($194,099–$16,536), the American Athletic Conference ($167,944–$15,946), the Mountain West Conference ($99,474–$14,373), Conference USA ($97,432–$12,280), the Sun Belt Conference ($77,107–$10,419), Independent schools ($76,113–$15,598), and the Mid–American Conference ($71,042–$15,509).[60]

Ah, the casual reader of these figures might mutter, at least the teams in the weaker conferences keep things in something approaching perspective: the ratio of expenditures on football players versus plain old students is less obscene in the Mid-American Conference (4.6–1) than in the Southeastern Conference (19.3–1). But the difference is not for lack of trying or purity of heart. The MAC schools are the champs when it comes to extorting money from students via athletic fees. Journalist Gilbert M. Gaul notes that at Penn State, students admitted to its prestigious Honors College, which requires a 1400 SAT and 4.0 GPA, receive scholarships in the amount of $4,500, while a football scholarship for a Nittany Lion player (whose SAT score is almost certainly a fraction of that of a typical Honors College student) is worth $50,000 annually.[61]

Money, though, cannot buy time. Division I athletes have 20 fewer hours per week to study than nonathletes, per NCAA rules, and that's not even counting games and travel time. Given the scant academic preparation many top jocks have gotten in high school, it's a miracle (or an indication of the remarkable relaxation of standards at many universities) that the graduation rate is as high as it is. That figure of 20 hours is a rule more flexible than Gumby. It barely even attains the status of a bad joke. The limit of four hours a day, 20 hours a week, that may be devoted to NCAA sport excludes "voluntary" activities such as "informal practices, weight-training, conditioning, et cetera."[62] You could drive a tank through that loophole. Despite this cap on mandatory practice and playing time, a 2006 survey of 21,000 NCAA athletes revealed that football players spent, by their own reckoning, an average of 44.8 hours a week "practicing, playing or training for their sport." Golfers were second, at 40.8 hours per week, baseball players third at an even 40 hours, and softball players led all women athletes with a reported weekly average of 37.1 hours spent on their sport. Curiously, football players also claimed to spend more time than other athletes (39.5 hours per week) on academics—for an 84-hour workweek.[63] Harry Edwards, the venerable sociologist of sport, estimates that Division I football and basketball players spend from 50–60 hours a week on athletics, leaving no time for academic work outside of perfunctory, if even that, classroom attendance.[64]

There is, of course, no rule preventing a university from imposing a more stringent limit on the hours that an athlete devotes to his or her sport. It's a cop-out when college presidents bewail the excessive practice time in athletes' schedules. They could, if they wished, free up more time for the linebacker to study English lit, or the power forward to read Kant. But that would be the dreaded unilateral disarmament. A Division I college basketball season can last from the first practice in early October until the championship game in early April—that is, the majority of the fall and spring semesters, leaving pitifully little time for players to devote to study. Football encompasses spring practice and a season that often begins the final weekend of August and can go into the bowl championship of early January. With ESPN-driven bowl games proliferating like mushrooms, and even teams with sub-.500 records going bowling, the majority of FBS players are now engaged in the sport into at least late December.

Weeknight games exist because of television, and in particular the noxious weed known as ESPN. These disrupt study schedules for non-athletes who wish to watch the game (and participate in the rituals surrounding the contest) and they make it difficult or impossible for athletes, who typically have to schedule all their classes before early afternoon so as not to miss practices, to keep anything like a good attendance record. No one puts a gun to the head of the MAC commissioner demanding that he schedule Akron versus Northern Illinois on a Tuesday night;

clearly the MAC sees this as an opportunity to have the spotlight all to itself, albeit on a night few associate with football, and ESPN is always voracious for programming. Forsaking such games—not only in football but, more controversially, in basketball, would leave money on the table, to use the gambler's term, but it would ensure that the "student-athletes" not miss valuable class time and, in truncating and compacting the schedule, it would also encourage the re-regionalization of college sports.

Let's not put all the blame on the MAC and other strivers. Alabama's legendary football coach Bear Bryant said in 1969, "We think TV exposure is so important to our program and so important to this university that we will schedule ourselves to fit the medium. I'll play at midnight if that's what TV wants."[65] If even the Bear is willing to prostrate himself before the great god of television, what chance does the AD at Eastern Michigan have? Far from being helpless victims of television, college football and basketball have been entirely willing. They have become entwined in the nexus of athletic, media, and corporate interests that Howard L. Nixon II, a professor of sociology at Towson University and confessed sports fan, labels "the intercollegiate golden triangle," or trap, in which schools pursue prestige, alumni donations, and increases in applications in exchange for—all too often—their integrity.[66] The lure of money and televised glory is strong. And given that the number of schools whose athletic departments do not require subsidy seldom exceeds 20, this is a fool's trade-off.[67]

Research suggests that while athletes may graduate at a rate similar to or even higher than that of nonathletes, the graduation rates in the money sports of FBS football and Division I men's basketball are generally lower and often absymal. In one typical study, "Are Athletes Also Students? The Educational Attainment of College Athletes," by Dean A. Purdy, D. Stanley Eitzen, and Rick Hufnagel, the authors reported the results of their investigation into "the academic achievements of athletes at Colorado State University from the fall of 1970 through to the spring of 1980." They found that CSU athletes entered school with academic records inferior to those of other students, posted lower grades than those of other students, and graduated at a lower rate as well. Nonscholarship athletes or those with partial scholarships did better than scholarship athletes, and athletes in sports other than football and basketball exceeded the academic accomplishments of football and basketball players.[68]

John Fizel and Timothy Smaby, in "Participation in Collegiate Athletics and Academic Performance," sampled almost 20,000 students, including 583 varsity athletes, at Penn State in the spring of 1995. Athletes entered with somewhat lower SAT scores (average 989) than the overall student body (1030). The lowest average SAT scores were tallied by the women's basketball team (877) and the football team (914). Athletes were also likelier to take "easier" courses: that is, they were disproportionately represented in the two Penn State colleges with the highest average GPAs, Education and Health and Human Development.[69]

These studies are of the dog-bites-man variety. No one who has observed, even casually, the development of intercollegiate sports over the last century-plus would be surprised in the least. Charles T. Clotfelter, a professor of public policy and economics at Duke University, analyzed mission statements from 52 universities from the major athletic conferences. Only five of these even mentioned athletics. Most bold was Ohio State, whose mission statement declared, "Our intercollegiate athletic programs will routinely rank among the elite few."[70]

Jimmy Valvano, the late and beloved basketball coach at North Carolina State, once boasted to a reporter:

> I work for the N.C. State Athletic Association. That has nothing to do with the university. Our funding is totally independent. You think the chancellor is going to tell me what to do? Who to take into school or not take into school? I doubt it. I'm paid to win games. If I say a kid can help me win, I'll get him. It's the same at 99 percent of the places in the country.

And this was *before* NC State captured the hearts of basketball fans with a magical NCAA championship in 1983. (That team had a cumulative 1.67 grade average out of a possible 4.0.)[71]

Sanity appears, briefly

It's not as if these problems are unknown to those who supervise and administer intercollegiate sports. There have been efforts for many decades to at least improve matters along the margin. Radical actions—that is, those that cut to the root of the problem—are rare, but moderate reform is always just around the corner. Alas, reformers of college athletics, concluded NCAA executive director Walter Byers in retirement, "never reformed much of anything."[72] It's an old, old story. The first 40 years of the NCAA had been marked by a fairly *laissez-faire* posture, as it respected the principle of home rule for colleges, or allowing individual schools to regulate their own affairs, leaving to the NCAA the establishment of agreed-on rules for the games themselves.

Internal pressure for a more activist role grew when in 1935 the Southeastern Conference permitted full athletic scholarships, which seemed to many a form of payment to athletes and violation of amateur principles. Other conferences objected, contending that this put them at a competitive disadvantage against the mercenaries of the SEC. In 1939 the NCAA set down a policy formally rejecting athletic scholarships, but enforcement was left to the schools, and the NCAA had no real investigative abilities, especially during wartime. (In wartime, freshman eligibility was restored briefly to fill out depleted teams. Freshman eligibility rules waxed and waned throughout twentieth century, with frosh returning to football and basketball varsity teams in 1972, though by the 1980s some influential voices— Joe Paterno, Tom Osborne, John Thompson—proposed a return to barring freshmen, to no effect.)

Prior to 1948, the NCAA had no real method of enforcing its rules. Individual school and conferences were their own policemen. But just as the post-World War

II federal government enjoyed, and used, expanded powers, so did the NCAA. Its first initiative was to establish association-wide grants-in-aid standards. Or, in plainer English, to ban athletic scholarships by limiting financial aid to athletes to those with demonstrated need. In 1946, a gathering of conference officials of NCAA schools began the approval process of the primly named Purity Code, formal name "Principles for the Conduct of Intercollegiate Athletics," which among other things barred athletic scholarships, off-campus recruiting, and special admissions standards for athletes. The phrase *Purity Code* reeked of faux-virginal sanctimony and Puritanism, so it was renamed the Sanity Code (which, even more offensively, implied that critics or nonadherents were insane). The Sanity Code permitted student-athletes to receive tuition and fee waivers (not room and board) as long as they had financial need and satisfied the school's admission policies for non-athletes. Such aid, once awarded, could not be withdrawn if an athlete were injured or just didn't feel like playing anymore.

The impure or insane SEC, however, was unswayed. Its secretary declared, "The N.C.A.A. doesn't want the schools to pay the room and board of athletes. We in the S.E.C. think we should pay them."[73] Nevertheless, the Sanity Code was formally enshrined in the NCAA Constitution in 1948, along with enforcement mechanisms. Southern schools, which had been awarding athletic scholarships for over a decade, balked. The University of Virginia, one of the most academically distinguished big-time Southern football schools, threatened to withdraw from the NCAA if it were not allowed to provide athletic scholarships. UVA was acting in the Jeffersonian tradition of its founder, who believed that policies ought to be made at the most local or individual level—in this case, by the institution or the conference. In 1950, the "Sinful Seven," a motley septet of mostly football weaklings (Boston College, Citadel, University of Maryland, University of Virginia, Villanova, Virginia Military Institute, and Virginia Polytechnic) were threatened with expulsion from the NCAA for disregarding the Sanity Code. The vote to expel failed, 111–93 (it needed two-thirds), and the Sanity Code died as effectively unenforceable.

By 1956 purity, or sanity, or both, were abandoned, and full athletic scholarships were permitted. These covered tuition, room, board, fees, books, and $15 per month for "laundry money." (That's a lot of quarters, given that college students traditionally keep a distant relationship with their local washer and dryer.) The full-ride scholarship was born. The hope was that this would usher in an era of honesty and transparency. Yet there was something faintly risible about this whole episode, since numerous press accounts of the time and in later years established that football players were being paid handsomely under the table by boosters. That's one illicit act that never goes out of style. As Bobby Knight, Indiana University basketball coach, said in 1985: "some basketball players are being paid more money to attend college than the professors who teach at the schools they attend."[74] The Big Ten held the line against athletic scholarships until 1961, awarding them only on the basis of need. But when the brawn drain from the Midwest reached critical proportions, the Big Ten relented.

Putting athletes to the test

Richard Snyder, director of admissions at Stanford, played the Cold War card that so many advocates of an increased federal role in education were playing during the Eisenhower years. In 1959 he told the NCAA convention, "The age of rockets and of satellites will not accept the free ride for an athlete of limited academic potential while the physicist with only moderate physical prowess goes unaided."[75] The solution? Subsidize science education, and impose national academic standards for athletes, enforced by the NCAA.

The Atlantic Coast Conference, surprisingly, was first out of the gate when in 1960 it established minimum academic requirements for scholarship athletes: a combined math and verbal score of 750 on the SAT. (This was boosted to 800 in 1964.) Contemporaneously, the NCAA approved a rule limiting athletic scholarships to those whose high school grades and SAT/ACT (American College Test) scores predicted a freshman GPA of at least 1.600 on a 4.000 scale. The 1.600 rule drew criticism from partisans of home rule, especially members of the Ivy League, and, soon enough, from those who argued that it would disproportionately harm African Americans. As Ronald Smith points out, when the ACC adopted its minimum SAT requirement the league had no African American football players and the percentage of African Americans playing intercollegiately outside the South was rather small, so these early academic rules had no intended racial effect. Nevertheless, the 1.6 GPA threshold came under increasingly harsh criticism as a weapon of racism, and it fell in 1973, supplanted by the 2.0 Rule, which sounds stricter but in fact required only that a high school student present a 2.0 GPA to be eligible for collegiate athletics. "Losing the 1.600 rule was one of the most painful experiences in the 22 years I had then served as executive director," said Walter Byers. "It was a terrible day for college athletics."[76]

The problem with privileging the high school GPA in admissions decisions is that "grade inflation is greatest for students with low to average standardized test scores," as University of Oklahoma researchers Carla A. Winters and Gerald S. Gurney explained in their 2012 study of special admissions policies. High school grades have become "less indicative of cognitive ability" than in the past. Working with a sample of special admits at a large midwestern university, the authors found that those special admits who scored low on the ACT or SAT and gained admittance thanks to their high school GPA exhibited significantly inferior skills in "word recognition, sentence comprehension, and spelling" compared to other special admits who had higher standardized test scores.[77]

The NCAA is not unmindful of the problems, public relations and otherwise, produced by the collision of scholarship athletes with academics. The first time the NCAA compiled graduation rates, it reported that 56 percent of recruited Division I athletes who enrolled in the fall of 1984 were graduated within five years, compared to 48 percent of all students. Yet within the rather broad category of recruited Division I athletes there were significant divisions by sport. Just 47 percent of recruited football players were graduated within five years, and the figure was most dismal (39 percent) for men's basketball players.[78] (The five-year standard is not a reflection on an athlete's lack of academic capability. Rather, it is an acknowledgement of the widespread practice of redshirting, or sidelining an athlete for his or her freshman year in order to enable him or her to mature, thus extending the college career to five years. Redshirting began in the 1950s.)

The next flashpoint in the debate over academic standards at big-time sports universities was known as Proposition 48. Proposition 48, which took effect in 1986, required freshmen athletes at Division I schools to have achieved a 2.0 high school grade point average while taking a set of prescribed courses that included math, English, social studies, and science. They also had to have a combined score of 700 on the verbal and math sections of the SAT or a 15 (out of a possible 36) on the ACT. These were hardly exacting standards, but they called forth howls of outrage from some African American administrators, particularly those representing historically black colleges and universities. Dr. Jesse N. Stone, Jr., president of the Southern University System of Louisiana, said of Prop 48:

> The end result of all this is the Black athlete has been too good. If it is followed to its logical conclusion, we say to our youngsters, "Let the White boy win once in a while." This has set the Black athlete back 25 or 30 years. The message is that White schools no longer want Black athletes.

Nonsense, replied Harry Edwards, the UC Berkeley African American sociologist of sport, inspiration for the protests by African American athletes at the 1968 Mexico City Olympic games, and a supporter of Proposition 48. Edwards pointed out, at the time of Prop 48's enactment, that "55% of black students generally score lower than 700 on the SAT and 69% score lower than 15 on the ACT."[79] Edwards agreed that the 700 SAT and 15 ACT minimums were arbitrary, but he contended that "they are arbitrary and so *low* as to constitute virtually no standards at all."[80] African American educationists were selling African American athletes short. A combined SAT score of 700 isn't Einstein territory; it is in fact well below average, and any student of even modest intelligence, if he or she puts his or her mind to it, can achieve it.

If he did not support Proposition 48, Harry Edwards wrote in 1984:

> I would risk communicating to Black youth in particular that I, a nationally known Black educator, do not believe that they have the capacity to achieve a 700 score on the SAT . . . where they are given a total of 400 points simply for filling out the biographical information . . . Black parents, Black educators, and the Black community must *insist* that Black children be taught and that they learn *whatever* subject matter is necessary to excel on diagnostic and all other skills tests.[81]

Penn State football coach Joe Paterno echoed Edwards:

I am surprised that so many black educators have gotten up here and kind of sold their young people down the river. You have sold them short. I think you have underestimated what great competitors the young black people are today in all areas . . . If it takes 700 in the SAT to compete and we give them time to prepare, they will be prepared.[82]

(In light of subsequent events, Paterno might have chosen his words more carefully when he also said, "For at least the last two decades we've told Black kids who bounce balls, run around tracks and catch touchdown passes that these things are ends unto themselves. We've raped them.")[83]

Proposition 48 seemed to work: during its operation, as Jill Singleton points out, the five-year graduation rate of African American athletes increased by fully one-third, from 30 to 40 percent, and the graduation rate of white athletes edged up from 54 to 60 percent.[84] But it ran into trouble almost from the start, as a vastly disproportionate number of those made ineligible by its provisions were African American. African American athletes constituted 81 percent (1986), 80 percent (1987), and 87 percent (1987) of the ineligibles in its first three years of operation. The four schools with the most Prop 48-ineligible football players in the 1988 season were all predominantly African American institutions: Alcorn State, Bethune-Cookman, Alabama State, and Grambling.[85]

The race card ought to carry little weight in this debate. As John R. Thelin writes, as far back as the 1970s:

For a coach to claim that an athletic scholarship was the only or the best way for a black student to gain access to higher education was patently incorrect— and often dysfunctional, when one considers the tendency for big-time programs to isolate student-athletes from the general student body. It also did a disservice to those minority students who had educational aspirations apart from athletics.[86]

A school seeking to increase its African American student population would be better advised to court accomplished students who might major in math, English, history, or engineering rather than poorly prepared or indifferent students whose focus is football, not books.

The late Barbara R. Bergmann, Distinguished Professor of Economics at American University and president of the American Association of University Professors, made much the same point in a 1991 article on the unprofitability of athletics at the University of Maryland. Awarding scholarships for athletes in the money sports, many of whom are African American, "diverts support from academically able students from poor backgrounds who could benefit from a regular education and shifts it to athletes who principally devote their ability, interests, talent, and time to nonacademic pursuits."[87] The budding young African American astronomer or mathematician or biologist is shafted in favor of the linebacker who skates through no-show independent study classes and never composes anything longer than a tweet.

Nevertheless, Proposition 48 fell victim to what Murray Sperber called "the phony grounds of political incorrectness."[88] It would be superseded by Proposition 16, adopted in 1992, effective 1996, which increased the number of required high school core courses from 11 to 13 but permitted those with extremely low SAT or ACT scores to become eligible for intercollegiate competition if their grade point average reached specified points on a sliding scale. This, too, was denounced as racist, since it did not entirely eliminate standardized test scores, which some argued were culturally biased. In subsequent years the number of core courses has risen to 16 and the SAT and ACT have faded ever more fully into irrelevancy, to the point that an athlete could score a combined 400 on the SAT—that is, he could get every single answer wrong—yet still be eligible. (A 3.0 high school GPA will make eligible an athlete with a 620 SAT.)[89]

The next round of NCAA reforms created an Academic Progress Rate (APR), effective 2004. The APR is a measure taking into account graduation and retention rates, eligibility, and progress toward a degree to assess the success or failure of schools in keeping students eligible or on track to graduate. The APR rewards teams whose members remain academically eligible and stay in school; the formula, reduced to its essence, is intended to punish via disapprobation and then sanctions any team whose graduation rate falls below approximately 50 percent. Still, the penalties are hardly onerous: the first time a team's four-year average falls below the minimum acceptable APR, it receives "a public warning letter for poor performance."[90] Restrictions on recruiting and practices follow the second year's failure to meet the minimum, and in the third year a postseason ban is applied. A fourth year of failure brings stricter sanctions involving NCAA membership.

The new rules made athletic eligibility depend on a student-athlete completing at least 40 percent of his or her work toward a degree within the first two years, 60 percent within three years, and 80 percent by the end of year four. (This was up from a previous floor of 25–50–75.) This may not sound onerous, but as Georgia Tech men's basketball coach Paul Hewitt described the reaction of his fellow ACC coaches, "almost every coach said, 'We're going to encourage our kids to take the easiest path to eligibility.'"[91] Molders of men indeed! The APR therefore encouraged schools to funnel athletes into the easiest courses and channels, a practice known as "clustering." The ever-diligent *USA Today* sports team found that athletes in the money sports majored disproportionately in what one may safely assume are the easiest fields in their particular schools. Every one of the 2007 University of Texas-El Paso men's basketball team's seven juniors and seniors were majoring in multidisciplinary studies. At Paul Hewitt's Georgia Tech that year, 63 percent of the men's team were management majors. Sixty-five percent of Colorado State's football juniors and seniors majored in liberal arts, compared to 2 percent of the juniors and seniors in the general population.

At Kansas State, the one-time cupcake that has in recent years become a football powerhouse, 34 percent of the 2007 football squad's juniors and seniors majored in social science, compared with 4 percent of the general junior and senior population. Steven Cline, a former Kansas State player, regretted the clustering. "I look back and say, 'Well, what did I really go to college for? Crap classes you won't use for the rest of your life?' Social science is really nothing specific . . . I was majoring in football." Boise State footballer Marty Tadman, who like 48 percent of the Broncos' juniors and seniors majored in communications, added, "You hear which majors, and which classes, are the easiest and you take them. You're going to school so you can stay in sports. You're not going for a degree . . . It's a joke."[92]

At Auburn, the football players were funneled into sociology; at the University of North Carolina it was that school's infamous Afro-American Studies department. Sport management is a favorite at many schools. Researchers have yet to find clustering of athletes in physics, optics, or mechanical engineering. It's not like no one saw this coming. When the new rules were promulgated in 2003, amidst much self-congratulatory hot air by administrators, a Syracuse University swimmer, Dylan Malagrino, head of the NCAA Student-Athlete Advisory Committee, observed that "coaches and academic administrators in the athletic department might be strongly encouraging students to take easier majors or to choose a major and never switch."[93] Ah, but what did a mere swimmer know when compared with such savants as NCAA president Myles Brand, who confidently assured one and all that a new day was dawning?

Brand called the new rules "dramatic" and "nothing less than the beginning of a sea change in college sports." Henceforth, said Brand, a philosopher who served as president of the Universities of Oregon and Indiana in addition to helming the NCAA, participants in college sports would be "students first, then athletes." When the Drake Group, which grew out of a meeting of faculty reformers convened by Drake University provost Jon Ericson, expressed its doubts about the latest deck-chair shuffling, Brand dismissed them as "self-appointed radical reformers and incorrigible cynics" and "a small number of faculty members who with an eye for publicity" wish to "end university support of intercollegiate athletics"— as if this venerable position were so far beyond the pale of discussion as to be unthinkable.[94] In fact, although the Drake Group has favored federal law as a corrective as opposed to reforming the system from within, its recommendations are hardly radical: a return to freshman ineligibility, a 2.0 GPA to remain eligible (which, critics say, only leads to cheating), the transfer of counseling from the athletic department to the university, and the publication of team GPAs, majors, and other indicators of academic seriousness. If Myles Brand found this outside the pale, what would he have thought of Harvard president Eliot or Chicago president Hutchins? (We know what they would have thought of him.)

Donning his philosopher's cap, Brand said that the Drake Group's contention that the rule requiring athletes to show annual progress toward a degree would encourage academic fraud was a "remarkably unsound argument" that "gives sophism a bad name."[95] A company line was being spelled out. Flattering articles in the education trade press speculated that a new day was dawning, as "the campus eggheads now feel emboldened in their fight against the jocks," what with a groundswell of faculty resistance to the Sports Behemoth and the elevation of Myles Brand to the NCAA presidency. Why, with this philosopher-king on the throne and his acolytes achieving increased prominence, we might well soon see a day when:

> [T]elevision networks will have less influence in things like the number of football and basketball games and their scheduling, corporate logos will be less commonplace on uniforms and in stadiums, and the colleges will pay less heed to keeping up with the Joneses through construction projects with opulent amenities like luxury boxes.[96]

It was a nice dream, but did this happen? No, no, and no.

In her Ph.D. dissertation in Education and Human Development at George Mason University, Jill A. Singleton, examining the 117 BCS schools in the 2004–5 season, found that the APR did not lead to an increase in graduation rates, nor was it an effective way to calculate academic success. Admissions standards were a much better predictor, as was the amount of money a school spent on athletics. Football, she found, was the most problematic sport in the area of reform, in part because its athletes score so much lower on the SAT (as high as 300 points at some FBS schools) than do non-athletes.[97] As predictable as a Woody Hayes-called quarterback sneak on fourth and inches, an endless line of new tweaks to NCAA academic standards will come and go, come and go.

Cheaters never win (except when they do)

If, as Ecclesiastes tells us, nothing is new under the sun, nor is anything new under the dome or under the Saturday night lights. The same complaints against the unethical and anti-academic nature of big-time college sports have been voiced in every generation for well over a century. From purists like Presidents Eliot and Robert Maynard Hutchins to earnest reformers like Howard Savage to establishment platitude-dispensers like John Hannah of Michigan State, the song remains the same. Thus one can read a major cover story on "The Shame of College Sports" published in *Newsweek* in 1980 with the authorship of four correspondents, foremost Pete Axthelm, and its content is akin to that of a 1920s piece in the *Saturday Evening Post* or today's *Chronicle of Higher Education*. "Cheat more and survive. Or quit," as Axthelm quotes Auburn head coach Doug Barfield as cracking bitterly.[98]

In 1985, the NCAA instituted a breathlessly titled "death penalty" for rule violations of such enormity that only the quietus will do. (Twice previously—for the 1952 University of Kentucky men's basketball team and the 1973 University of Southwestern Louisiana men's basketball team—teams had been barred from competition for at least a year under a different set of rules.) The death penalty has been applied to a Division I school only once: the Southern Methodist University football program, which was found to have paid 13 players at least $61,000 in 1986, was prohibited from intercollegiate play in 1987 and forced to play a reduced schedule of seven away games in 1988. SMU, once a mainstay of the corruption-dripping Southwest Conference, has yet to really recover. (Though, come to think of it, few ever do after receiving a penalty of death.) The team now plays in the mid-tier Conference USA. Since returning from the dead, SMU has compiled a record of 106–227–3.[99]

Curiously, or perhaps depressingly predictably, schools that have been slapped with punishments (shy of the death penalty, of course) for NCAA violations actually have shown, on average, greater profits from the revenue sports. After all, they have placed them on a pedestal.[100] Yet, reformers continue to believe that changing things at the margin, or making incremental improvements, can make big-time sports compatible with higher education.

In October 1989, the John S. and James L. Knight Foundation, a nonprofit endowed by the brothers who once published Knight Newspapers, established a Commission on Intercollegiate Athletics, under the direction, though not exclusive membership, of university presidents. This was no revolutionary tribunal; the Knights were sports fans whose goal was to clean up what had obviously become a rather shoddy environment surrounding top-level football and basketball. The majority of then-NCAA Division I football schools (57 of 106) had been "censured, sanctioned or put on probation" by the NCAA during the 1980s, and not for the sorts of petty rule violations (until 2014 schools couldn't give athletes unlimited food service, for instance) that coaches like to complain of.[101] Forty-eight of those 106 schools graduated less than 30 percent of their men's basketball players.[102]

Chairmen of the Knight Commission, which produced reports on big-time college football and basketball in 1991, 1992, 1993, and 2001, were president emeriti of two intercollegiate athletic titans: William C. Friday of the University of North Carolina and Rev. Theodore Hesburgh of the University of Notre Dame. The Knight Commission's "Keeping Faith with the Student-Athlete" loftily declared:

> Athletics programs are given special, often unique status within the university; the best coaches receive an income many times that of most full professors; some coaches succumb to the pressure to win with recruiting violations and even the abuse of players; boosters respond to athletic performance with gifts and under-the-table payments; faculty members, presidents, and other administrators, unable to control the enterprise, stand by it as it undermines the institution's goals in the name of values alien to the best the university represents.[103]

Friday had been president of the North Carolina system while Jimmy Valvano, as coach of North Carolina State, was making a mockery of every jot and tittle of the rules. The sheer cheek of a former University of North Carolina official dispensing sanctimonious platitudes was enough to make one long for out-and-out rogues like Jerry Tarkanian and Norm Ellenberger.

Disgorging its findings and recommendations in a series of reports, the Knight Commission urged greater presidential control of athletics, a chestnut of dubious utility. In fact, in 1997 the NCAA did empower presidents with governance of intercollegiate athletics, to no great effect. Overall, its product was "woefully inadequate," as Ronald Smith judged.[104] The establishment was hardly panicked. Bo Schembechler, the blunt-spoken former football coach at Michigan, scoffed that "by the turn of the century . . . [t]his hubbub will pass, as will the so-called reformers."[105] The Knight Commission on Intercollegiate Athletics revived in 2001 for a fresh look at what had become a stale subject and issued more far-reaching recommendations. Voicing alarm that the "problems of big-time college sports have grown rather than diminished" since 1989, the twenty-first century Knight Commission rehearsed the ills that were obvious to any observer: Athletics departments operated "with little interest in scholastic matters beyond the narrow issue of individual eligibility." Crossing over into the realm of alternative spec- ulative history, the commissioners mourned that the "historic and vital link between playing field and classroom is all but severed in many institutions."[106] (When, precisely, in the modern era did this link exist?)

The solution? A "Coalition of Presidents" from the power conferences who would spearhead academic reform, de-commercialization, and a slackening of the athletics arms race.[107] The Commission proposed a number of no doubt sincere moderate reforms directed to these ends—all of them having been proposed many times before, and futilely. Besides co-chairs President Emeritus Friday of the Uni- versity of North Carolina and Father Hesburgh of Notre Dame, institutions represented on the 2001 commission included the Universities of Georgia, Florida, Iowa, Tufts (Tufts?!), Penn State, Kent State, Utah, Nebraska, Southern Methodist, and Ithaca College. (Ithaca's rep was a lunch companion for the fellow from Tufts, one assumes.) Given that these schools, Division III Ithaca and Tufts excepted, are deeply embedded in the system they propose to refresh, one wonders why they have exhibited not the least iota of resistance to the trends they decry. They have not, for instance, voluntarily shortened the distended football season by refusing to play a 12th regular season game or rejecting bowl bids. And even those in whom these reformers reposed confidence despaired of setting things aright: a 2009 Knight Commission survey found that 80 percent of FBS school presidents did not think they could limit or reverse the commercialization of big-time inter- collegiate sports.[108] Most college presidents are not starry-eyed fanboys or fangirls. They understand that big-time athletics subverts the university's mission and, unless you are at the helm of an Alabama or Texas A&M, is a financial burden. But the edifice of Division I sport is by now so built-up, so massive, so comprehensive, that even the most idealistic presidents despair of effective reformation. Just as the financial institutions during the Crash of 2008 were said by champions of subsidy to be "too big to fail," so are these programs too big to reform, except at the margins. The cleanest and purest solutions—abolition, à la the University of Chi- cago; or club sports—are discussed in the coming pages, though pursuit of such changes at most big-time athletic schools would be audacious, preternaturally courageous, and in some cases tantamount to career suicide. And the suicidally courageous tend not to rise to the position of college president in the first place.

The scandals

> If the top hundred or so high school football and basketball players each year are worth hundreds of thousands of dollars per year to a university, but can be acquired for a scholarship paying $5,000 to $20,000 [in late 1980s dollars], it is obvious that colleges will have a very strong incentive to acquire these players . . .

by means fair, foul, and everything in between, observed Stanford economist Roger Noll. The best players "are worth far more than they are paid through NCAA scholarships." Given that a coach's job depends upon his win-loss record, and that record depends on the recruitment and maintenance of the best players, "the incentive to break the rules is great. If the probability of getting caught is sufficiently low, cheating is worthwhile." (If immoral.)

Consider three-time Pac-12 men's basketball Coach of the Year Sean Miller of the University of Arizona. In 2018, it was revealed that FBI wiretaps captured Miller discussing a $100,000 payment to ensure the recruitment of a future superstar named DeAndre Ayton. The university tapped him lightly on the wrist, requiring him to sit out one whole game, before reinstating Miller. Ayton, his prize player, attended Arizona for one year before leaving to become the first pick in the 2018 NBA draft. He now plays for the Phoenix Suns, just up the road from Coach Miller, who remains on the bench in Tucson at a salary of over $4 million. Ask Coach Miller if cheating paid off for him. Professor David Berri of Southern Utah University estimated that Duke University's 2014–15 national championship team earned $33.7 million for its school. Had the players received half of this revenue in compensation, each would have been awarded $1.4 million. The best players, says Berri, are worth double that amount to their schools. He told the *Washington Post*, "If you're paying $100,000 to get one of these players on campus, that's a good deal."[109]

That big-time athletics has sullied, besmirched, even poisoned higher education in America is a truism that would make the most diligent producer of platitudes blush. It is simply accepted by all involved—if not articulated—that a large portion of FBS and D-I basketball athletes are incapable of doing college-level work in even the most lax definition of the term. Tates Locke, disgraced former coach of Clemson basketball in the 1970s, complained that the ACC's then-requirement that an athlete must have scored at least an 800 on the SATs made it "practically impossible to recruit a kid from the South."[110] Not since caustic social critic H.L. Mencken mocked the "Sahara of the Bozart" has Dixie taken it on the chin like that.

If only our competition played fairly! This is a constant theme of those who at least feel a twinge of embarrassment over the drastic lowering of their admissions standards in order to accommodate athletes. Sure, nothing is keeping schools from hiking admissions standards for athletes, but the mere suggestion brings scoffing dismissals: no one wants to unilaterally disarm. Former Harvard president Derek Bok commented on this sempiternal excuse of the un-level playing field:

> If some institutions choose to ignore admissions standards for athletes and are indifferent to whether their athletes ever graduate, other colleges will find it hard to compete with them on the playing field. In a world in which television revenues are so lucrative, alumni and legislators care so much about winning, and gate receipts are so important in meeting athletic costs, many institutions will find it very hard to maintain reasonable academic standards if their competitors refuse to do likewise.[111]

In 1981, Jan Kemp, coordinator of the English section of the University of Georgia's Developmental Studies Program, blew the whistle on the improper passage of nine football players from remedial courses (which they had not passed) to regular courses. For her honesty she was fired; a court later awarded her $2.58 million in damages, still later reduced to $1.08 million. Among the trial's revelatory moments was the release of a transcript in which Leroy Ervin, Kemp's boss and head of the remedial learning program, was secretly taped admitting of Georgia's athletes:

> [T]hese kids are not taught in high school. They aren't. We try to teach them here, but there is no way to do it. The majority of these kids are black [as was Ervin] that are coming in, and it kind of rips in at me at the insides, and I take it very, very personal. I know for a fact that these kids would not be here if it were not for their utility to the institution. There is no real sound academic reason for their being here other than to be utilized to produce income. They are used as a kind of raw material in the production of some goods to be sold . . . and they get nothing in return.[112]

Kemp was driven to two suicide attempts by this ordeal. She was reinstated at the University of Georgia and died of complications of Alzheimer's at the age of 59.[113] She serves as an example of the price a mid-level employee pays for blowing the whistle. (As an example of just how rigorous an academic regimen the University of Georgia put its athletes through, a 2004 course in "Coaching Principles and Strategy of Basketball," taught by the son of the UGA head coach, included these questions on its final exam: "How many goals are on a basketball court? How many points does a 3-point field goal account for in a basketball game?"[114] Now just how much is that UGA diploma worth?)

Just to the west of Athens, Georgia, in that football-worshiping church known as the Southeastern Conference, Auburn had its own whistle-blower: Professor James Gundlach, director of the Sociology Department, who was alerted to the rampant corruption within when he saw during a televised game that one of Auburn's players was the scholar of the week. This scholar was a sociology major, and yet Gundlach and two associates had no idea who he was. It turns out that he, and 17 other members of the undefeated and #2 ranked 2004 Auburn Tigers squad, had taken 97 hours of independent study with Professor Thomas Petee; their average GPA in those classes was 3.31. Auburn's star player, running back "Cadillac" Williams, took only two courses in his last semester at Auburn: both independent studies with Professor Petee. Professor Gundlach chose not to defer to the behemoth of Auburn football but rather to fight the power. He compiled documentation of the independent-study farce at Auburn and went to the press. "We were getting sociology majors graduating without taking sociology classes," he told the *New York Times*. The "corruption," he said, "runs the full gauntlet of the administration."[115] Auburn had to do something; the story made national headlines. So it suspended Professor Petee, who in response sued the school.[116] At this writing, ten years later, Dr. Petee is the senior consultant at the Auburn University Montgomery Center for Government. And the Auburn Tigers are ranked, once again, in the Top Ten.

Of course Southern schools hardly have a monopoly on dirty pool. In 1999, Jan Gangelhoff, the former executive secretary of the University of Minnesota men's basketball team, confessed that between 1994–8 she had written 400 papers in her side role as a "tutor." Her revelations won a Pulitzer Prize for the St. Paul *Pioneer-Press* reporter who broke the story and got coach Clem Haskins fired.[117]

Perhaps the most astounding scandal of recent years concerned academic fraud on a massive scale at one of the most distinguished public universities in the South. Over a period of almost a quarter century—1990–2013, though cases of fraud doubtlessly extend both prior and subsequent to those years—officials at the University of North Carolina at Chapel Hill:

> [K]nowingly and eagerly admitted athletes with poor academic training or little to no interest in school and further served the needs of the athletic program by creating paths to academic eligibility that kept these athletes on the field year after year,

according to Jay Smith, a professor of history at UNC Chapel Hill, and Mary Willingham, the counselor in Chapel Hill's Center for Student Success and Academic Counseling who was at the center of the maelstrom.[118] The scandal broke in 2010. Mary Willingham, who had worked with some of the most academically marginal athletes, was interviewed by UNC investigators in September of that year. She told them what she had seen: blatant cheating and plagiarism and improper benefits for athletes. Chancellor Holden Thorp was remarkably uninterested in pursuing this line of inquiry. The administration swept Willingham's charges under the rug, and it took an investigative reporter for the Raleigh *News & Observer* to bring Willingham's story to light. The November 2012 story by the *News & Observer*'s Dan Kane "left UNC's leaders defensive and speechless."[119]

The unqualified UNC admittees were, overwhelmingly, football and men's and women's basketball players. Athletes in the so-called Olympic sports—also known as the sports without spectators—were generally up to academic snuff, and in fact at most schools these athletes rack up higher graduation rates than do non-athletes. Willingham was less a tutor, she said, than an "eligibility specialist" who assisted her charges as much as possible "without actually doing the work for them." The absurdity of her task soon became clear: she was being asked to help athletes whose verbal skills were at an elementary school level do college work at a well-regarded university. It could not be done.

At the center of this mess were African- and Afro-American Studies curricular chair Julius Nyang'oro, a Tanzanian scholar, and his assistant, Debby Crowder. They oversaw independent study courses that football and basketball players took; it is barely an exaggeration to say that one could pass these courses with flying colors simply by signing one's name. As Willingham says, "We put athletes in the paper classes specifically because they didn't meet. Any kind of paper got an A or a B grade. It wasn't clear whether anyone was even reading the papers."[120] One unnamed student's final essay for an Afro American course in which he received a grade of A- went viral. It was, as essays, go—brief. One hundred forty-six words brief, to be exact. Now, pith is often superior to prolixity, and President Abraham Lincoln's immortal Gettysburg Address was just 272 words, but this was, well, here it is:

> On the evening of December Rosa Parks decided that she was going to sit in the white people section on the bus in Montgomery, Alabama. During this time blacks had to give up there seats to whites when more whites got on the bus. Rosa parks refused to give up her seat. Her and the bus driver began to talk and the conversation went like this. "Let me have those front seats" said the driver. She didn't get up and told the driver that she was tired of giving her seat to white people. "I'm going to have you arrested," said the driver. "You may do that," Rosa Parks responded. Two white policemen came in and Rosa Parks asked them "why do you all push us around?" The police officer replied and said "I don't know, but the law is the law and you're under arrest."[121]

Four-fifths of the starters on UNC's 1993 national championship basketball team were African or Afro-American Studies majors. By 1997–8, 50 students were taking independent studies in AFRI/AFAM—almost all from Professor Nyang'oro—up from the "handful" who had taken such courses prior to the professor's ascent. By 1999–2000, 86 young scholars were engaged in AFRI/AFAM independent study, and the number skyrocketed to 175 in 2001–2, 238 in 2002–3, and 291 in 2003–4. For one man to direct 291 independent studies courses is a feat that puts Mr. Chips and Mr. Holland to shame. Players on the 2005 national championship basketball team took a total of 31 "paper classes"—that is, classes that existed only on paper, and dispensed with the requirement that a "student" actually show up and do any work. "All 31 grades awarded, without exception, were either A or A-," write Smith and Willingham.[122]

The notorious Swahili 403 was an upper-level class which was, as Smith and Willingham write, "instructorless; no faculty member in the department had ever admitted responsibility for the course, and no instructor has admitted assigning a grade."[123] All those As and A-minuses were conceived in thin air. Defensive tackle Marvin Austin, who went on to be a second-round draft pick of the New York Giants, received a B+ in "Bioethics in Afro-American Studies" while "taking" it in the summer prior to his freshman year—and this despite Austin not yet taking the remedial composition class to which he had been assigned.[124] Jon Ericson, who founded the reformist Drake Group in 1999, observed, "You don't start at the senior level seminar and then work your way down to remedial writing."[125] Unless, that is, you are a star football player at the University of North Carolina. (The UNC Swahili fiasco resembles, strangely enough, a similar scandal at the University of Washington in the summer of 1992, when quarterback Billy Joe Hobert's eligibility was preserved thanks to the hard-partying young scholar earning 15 credits through Swahili courses.)[126]

Even more remarkable, a number of the athletes who passed Professor Nyang'oro's "classes" with flying colors had scored below 300 on the SAT reading section, and, according to Smith and Willingham, "at least one" achieved the perfectly null score of 200.[127] The professor, whose salary was $171,000, eventually retired.

UNC administrators shillied and shallied, one minute pronouncing themselves deeply disappointed and the next minimizing the extent of the scandal. Former Governor James Martin, whom Chancellor Thorp had asked to lead an investigation, asserted, with a politician's lack of veracity, "This was not an athletic scandal. It was an academic scandal, which is worse; but an isolated one."[128] Isolated? When the Department of African, African American and Diaspora Studies "offered more than 200 lecture courses that never met"?[129] That's a strange kind of isolation. Governor Martin never even bothered to look at student transcripts, lest knowledge of Swahili 403 and other paper courses complicate his simple narrative. Nor did he speak with any former or then-current basketball players.[130] The fear underlying this half-hearted investigation, speculated Jay Smith, was that the Tar Heels' 2005 and 2009 basketball national championships were won by players who took no-show classes.[131]

The UNC scandal exploded under football coach Butch Davis, formerly head honcho of the University of Miami Hurricanes and the NFL's Cleveland Browns. Davis was fired, though he disclaimed any knowledge of the avalanche of improper gifts, academic malpractice, and serial dishonesty plaguing the football program. His buyout package of $2.7 million cushioned the blow, to be sure, and by 2017 he was back on the sidelines, coaching at FBS school Florida International. Athletic director Dick Baddour was forced into early retirement, and UNC chancellor Holden Thorp retired. Hodding Carter, professor of Leadership and Public Policy at UNC and once President Jimmy Carter's press secretary, had taken issue with Chancellor Thorp's contention that athletic directors should be the ones to clean up athletics: "you don't get control of it by letting the guy who raised Godzilla become the person who is now supposed to supervise Godzilla."[132]

Thorp was succeeded by Carol Folt; among Chancellor Folt's first actions was the creation of five new Title IX compliance positions.[133] The school also created a new title: Vice Chancellor for Communications and Public Affairs, for which they hired a former Disney flack at $300,000 a year.[134] Panels were appointed, reports were submitted, rear ends were covered. Chancellor Thorp had the nerve to charge one investigative body, the Rawlings Panel on Intercollegiate Athletics at the University of North Carolina at Chapel Hill, with "provid[ing] ideas to other universities that are willing to tackle, what most agree is, a challenging issue for all of higher education"—as if UNC were not a gross offender but a wise instructor![135] There was much high-minded rhetoric about the primacy of academics, the necessity of reform, and the need for new approaches, always with the assurance that this problem was not peculiar to UNC but rather epidemic among D-I schools. Yet the Rawlings Panel, chaired by Association of American Universities president Hunter Rawlings, expressed confidence that North Carolina could "continue to pursue a high degree of competitive success on the playing field" without "compromising its institutional identity as a world class public university."[136] Timid suggestions of the "UNC should consider" variety, such as requiring freshman special admits to sit out of competition for a year, and reducing the number of hours athletes devote to sports, had a shelf life shorter than a plate of steaks at a football training table.[137] Roy Williams, the UNC men's basketball coach, is not about to have an incredibly talented freshman sit out for a year just because some tweedy Mugwumps issued a sententious letter. As one anthropology professor joked on the release of the Rawlings Panel report, "I was struck with a feeling of déjà vu—I would like to find out more about 'where are we on the recommendations of the 1989 report?'"—a similarly high-minded set of recommendations that are moldering in the dead letter file in the athletic department's basement.[138]

A subsequent investigation by Kenneth Wainstein, an ex-federal prosecutor, determined that from 1993–2011, no-show classes, plagiarized papers, and unethical assistance from teachers and tutors enabled 329 athletes to retain their eligibility. So did UNC de-emphasize big-time sports after this humiliating episode? Of course not. Dozens of academically unqualified athletes—overwhelmingly football and basketball players—continue to be awarded special admittances. (Chancellor Carol Folt, facing questions about a gap of over 300 between the average SAT scores of football players and non-athletes, fell back on the false statement that SAT scores are "not a very good predictor" of academic success.)[139] Coaching salaries almost doubled in the ten years between 2005 and 2015, from $17 million to $31 million. Over that same period, writes Logan Ulrich in *The Daily Tar Heel*, UNC athletic revenue rose from just less than $55 million to almost $90 million, but student athletic fees ballooned by 250 percent, to almost $250 per student. For the 2017–18 academic year, the undergraduate fee was $279.[140] In return, students get free access to athletic events: a fair trade for sports fans, but a rip-off for those who don't care if the Tar Heels are playing Wake Forest or Sherwood Forest. As Jay Smith told Ulrich, "They rake in millions year after year, but yet they keep coming back . . . and asking for support from students. At some point, doesn't something have to give?"[141]

Though UNC was a particularly egregious offender, countless Division I schools engage in similar charades. University of Missouri wide receiver Sean Coffey recalled that when he played for the Tigers (2002–5), his "academic" counselors steered him toward agricultural studies, despite the fact that he was a city boy who had no interest in animal husbandry or crop rotations. When his dissatisfaction became a little too manifest, he was flipped onto a hotel and restaurant management track, which was equally remote from his interests. All that mattered, said Coffey, was maintaining eligibility. The academic advisers "know every class and which ones are easiest."[142] Wayne Yates, formerly basketball coach at Memphis State, once remarked, "I've heard an academic counselor say he could keep a cockroach eligible for two years. That's true." Yates coached Memphis State from the 1974–5 through the 1978–9 seasons; as Murray Sperber notes, Memphis State did not graduate a single African American player from its predominantly African American basketball teams from 1972 through 1985.[143]

Connoisseurs of the genre still marvel over the case of DeShawn Stevenson, a highly prized recruit of the University of Kansas, who scored an almost impossibly low 450 combined math–verbal on his SAT.[144] When he took it again, he miraculously tallied an 1150. Alas, that 1150 was scored in North Carolina, and DeShawn was resident in Fresno, California. Kansas coach Roy Williams (later coach of the University of North Carolina) groused that Stevenson had gotten a "raw deal." So he took it a third time—and scored less than 650. The Kansas Jayhawks were thus deprived of his services, so Stevenson went into the NBA Draft, was chosen by Utah in the first round, and enjoyed a 13-year NBA career.[145] DeShawn Stevenson succeeded in a lucrative business: why the need for the scholastic sham?

In 1985, Chris Washburn, a basketball prodigy, entered North Carolina State with a subterranean SAT score of 470 (270 verbal, 200 math). Chancellor Bruce Poulton, defending N.C. State's decision, said, "We admitted Mr. Washburn because we honestly thought and believed he could do the work here, and his work here certainly vindicates that judgment."[146] Poulton spoke too soon: Washburn got off on the wrong foot when he stole a fellow athlete's stereo. He dropped out of school, played two unremarkable seasons in the NBA, and endured a long struggle with drug abuse. Poulton's puling defense of Washburn's admission pales before Donna Shalala's remarks on the 2004 admission to the University of Miami (FL) of Willie Williams, a phenomenal high school football player who had already racked up 11 arrests in five years. Shalala, who had been the Secretary of Health and Human Services under President Clinton before taking the Miami job, said of Williams:

> This is hardly a perfect applicant to the University. Oh, how we love perfection—perfect grades, perfect character, and perfect recommendations. Those are the easy ones! This young man is not perfect and has made some bad

decisions—in friends, in behavior, etc. However, he is young, and his file reveals academic talent as well as the better-known athletic ability.[147]

Willie Williams was no dummy. He had scored a 1070 on his SAT, which is a golden ticket to anywhere if you're a good football player. But there was the small matter of those 11 arrests. Williams washed out of Miami; after a series of transfers to ever more obscure schools and run-ins with the law, he wound up doing 15 years for burglary in a Kentucky prison.[148]

The hard truth, says Richard Southall, director of the University of South Carolina's College Sport Research Institute, is that:

> We pretend that it's feasible to recruit high school graduates with minimal academic qualifications, give them a full-time job as a football or basketball player at a Division I NCAA school, and somehow have them get up to college-level reading and writing skills at the same time that they're enrolled in college-level classes.[149]

It's an impossible dream.

A year-long investigation by the *Atlanta Journal-Constitution*, using data from the NCAA certification process covering 54 Division I football or basketball schools, revealed a significant "admissions gap" separating scholarship athletes and regular students. The average combined math and verbal SAT score for all freshmen at the 54 schools in the survey was 1161. The average for athletes was 1024, for football players 941, and male basketball players 934. At some schools the gap resembled a grand canyon: the difference between the average SAT score of men's basketball players and the student body was 433 points at the University of Texas, 396 points at Georgia Tech, 369 points at the University of North Carolina, and 350 points at the University of California, Berkeley. The smallest gap was just 27 points, at Washington State. The largest chasms between average SAT scores for the student body and football players were the University of Florida (346 points), UCLA (340 points), and good old UC Berkeley (331 points).[150]

This gap was not always thought to be unbridgeable, or even to exist. Howard Savage, in his 1929 Carnegie report, wrote:

> The common notion that athletes in general are poorer students than non-athletes is erroneous. On the other hand, participation in sports that require very hard training and long practice hours impairs the academic standing of certain athletes . . . The causes of this condition are ascribable not to an inferior mental equipment among college athletes . . . but to the conduct, emphasis, and values of modern college sport.[151]

Fix the flaws in intercollegiate sport and its gladiators will win acclaim in the classroom, too.

President? Faculty?

But who will fix the flaws? In his 1929 Carnegie Report, Howard Savage placed the responsibility squarely on the shoulders of the president and the faculty of the colleges. It is not a responsibility that has been borne manfully, or womanfully, or at all satisfactorily. Ninety years later, Savage's challenge has been evaded, if not subverted.

Among the most insightful insider critiques of big-time college sports was that of former University of Michigan president James J. Duderstadt in *Intercollegiate Athletics and the American University: A University President's Perspective* (2003). Duderstadt accepts sports as a legitimate activity of the university and considers swimmers, rowers, gymnasts, and others who engage in "minor" sports to be active participants in the life of the university. But football and basketball "threaten not only the academic welfare of their participants but the integrity and reputation of the very institutions that conduct them, our colleges and universities." Indeed, "Any educational mission" connected with football or basketball "has been subverted if not destroyed entirely."[152]

The fault, he says, "lies at the academic heart of the university itself, with its faculty, its governing boards, and, perhaps most of all, with its presidents." The faculty has "abdicated its responsibility for student activities beyond the classroom," the governing boards bow to the demands of boosters and TV, and the university presidents "succumb to timidity and procrastination," issuing high-minded proclamations but never actually taking steps to curb the wretched excesses, let alone achieve fundamental reforms.[153] A recent *Chronicle of Higher Education* exploration found that not a single president or chancellor of the 25 largest athletic departments had language in his or her contract giving him or her oversight of athletics. About the only mention of athletics in any of these contracts was the provision of free tickets (for life!) to campus sporting events or postseason games.[154]

In collegiate governance, faculties have become, as social critic Thorstein Veblen said long ago, "deliberative bodies charged with power to talk."[155] Athletic departments are largely autonomous; faculty control is minimal. Athletic directors, and not faculty or university presidents, oversee athletics: the hiring, the firing, the NCAA compliance, the scheduling, the conference relations. At most schools, all the faculty can do is sit on the sidelines and bewail the passing parade. In 2013, at Bowling Green, athletic spending had increased by 42 percent over the previous decade while academic spending per student had fallen by 13 percent. So when the school announced that it was going to cut 40 faculty positions, journalism professor Dave Sennerud, who was making all of $40,000 and was among those on the chopping block, asked reporters, "Are they looking to put out semi-pro football teams or educate students? What about academics? What is our purpose?"[156] It's a question that is frequently asked and seldom answered, except in the most hackneyed phrases. Until it is answered, the prospects of real reform are about as bright as Bowling Green's chance to be crowned next year's FBS champions.

Just say no

If cosmetic reforms are inadequate, as they clearly are, what of the nuclear option: abolition? Where are the Robert Maynard Hutchinses of our day? Many are called, but few choose this path.

One that almost did was Maryland's Towson State, which now goes by Towson University. Towson plays in the FCS, which is not exactly big-time: about 85 percent of its athletic budget is a university subsidy, mostly from student fees. Brit Kirwan, chancellor of the University System of Maryland, explained: "Towson is an example of a school that wants to play big-time football but can't generate enough revenue from external forces. The sad part is there are probably a hundred and fifty other schools out there just like it."[157] The Towson school administration considered dropping football in 1990, amid grumbling over a student fee hike.[158] Football survived, thanks to a University Senate vote of 12–6 (student representatives were unanimously pro-football; the faculty reps split), and on the field, at least, things improved: the Towson Tigers were occasionally nationally ranked in FCS polls as members of the Colonial Athletic Association.[159] But the team today remains heavily dependent on student subvention in the form of a $435 per term athletic fee assessed on all students taking at least 12 units.[160]

Towson announced in October 2012 that it would drop baseball and men's soccer in 2013. Ironically, this came just "three days after taking home a check for $510,000 from its nationally televised football game at LSU"—one of those sacrificial-lamb-for-pay days that plenish the coffers of the non-elite.[161] (The LSU Tigers struggled to beat the Towson Tigers, 38–22, in a great moral victory for the underdog.) At the time, the athletics fee was $798 per year ($399 per term), and Towson president Maravene Loeschke announced that "I am not willing to allow Towson students to bear the burden of a significant fee increase to support our athletic programs."[162] Baseball was restored thanks to a fundraising campaign and a 1 percent increase in the athletics fee, but men's soccer was eliminated, just as men's indoor track, outdoor track, cross country, and tennis had fallen to budget cuts and (ostensibly) Title IX compliance in the several years previous.[163] Towson currently offers just six men's and 13 women's varsity sports. In 2016, Towson's athletic budget was $19.9 million, of which $15.78 million was supplied by the student athletics fee.[164] There is no realistic chance that the basic contours of the budget will change any time soon.

It's one thing for FCS schools to drop football, as happens on occasion. Towson drew back from the brink, but in a two week span in late 2009, fellow FCS members Northeastern and Hofstra Universities announced that they were pulling the plug on their programs. Stuart Rabinowitz, president of Hofstra, said that football's $4.5 million annual budget—one-quarter of the entire athletic budget—would be redirected toward academic programs and scholarships. He dismissed one admittedly long-shot option: a move up the ladder to the FBS. Though Hofstra had a proud tradition and had sent several players to the NFL, it attracted an average of just 4,260 fans in its final season, and as President Rabinowitz said, "The

Southeastern Conference and the Big Ten weren't calling us."[165] At Northeastern, a school better known for its Division I men's hockey team, athletic director Peter Roby said of football that "It was a $20-million-plus situation, and that, to me, was not tenable."[166] Coincidentally or not, in the years since Northeastern has become a "hot school," rather like NYU and George Washington University—and not one of that trio fields a football team.

Perhaps the most amusing, and certainly the most ill-timed and sanctimonious, reaction to football's demise at Hofstra and Northeastern came from Ohio State president E. Gordon Gee, whom the *New York Times* identified as "an outspoken supporter for reform in college athletics." From atop his ivory tower, President Gee pontificated, "I expect you will see these types of decisions accelerate at smaller institutions as they must make critical decisions. In times of economic distress, academic programs should and will win out."[167] The very next year, 2010, Ohio State's 12 football victories were retroactively annulled by the NCAA due to numerous violations of NCAA rules. Gee, meanwhile, was making a serious bid for retiring the trophy in the hypocrisy sweepstakes. While tut-tutting in favor of belt-tightening in times of economic distress, Gee was, according to a *Dayton Daily News* investigation by Laura A. Bischoff, pulling down a munificent $8.6 million in salary and compensation, giving him the dubious distinction of being the highest-paid public university president in the country. OSU also provided a mansion for Gee: a 9,600 square foot palace at which he entertained lavishly. Bischoff reported that Gee's annual expenses totaled $7.7 million, as Mr. Tighten Your Belt "stayed in luxury hotels, dined at country clubs and swank restaurants, threw lavish parties, flew on private jets, and handed out thousands of gifts—all at public expense."[168]

Oh, and that description by the *Times* of Gee as "an outspoken supporter for reform in college athletics"? It came from Gee himself, who in 2005 told the *Phi Kappa Phi Forum* that in his then-position as Chancellor of Vanderbilt University he was "viewed by some as a reformer in intercollegiate athletics." The bow-tie-wearing Gee is fluent in high-flown and self-congratulatory rhetoric; he boasted that at Vanderbilt, "our student-athletes take real classes . . . they attend those classes . . . their grades stay healthy, and . . . they graduate."[169] Gee cannot be blamed for the moral collapse of the Vanderbilt football program several years later, when three players were convicted of raping a 21-year-old neuroscience student in 2013, but let us say that his reforms didn't exactly stick.[170]

On the exceedingly rare occasion when an FBS school opts out of football, the howls of outrage can be deafening. In December 2014, University of Alabama at Birmingham president Ray Watts, a noted neurologist, using as ammunition a report from Carr Sports Consulting, announced that the football, bowling, and rifle teams were being cut for budgetary reasons. Two-thirds of UAB's athletic expenses were being subsidized by either student fees or the university, and it was hard to envision a path to anything approaching self-sufficiency, given UAB's lower-level conference, lack of football tradition, the presence of Goliath (the University of Alabama) down the road, and projected cost increases in maintaining a football program.[171] Retaining football would require an additional $49 million from the university over the next five years, money that President Watts believed could be better spent on academic offerings. The nerve of that egghead neurosurgeon! The faculty senate cast a vote of no confidence in Watts. The national sports press roasted him. Six months later, after a fundraising drive raised over $20 million in pledges, President Watts reversed field. Football would return. And in the fall of 2017, after a two year hiatus, the UAB Blazers were back on the field as part of the FBC Conference USA.[172] They posted a decent record of 8–5, followed by a surprising 11–3 in 2018. UAB rifle, a coed sport, and women's bowling also survived, with rather less fanfare.

The folks at Wichita State drew a different lesson from their experience *sans* football. The Shockers had fielded a team since 1897, but at the end of the 1986 season the administration, faced with mounting debts from a program that had had just two winning seasons in the quarter century since 1962, announced that it was indefinitely suspending football.[173] Surely that tornado-colored Kansas sky would collapse on poor WSU! "There were warnings that enrollment would drop and that fund raising would fall off," Robert F. Hartsock, vice president for development and alumni affairs, told the *Chronicle of Higher Education* a year later. Instead, enrollment and annual giving actually *increased* the next year.[174]

Since Wichita State departed the field, the subject of a return to the gridiron has come up on occasion. A 1992 study reported that bringing the school's football stadium up to Division 1-A standards would cost $24 million. In 1998, an advisory committee urged Wichita State to field a team again, but nothing came of this suggestion.[175] A 2016 study pegged the cost of renovating the stadium and constructing practice facilities at between $42 and $49 million. So this is on the minds of some influential people at Wichita.[176] For now, at least, there are no plans to revive the program. Wichita State did not inspire a legion of followers, though here and there one encounters lonely voices calling for abolition of football, or at least its de-emphasis.

Perennial doormat Eastern Michigan subsidizes 85 percent of its athletic budget with student fees and general revenue from the school and runs a $20 million athletic deficit. EMU Accounting professor Howard J. Bunsis says:

> The board has this belief that football is the window to the university. If we just put the resources into football, we will really help enrollment. I think they are wrong. We are stuck. We really can't be successful at D-I. We need to get out.[177]

They have not gotten out. Eastern Michigan remains an also-ran member of the MAC. For Power Five conference teams, dropping out of the FBS is as unthinkable as inviting Donald Trump to be the commencement speaker.

Less than 50 miles from the aforementioned Towson is the University of Maryland in College Park. Towson, the second largest school in the Maryland university system, is but a poor stepsister to the Maryland Terps. But the Big Brother in College Park has never developed the generous and fanatical alumni base of other flagship state schools, so it, too, ran into financial trouble earlier in this century. A $1.2 million athletic department budget deficit in 2010–11 put the most vulnerable of the University of Maryland's 27 teams on the chopping block. A 24 percent reduction ($13 million to $9.9 million) in athletic donations over the previous three years, coupled with a decline in football attendance from an average of 49,393 to 39,169 over the previous five years, made a lie of earlier claims that a $50.8 million stadium expansion would pay for itself with increased revenues. Years of football mediocrity were taking its toll.[178]

Women's sports were less vulnerable than men's, due to Title IX. So in November 2011, Maryland president Wallace D. Loh announced that eight sports—men's cross country, indoor and outdoor track, and tennis; men's and women's swimming and diving; and women's acrobatics and tumbling and women's water polo—would be dropped at the end of the school year.[179] This reduced the number of intercollegiate UM squads from 27—quite high for Division I—to 19. Squeals of protest were not overly audible, except, understandably, from the athletes affected. Several of the dropped sports resurfaced at the more human-scale club sports level, joining such other UM club offerings as badminton, boxing, cricket, dodgeball, ice hockey, paintball, rugby, sailing, and wushu.[180] (See Chapter 8 for more on club sports.) Despite the reductions, the University of Maryland maintains an athletic fee of $203.19 per semester.

The school also found a new home—or at least a temporary residence. Trawling for cash, Maryland met a conference—the Big Ten—that wanted to increase its exposure in the Middle Atlantic/DC area, and a marriage of convenience was born. In late 2012 the University of Maryland announced that as of 2014 it was abandoning the Atlantic Coast Conference, its home for almost six decades, and joining the Big Ten. This was an act of geographic incoherence: the Big Ten is and always has been a Midwestern conference. But loyalty and history add up to nothing when placed against the prospect of a fatter cut of conference payouts.[181] The Terps are getting clobbered on Big Ten football fields, but football's privileged position in the Maryland athletic department is safe.

Rutgers, a fellow latecomer to the Big Ten, also faces perennial shortfalls in its athletic department budget. But unlike Maryland, it also faces persistent in-house criticism. In the 1990s, the Rutgers 1000 Alumni Council, a grouping of faculty, students, and alumni, campaigned for the school to leave Division I for Division I-AA or an even lower tier and concentrate on its academic mission.[182] The voices of sanity included that of Nobel Laureate Milton Friedman, who argued, in a full-page ad in the student newspaper in April 1998 sponsored by the Rutgers 1000, that "it is not the purpose of a university to generate publicity or to stimulate sports." As Friedman told *New York Times* columnist Robert Lipsyte, "as long as athletes are admitted on lower standards than other students, sports is a corruptive influence on higher education."[183] At the time, Rutgers was a member of the Big East Conference, which also included Virginia Tech, which had football players being investigated for such crimes as rape and assault; and the notorious "U," the

University of Miami, whose outlaw program, awash in drugs and payoffs to players, didn't even bother to hold up a fig leaf of respectability.

William C. Dowling, a Rutgers professor of English and American literature, argued in the *Chronicle of Higher Education* that the problem with big-time sports went much deeper than NCAA violations, or even the long-settled question of the propriety of athletic scholarships. Dowling took aim at the very idea that athletes should be "recruited on the basis of physical skills rather than for academic or intellectual ability." In fact, given the inordinate number of hours that any college athlete must devote to his or her sport, it made sense, said Dowling, that "only students with SAT scores above the average for their entering class would be permitted to play basketball or football." Average or below-average students, he said, are incapable of performing acceptable academic work while spending 40 or more hours a week at their sport.[184]

The campaign of the Rutgers 1000 was noble but doomed. Dowling kept up the agitation, though, getting in hot water when in 2007 he told the *New York Times*, responding to a question about the impact reform would have on minority athletes:

> If you were giving the scholarship to an intellectually brilliant kid who happens to play a sport, that's fine. But they give it to a functional illiterate who can't read a cereal box, and then make him spend 50 hours a week on physical skills. That's not opportunity. If you want to give financial help to minorities, go find the ones who are at the library after school.

Rutgers athletic administrators jumped on these comments, deeming them racist, which outraged Downey, who had marched for civil rights in the 1960s.[185] All the while, Rutgers kept on spending. An expansion of the football stadium spurred an increase in facilities spending from $2 million in 2005 to $11 million a decade later, the bulk of it due to $6.5 million in annual debt service for the stadium.[186]

Things got especially dicey for Rutgers in 2011–12, when a spate of articles highlighted the school's dependence on institutional subsidies and student fees—in sum, though not in percentage, the highest at any public school in the nation. Year in and year out, institutional subsides accounted for over 40 percent of the athletic budget.[187] (The Scarlet Knights have since been eclipsed for this dubious honor by UConn, though Rutgers still receives more than one-third of its athletics revenue from institutional subsidies, which is extremely high for a member of a Power Five conference.) Making the Rutgers subsidy even more galling was the fact that the school is among the most expensive public schools for in-state students in the nation.[188] For the 2017–18 school year, tuition and mandatory fees for New Jersey residents attending Rutgers were $14,638.[189]

Professors have led the Rutgers protests. "[T]he core mission of the university is to teach, do research and then provide service to the state of New Jersey, and ancillary enterprises such as athletics should not be the top priorities," said Patrick Nowlan, executive director of the Rutgers American Association of University

Professors-American Federation of Teachers. Among their chief beefs was that football coach Greg Schiano (since fired) was pulling down $1.9 million annually, making him the highest-paid coach in the Big East, in an era of salary freezes for non-football-related staff.[190] The Rutgers faculty council voted in March 2012 to demand athletic spending cuts and a referendum on student fees, the latter a nice piece of idealism that the university was not about to consent to. ("Ninety-nine percent of students don't know" that they're paying such high fees, said Kristen Clarke, the nonvoting student rep on the Rutgers Board of Governors.)[191]

The university's president, who liked to point out that athletics constituted only about 1 percent of the school's total budget, promised to reduce the institutional subsidy, and when the Big Ten admitted Rutgers in 2014, hoping to expand its footprint on the East Coast, it appeared as an answered prayer. "The Big Ten is the ultimate academic neighborhood to live in, and we're now in that neighborhood," said athletic director Tim Pernetti, but this was window dressing: the real lure of the Big Ten was not the chance to bask in the reflected academic glory of such mid-level schools as Ohio State and the University of Minnesota but rather to share in the munificent bowl and television contract payouts.[192] Rutgers has since reduced, by a small margin, its reliance on institutional subsidies, but the student athletics fee of $363.50 per year is not going anywhere but up, at least for the time being. Rutgers will not fully share in revenue distributions from the Big Ten until 2022, but even then, realists expect the student subsidy to survive.

As New Jersey State Senator Ray Lesniak, Rutgers alum and fervent booster, said, "We're in the Big Ten. We should act like it."[193] Fiscally responsible Big Ten members like Purdue to the contrary, *acting like it* apparently means spending without limit, and without regard to the capacity of students to handle the necessary fees. Not that the students are in the vanguard of protests. Matt Panconi, student body president, said in 2016:

> No students are thrilled about any student fee. However, I don't think that's of much concern because I think students understand the importance of Big Ten athletics. I think students are excited about the future and potential of Rutgers athletics, for the most part.[194]

For the most part. That last qualifier is important. Rutgers athletics has attracted more sustained protest over spending than that of any other major college sports program. The football team remains mired in the Jersey muck: its 2017 record was 4–8, and it is a punching bag for its new opponents in the Big Ten.

In the neighboring football non-hotbed of New York State, SUNY Buffalo announced in April 2017 that it was dropping four sports—baseball, men's soccer, men's swimming and diving, and women's rowing—bringing it down to the minimum of 16 teams which the NCAA requires of FBS schools. UB's $31.9 million athletic budget ranked third in the 12-team MAC. School president Satish K. Tripathi acknowledged that the size of the institutional subsidy for UB sports—$24 million, or about three-quarters of the athletic budget, which put UB in the nation's Top Ten in subsidies, if not football or basketball prowess—was a factor in the decision.[195]

Kenneth Dauber, a professor of English at SUNY Buffalo, told the *Buffalo News* that UB's $24 million athletic subsidy could have paid for 225 new faculty members or a $1,000 reduction in tuition for its students. Neither item, however, was on the school's agenda. Instead, President Tripathi dreamily predicted that "The investment from UB central is going to go down, as we are able to really develop the program to a prominence in the MAC, we are able to attract more ticket sales and so on." This is, of course, not true for any other school in the MAC, and saying it will not make it so. Ticket sales will make no dent in the $534 per student athletic fee. About $8.2 million, or 93 percent of funds raised by the fee, went toward intercollegiate athletics, while the remaining 7 percent ($620,000) was spent on club and intramural sports, which, as the *News* noted, have thousands of participants, as compared to the 525 UB varsity athletes. This really "grinds the gears of a majority of students," said Joseph Pace, treasurer of the UB Student Association. Among the students quoted in a *Buffalo News* story about UB's athletic subsidies was Rayna Moncrieffe, a basketball fan and member of the UB Step Troupe, whose 53 members were subsidized to the tune of $77 apiece, for a total of $4,100—which means, as the reporter noted, that UB "spends 10 times the amount the entire Step Troupe received on a single athlete."[196]

Buffalo News columnist Jerry Sullivan pointed out the elephant in the room:

> Cut through all the scholarly rhetoric and it comes down to one sickening reality: This is the inevitable consequence of UB pretending to be a major college football program, which seems more and more a fool's errand with each passing year.

Football consumes $7.53 million, or about one-quarter of the athletic budget; it is, says UB soccer player Vinny DiVirgilio, a "bottomless pit."[197] Baseball's budget, according to the *Buffalo News*, was $600,000 annually, or "by far the smallest in the conference." This included scholarships: while conference teams are permitted to award the equivalent of 11.7 free rides (often distributed among twice as many players), UB gave out just 6.5 scholarships yearly.[198]

Football was never considered for the chopping block. And yet the perpetually poor Bulls teams had given this generally fine university a national reputation as "Loser U," in Murray Sperber's pungent phrase.[199] Buffalo's promotion into the big time was supposed to provide what school president William Greiner called "a major contribution to the total quality of student life and the visibility of your institution." (Sperber interpreted the phrase as code for "student partying in conjunction with college sports."[200]) Instead, UB, a perfectly respectable academic institution, took on the aura of a whipped cur. Its football teams were regularly ranked in the Bottom Ten whenever sports writers surveyed the dregs of the D-I world. One Buffalo professor termed this the "negative halo effect."[201] *Loser U* is emphatically *not* the sobriquet UB was aiming for when it joined football's top division in 1998, but then you can't always get what you want. (Buffalo rebounded to a fine 10–4 record in 2018, though this may prove to have been an anomalous year.)

On occasion, wisdom triumphs. In 2004, trustees at Winston-Salem State University in North Carolina, a historically African American school, voted to move its teams from Division II to Division I (football would, at first, join Division I-AA). The hope, as Chancellor Harold Martin explained, was that:

> Moving up to NCAA Division I advances our university's strategic plan and will offer our talented student–athletes even more challenging competition. Specifically, competing on a larger stage will elevate awareness of WSSU and our reputation for excellence regionally and nationally, while creating opportunities to generate even more revenue from our athletic programs.

Well, that was the hope anyway. The reality was different. Winston-Salem State soon learned the cost of "moving up." The NCAA mandated over $10 million in athletic facility upgrades.[202] Three years into its D-I transition, which spanned the seasons from 2007–8 to 2009–10, WSSU pulled the plug. Donald Reaves, the new chancellor, predicted an athletic department deficit of $15 million. The football team was staggering through a 1–10 season. The envisaged elevation of the school's reputation was nowhere in sight. So Winston-Salem State returned to Division II, balanced its greatly reduced athletic department budget, and by 2012 its football team was playing for the NCAA Division II national championship: the first historically black college ever to do so.[203]

Charles Clotfelter found that of the 100 largest college football programs in 1920, 60 were still among the 100 top spenders on athletics in 2009. He observed, "One would be hard pressed to find many markets for consumer goods or services in which 60% of today's most successful firms or products had also been among the most successful 90 years before."[204] Of the 40 schools that had dropped from the Top 100, three (West Point, Navy, and Utah State) still competed at the top level (Division 1 or FBS), though their athletic budgets were just outside the pale. Twenty-eight were "private liberal arts colleges or regional universities," 24 of which competed in 2009 at a lower level. Seven were members of the Ivy League, which dropped to the Division 1-AA or FCS tier. And just two—the University of Chicago and Washington University of St. Louis—were national universities that dropped football. (Washington dropped the sport briefly, from 1943–6, and now competes in Division III. And even Robert Maynard Hutchins's university returned to Division III in 1973. Hutchins, who died in 1977, thus lived to see football's rebirth.[205])

One that did drop football, and seemingly for good, was the University of Denver, a private Division I school that fielded an 11 from 1885 until Thanksgiving Day, 1960, when the Pioneers packed it in due to annual losses of $100,000 or more and "crowds" averaging under 1,300 a game. (Before 1926, the team had been known as the Fighting Parsons or Fighting Ministers—names to strike terror into the hearts of the wicked, if not surly middle linebackers!) Football, said Chancellor Chester M. Alter, was "prohibitively expensive." The chancellor ought to have stopped there, but he added that it was a dying sport whose most popular days were in the rearview mirror.[206] Asked in 2004 whether he regretted the move, the 98-year-old Alter replied, "DU's still there, isn't it? It seems to have survived just fine."[207]

Chancellor Alter's successor, Maurice Mitchell, was hardly going to reverse his action. In fact, he had the football stadium razed to create more space for intra-mural sports. Mitchell encouraged widespread participation in physical activity and the cultivation of participants, not spectators. He was, perhaps, the most vocifer-ously anti-intercollegiate sports chancellor of his time. He scorned football and other major sports as "parasite[s] on an institution that does not need them, does not benefit from them, and is gravely debilitated by them." Swimming and its low-profile ilk were "cute little varsity sports that rattle around on a campus just to make it look as though football and basketball are simply two more parts of the program." If he hadn't made himself clear yet, he concluded in a 1982 essay, "[W]hat is the role of intercollegiate athletics in the university? There isn't any. They are an evil and a sin."[208] The Fighting Ministers proved to be a worthy scourge for the demon of big-time sports.

Notes

1 Robin Herman, "How the College Crowd Feels about It: Jeers Outscore Cheers," *New York Times*, March 15, 1974.
2 James H. Frey, "The Winning-Team Myth," *Currents* 12, No. 1 (January 1985): 33.
3 James Frey, "The Place of Athletics in the Educational Priorities of University Alumni," *Review of Sport & Leisure* 6, No. 1 (1981): 55.
4 Ibid.: 57.
5 Ibid.: 57–8.
6 Ibid.: 60.
7 Ibid.: 61.
8 Allen L. Sack and Charles Watkins, "Winning and Giving," in *Sport and Higher Education*, pp. 303–4.
9 Lee Sigelman and Samuel Bookheimer, "Is It Whether You Win or Lose? Monetary Contributions to Big-Time College Athletic Programs," *Social Science Quarterly* 64, No. 2 (June 1983): 349. See also George W. Brooker Jr. and T.D. Klastorin, "To the Victors Belong the Spoils? College Athletics and Alumni Giving," *Social Science Quarterly* 62, No. 4 (December 1981): 744–50.
10 Robert A. Baade and Jeffrey O. Sundberg, "Fourth Down and Gold to Go? Assessing the Link between Athletics and Alumni Giving," *Social Science Quarterly* 77, No. 4 (December 1996): 790.
11 Frank, "Challenging the Myth: A Review of the Links Among College Athletic Success, Student Quality, and Donations," p. 1.
12 Linda Myers, "Winning College Sports Teams Rarely Attract More Alumni Gifts or Better Student Applicants, Cornell Report Shows," *Cornell Chronicle*, September 7, 2004.
13 Maurice Mitchell, "Big-Time Sports Should Be Banished from Campus," *The Center Magazine* 15, No. 1 (January–February 1982): 23.
14 Robert A. Baade and Jeffrey O. Sundberg, "What Determines Alumni Generosity?" *Economics of Education Review* 15, No. 1 (1996): 80.

15 Jonathan Meer and Harvey S. Rosen, "The Impact of Athletic Performance on Alumni Giving: An Analysis of Micro Data," CEPS Working Paper No. 162, March 2008, pp. 10–12.

16 Ibid., p. 16.

17 Duderstadt, *Intercollegiate Athletics and the American University: A University President's Perspective*, p. 129.

18 Brad Wolverton, "Sharp Growth in Athletics Fund Raising Leads to Decline in Academic Donations on Some Campuses," *Chronicle of Higher Education*, September 25, 2007.

19 Brad Wolverton and Sandhya Kambhampati, "Colleges Raised $1.2 Billion in Donations for Sports in 2015," *Chronicle of Higher Education*, January 27, 2016.

20 Douglas Lederman, "Do Winning Teams Spur Contributions? Scholars and Fund Raisers Are Skeptical," *Chronicle of Higher Education*, January 13, 1988.

21 Frey, "The Winning-Team Myth," *Currents*: 34.

22 Lederman, "Do Winning Teams Spur Contributions? Scholars and Fund Raisers Are Skeptical," *Chronicle of Higher Education*.

23 Murray Sperber, *Beer and Circus: How Big-Time College Sports Is Crippling Undergraduate Education* (New York: Henry Holt, 2000), p. 256.

24 Brad R. Humphreys, "The Relationship Between Big-Time College Football and State Appropriations for Higher Education," *International Journal of Sports Finance* 1, No. 2 (2006): 121. See also Brad R. Humphreys, "The Relationship Between Big-Time College Football and State Appropriations to Higher Education," UMBC Economics Department Working Paper 03–102, July 7, 2003, p. 3.

25 Ibid., p. 1.

26 Humphreys, "The Relationship Between Big-Time College Football and State Appropriations for Higher Education," *International Journal of Sports Finance*: 121.

27 Ibid.: 126.

28 Irvin B. Tucker, "The Impact of Big-Time Athletics on Graduation Rates," *Atlantic Economic Journal* 20, No. 4 (December 1992): 71. For the argument that graduation rates are an unreliable indicator of a college's quality, see Stephen Burd, "Graduation Rates Called a Poor Measure of Colleges," *Chronicle of Higher Education*, April 2, 2004.

29 Jordan Weissmann, "The Real Crisis in College Sports: It's Wasted Money, Not Wasted Students," *The Atlantic*, January 24, 2012, www.theatlantic.com.

30 William F. Shughart II, Robert D. Tollison, and Brian L. Goff, "Pigskins and Publications," *Atlantic Economic Journal* 14 (July 1986): 48.

31 Clotfelter, *Big-Time Sports in American Universities*, p. 145.

32 Mike Dodd, "Winning One for the Admissions Office," *USA Today*, July 11, 1997.

33 "The Business of Being Cinderella; Mason Releases Study on Final Four Impact," George Mason University Media and Public Relations, March 14, 2008; see also Brad Wolverton, "George Mason U. Drew Big Spike in Interest Following Final Four Run," *Chronicle of Higher Education*, March 17, 2008.

34 Tim McGarry and Laken Litman, "A Cinderella Story: How Universities Benefit from Being an NCAA Tournament Underdog," *USA Today*, March 27, 2014.

35 Stu Woo, "The State of Affairs That Is Boise State," *Wall Street Journal*, October 19, 2012.

36 "Boise State University," *U.S. News & World Report*, www.usnews.com/best-colleges/boise-state-university-1616, accessed August 17, 2017.

37 "Census Day Profile of New Academic Freshmen: Fall 2016," Boise State University, https://enrollmentservices.boisestate.edu/wp-content/blogs.dir/1/files/2016/12/Fall-2016-Census-Day-Freshmen-Cohort-Profile.pdf.

38 "2017 Roster," Boise State Broncos, www.broncosports.com/sports/m-footbl/mtt/bosu-m-footbl-mtt.html, accessed August 17, 2017.

39 George A. Chressanthis and Paul W. Grimes, "Intercollegiate Sports Success and First-Year Student Enrollment Demand," *Sociology of Sport Journal* 10 (September 1993): 296.

40   Ibid.: 297.
41   Frank, "Challenging the Myth: A Review of the Links Among College Athletic Success, Student Quality, and Donations," p. 4.
42   Robert G. Murphy and Gregory A. Trandel, "The Relations between a University's Football Record and the Size of Its Applicant Pool," *Economics of Education Review* 13, No. 3 (1994): 265–70.
43   Brian Goff, "Effects of University Athletics on the University: A Review and Extension of Empirical Assessment," *Journal of Sport Management* 14 (2000): 95.
44   Michael L. Anderson, "The Benefits of College Athletic Success: An Application of the Propensity Score Design with Instrumental Variables," National Bureau of Economic Research, Working Paper 18196, June 2012, p. 18.
45   Irvin B. Tucker and L. Ted Amato, "A Reinvestigation of the Relationship Between Big-Time Basketball Success and Average SAT Scores," *Journal of Sport Economics* 7, No. 4 (November 2006): 428–40.
46   Devin G. Pope and Jaren C. Pope, "The Impact of College Sports Success on the Quantity and Quality of Student Applications," *Southern Economic Journal* 75, No. 3 (2009): 776.
47   Ibid.: 764, 768.
48   Brian Fisher, "Athletic Success and Institutional Rankings," *New Directions for Higher Education* 148 (Winter 2009): 49.
49   Ibid.: 50.
50   Dodd, "Winning One for the Admissions Office," *USA Today*.
51   Robert Kirby Goidel and John Maxwell Hamilton, "Strengthening Higher Education through Gridiron Success? Public Perceptions of the Impact of National Football Championships on Academic Quality," *Social Science Quarterly* 87, No. 4 (December 2006): 855–6.
52   Ibid.: 861.
53   Daniel I. Rees and Kevin T. Schnepel, "College Football Games and Crime," *Journal of Sports Economics* 10, No. 1 (February 2009): 69, 74.
54   Robert A. Baade, Robert Baumann, and Victor A. Matheson, "Down, Set, Hike: The Economic Impact of College Football Games on Local Economies," College of the Holy Cross, Department of Economics Faculty Research Series, Paper No. 07–02, February 2007, p. 2.
55   Dennis Coates and Craig A. Depken II, "Do College Football Games Pay for Themselves? The Impact of College Football Games on Local Sales Tax Revenue," North American Association of Sports Economists, Working Paper Series, Paper No. 08–02, June 2008, p. 10.
56   Murray Sperber, "College Sports, Inc.: The Athletic Department vs. the University," *The Phi Delta Kappan* 72, No. 2 (October 1990): K2.
57   Edward S. Jordan, "Buying Football Victories: The University of Minnesota," *Collier's* (December 2, 1905): 19.
58   Heather Long, "Is College Worth it? Goldman Sachs Says Maybe Not," *CNN Money*, December 9, 2015, http://money.cnn.com/2015/12/09/news/economy/college-n ot-worth-it-goldman/.
59   Gaul, *Billion-Dollar Ball: A Journey through the Big-Money Culture of College Football*, pp. 123–4. Bryan Graham, "Stanford is Recruiting Football Players with the Smartest Pitch Imaginable," *mic.com*, October 20, 2014.
60   "Athletic & Academic Spending Database for NCAA Division I, Football Bowl Subdivision," Knight Commission on Intercollegiate Athletics, http://spendingdatabase. knightcommission.org/fbs, accessed March 6, 2017.
61   Gaul, *Billion-Dollar Ball: A Journey through the Big-Money Culture of College Football*, pp. ix–x.
62   Sperber, *Beer and Circus: How Big-Time College Sports Is Crippling Undergraduate Education*, p. 31.

63 Brad Wolverton, "College Football Players Spend 44.8 Hours a Week on Their Sport," NCAA Survey Finds, *Chronicle of Higher Education*, January 14, 2008.

64 Sperber, "College Sports, Inc.: The Athletic Department vs. the University," *The Phi Delta Kappan:* K4.

65 Ernest L. Boyer, "College Athletics: The Control of the Campus," in *Sport and Higher Education*, p. 401.

66 Nixon II, *The Athletic Trap: How College Sports Corrupted the Academy*; and Tim Goral, "Escaping the Athletic Trap: How College Sports Has Led to an 'Arms Race' in which There Are More Losers than Winners," *University Business*, June 2014, www.universitybusiness.com.

67 In 1988, Beano Cook, college football maven and ESPN analyst, decried the idea of extending the D-I football season from 11 to 12 regular season games: "It's absolutely insane. No matter how much money they [college athletic programs] have, it's never enough." Sperber, *College Sports Inc.: The Athletic Department vs. the University*, p. 30.

68 Dean A. Purdy, D. Stanley Eitzen, and Rick Hufnagel, "Are Athletes Also Students? The Educational Attainment of College Athletes," in *Sport and Higher Education*, pp. 223, 231.

69 John Fizel and Timothy Smaby, "Participation in Collegiate Athletics and Academic Performance," in *Economics of College Sports*, pp. 166, 168.

70 Clotfelter, *Big-Time Sports in American Universities*, pp. 28, 252.

71 Malcolm Moran, "Backtalk: Smart Enough to Know Better, Funny Enough Not to Care," *New York Times*, May 2, 1993.

72 Byers with Hammer, *Unsportsmanlike Conduct: Exploiting College Athletes*, p. 337.

73 Smith, *Pay for Play: A History of Big-Time College Athletic Reform*, p. 94.

74 Zimbalist, *Unpaid Professionals: Commercialism and Conflict in Big-Time College Sports*, p. 24.

75 Smith, *Pay for Play: A History of Big-Time College Athletic Reform*, p. 128.

76 Byers with Hammer, *Unsportsmanlike Conduct: Exploiting College Athletes*, p. 165.

77 Carla A. Winters and Gerald S. Gurney, "Academic Preparation of Specially-Admitted Student-Athletes: A Question of Basic Skills," *College & University* 88, No. 2 (Fall 2012): 4, 7.

78 Douglas Lederman, "College Athletes Graduate at Higher Rate Than Other Students, but Men's Basketball Players Lag Far Behind, a Survey Finds," *Chronicle of Higher Education*, March 27, 1991.

79 Harry Edwards, "Educating Black Athletes," in *Sport and Higher Education*, p. 378.

80 Harry Edwards, "The Collegiate Athletic Arms Race: Origins and Implications of the 'Rule 48' Controversy," *Journal of Sport and Social Issues* 8, Issue 1 (1984): 15.

81 Ibid.: 18.

82 Jill A. Singleton, "A History of the National Collegiate Athletic Association's Academic Reform Movement and Analysis of the Academic Progress Rate in Division I-A Institutions," Ph.D. dissertation, George Mason University, 2013, p. 54.

83 Harry Edwards, "The Collegiate Athletic Arms Race: Origins and Implications of the 'Rule 48' Controversy," *Journal of Sport and Social Issues*: 14.

84 Singleton, "A History of the National Collegiate Athletic Association's Academic Reform Movement and Analysis of the Academic Progress Rate in Division 1-A Institutions," p. 68.

85 "Blacks Hit Hard by Proposition 48, Survey Shows," Associated Press, *New York Times*, September 8, 1988.

86 Thelin, *Games Colleges Play: Scandal and Reform in Intercollegiate Athletics*, p. 175.

87 Barbara N. Bergmann, "Do Sports Really Make Money for the University?" *Academe* 77, No. 1 (January–February 1991): 29.

88 Shannon Blosser, "NCAA Should Leave Academic Requirements to Schools," John William Pope Center for Higher Education Policy, July 27, 2006.

89 Jay Schalin, "The Biggest Games in College Sports Aren't Always Played on the Field," John William Pope Center for Higher Education Policy, January 5, 2009.

90 Singleton, "A History of the National Collegiate Athletic Association's Academic Reform Movement and Analysis of the Academic Progress Rate in Division 1-A Institutions," pp. 91, 93.

91 Jill Lieber Steeg, Jodi Upton, Patrick Bohn, and Steve Berkowitz, "College Athletes Studies Guided Toward 'Major in Eligibility,'" *USA Today*, November 18, 2008.

92 Ibid.; see also "Colleges Push Athletes Down Easy Path to Maintain Eligibility," *Sports Business Daily*, November 19, 2008, www.sportsbusinessdaily.com.

93 Jodi Upton and Kristen Novak, "College Athletes Cluster Majors at Most Schools," *USA Today*, November 18, 2008.

94 Smith, *Pay for Play: A History of Big-Time College Athletic Reform,* p. 192.

95 Myles Brand, "Backtalk; in Athletics, Level Field Must Begin in Classroom," *Chronicle of Higher Education*, May 9, 2004.

96 Bill Pennington, "Unusual Alliance Forming to Rein in College Sports," *Chronicle of Higher Education*, January 17, 2003.

97 Singleton, "A History of the National Collegiate Athletic Association's Academic Reform Movement and Analysis of the Academic Progress Rate in Division 1-A Institutions," pp. 156–9, 176.

98 Pete Axthelm et al., "The Shame of College Sports," *Newsweek*, September 22, 1980.

99 Jordan Hofeditz, "Death Penalty Killed Football, Saved SMU," *SMU Daily Campus*, May 3, 2009.

100 Arthur Padilla and David Baumer, "Big-Time College Sports: Management and Economic Issues," *Journal of Sport & Social Issues* 18, No. 2 (May 1994): 141.

101 Steve Berkowitz, "New Expenses Loom for Universities' Athletic Departments," *USA Today*, May 18, 2016.

102 "A Call to Action: Reconnecting College Sports and Higher Education," Report of the Knight Foundation Commission on Intercollegiate Athletics, June 2001, p. 9.

103 "Keeping Faith with the Student-Athlete: A New Model for Intercollegiate Athletics," Report of the Knight Foundation Commission on Intercollegiate Athletics, March 1991, p. 21.

104 Smith, *Pay for Play: A History of Big-Time College Athletic Reform,* p. 175.

105 "A Call to Action: Reconnecting College Sports and Higher Education," Report of the Knight Foundation Commission on Intercollegiate Athletics, p. 22.

106 Ibid., pp. 4, 14, 15.

107 Ibid., p. 26.

108 "Position Statement: Establishment of a Presidential Commission on Intercollegiate Athletics Reform," The Drake Group, p. 10. The Knight Commission continues to call for belt-tightening and a greater emphasis on the student half of the portmanteau phrase student-athlete, for instance by requiring that schools be on track to graduate at least half their players in order to be eligible for postseason play. "Restoring the Balance: Dollars, Values, and the Future of College Sports," Knight Foundation Commission on Intercollegiate Athletics, June 17, 2010, p. 14.

109 Roger Noll, "The Economics of Intercollegiate Sports," in *Rethinking College Athletics*, pp. 206–7.

110 Tates Locke and Bob Ibach, "Caught in the Net," in *Sport and Higher Education*, p. 70.

111 Derek Bok, "Presidents Need Power Within the NCAA to Preserve Academic Standards and Institutional Integrity," in ibid., p. 208.

112 William Nack, "This Case Was One for the Books," *Sports Illustrated*, February 24, 1986, www.si.com/vault.

113 Richard Goldstein, "Jan Kemp Dies at 59; Exposed Fraud in Grades of Players," *New York Times*, December 11, 2008.

114 Jay Schalin, "An Athletic Dilemma," John William Pope Center for Higher Education Policy, January 5, 2009.

115 Pete Thamel, "Top Grades and No Class Time for Auburn Players," *New York Times*, July 14, 2006.

116 Associated Press, "Suspended Auburn Professor Sues University," *AL.com*, June 14, 2007.

117 Sam Farmer, "A Losing Record for NCAA Whistle-Blower," *Los Angeles Times*, March 30, 2001.

118 Jay Smith and Mary Willingham, *Cheated: The UNC Scandal, the Education of Athletes, and the Future of Big-Time College Sports* (Lincoln, NE: Potomac Books, 2015), p. 1.

119 Ibid., p. 131.

120 Paul M. Barrett, "Bad Sports," *Bloomberg Businessweek*, March 3, 2014.

121 Tony Manfred and Peter Jacobs, "A UNC Athlete Got An A−? In A Fake 'Paper Class' with This Ridiculous One-Paragraph Final Essay," *Business Insider*, October 22, 2014, www.businessinsider.com/unc-athlete-essay-a-minus-2014-10.

122 Smith and Willingham, *Cheated: The UNC Scandal, the Education of Athletes, and the Future of Big-Time College Sports*, pp. 23, 24, 45.

123 Ibid., p. 56.

124 Ibid., p. 52.

125 Rob J. Anderson, *Tarnished Heels: How Unethical Actions and Deliberate Deceit at the University of North Carolina Ended the Carolina Way* (Rock Hill, SC: Strategic Media Books, 2014), p. 73.

126 Smith and Willingham, *Cheated: The UNC Scandal, the Education of Athletes, and the Future of Big-Time College Sports*, p. 215.

127 Ibid., p. 162.

128 Ibid., p. 132.

129 Barrett, "Bad Sports," *Bloomberg Businessweek*.

130 Smith and Willingham, *Cheated: The UNC Scandal, the Education of Athletes, and the Future of Big-Time College Sports*, p. 135.

131 Barrett, "Bad Sports," *Bloomberg Businessweek*.

132 Anderson, *Tarnished Heels: How Unethical Actions and Deliberate Deceit at the University of North Carolina Ended the Carolina Way*, p. 298.

133 Jenna A. Robinson and Jay Schalin, "UNC Budget Brawl Shaping Up," John William Pope Center for Higher Education Policy, March 10, 2014.

134 Murray Sperber, "Five Myths about College Sports," *Washington Post*, March 13, 2015.

135 "Letter of the Rawlings Panel on Intercollegiate Athletics at the University of North Carolina at Chapel Hill to Chancellor Carol L. Folt," August 29, 2013, p. 1.

136 "Report of the Rawlings Panel on Intercollegiate Athletics at the University of North Carolina at Chapel Hill," p. 10.

137 Ibid., pp. 13–14.

138 Jesse Saffron, "The Prospects for Athletic Reform," John William Pope Center for Higher Education Policy, September 30, 2013.

139 Jesse Saffron and Jenna A. Robinson, "The Biggest Lesson from the UNC Academic Scandal Has Been Ignored," John William Pope Center for Higher Education Policy, December 1, 2015.

140 "Student Fees," University of North Carolina at Chapel Hill, http://cashier.unc.edu/tuition-fees/student-fees/.

141 Logan Ulrich, "The Cost of Winning: UNC's Growing Athletic Budget Puts Students on the Hook," *The Daily Tar Heel*, December 1, 2016.

142 Michael Miner, "Trust Me, Academics Used to Be Important to Missouri," *Chicago Reader*, April 5, 2012.

143 Sperber, "College Sports, Inc.: The Athletic Department vs. the University," *The Phi Delta Kappan*: K5–6.

144 Murray Sperber notes that in the mid-1980s, Florida State admitted two football players whose SAT scores were an almost impossibly low sub-450—that's *combined* math and verbal. Sperber, *College Sports, Inc.: The Athletic Department vs. the University*, p. 218.

145 John Canzano, "Memphis Basketball Teaches the Wrong Lesson," *The Oregonian*, June 5, 2009, www.oregonlive.com/sports/oregonian/john_canzano/index.ssf/2009/06/m emphis_basketball_teaches_the.html.

146 "Poulton Defends Admission of Washburn," UPI, [N.C. St.] *Technician*, February 18, 1985.

147 Shannon Blosser, "Miami Places Winning above Character," John William Pope Center for Higher Education Policy, July 30, 2004.

148 Jeff Pearlman, "The Tragic Story of Willie Williams, College Football's First Celebrity Recruit," *Bleacherreport.com*, February 4, 2014, http://bleacherreport.com/articles/ 1943325-the-tragic-story-of-willie-williams-college-footballs-first-celebrity-recruit.

149 Barrett, "Bad Sports," *Bloomberg Businessweek*.

150 Doug Lederman, "The Admissions Gap for Big-Time Athletes," *Inside Higher Ed*, December 29, 2008.

151 Ellipses taken from Edwards, "The Collegiate Athletic Arms Race: Origins and Implications of the 'Rule 48' Controversy," *Journal of Sport and Social Issues*: 4.

152 Duderstadt, *Intercollegiate Athletics and the American University: A University President's Perspective*, p. x.

153 Ibid., p. xi.

154 Brad Wolverton and Andrea Fuller, "Who's in Charge of Sports?" *Chronicle of Higher Education*, September 3, 2012.

155 Smith, *Pay for Play: A History of Big-Time College Athletic Reform,* p. 24.

156 "Robin Hood in Reverse," *CityBeat*.

157 Gaul, *Billion-Dollar Ball: A Journey Through the Big-Money Culture of College Football*, p. 202.

158 Bill Glauber, "Money Woes May Sack Towson football: Higher Student Fee Linked to Survival," *Baltimore Sun*, October 10, 1990.

159 Kent Baker, "Towson State's Senate Votes to Sustain Football," *Baltimore Sun*, December 4, 1990.

160 "Fall Term," www.towson.edu/bursar/tuition/fall.html, accessed February 24, 2017.

161 Don Markus and Todd Karpovich, "Towson Athletic Department Recommends Cutting Baseball and Soccer," *Baltimore Sun*, October 2, 2012.

162 Maravene Loeschke, "Towson President Says Cutbacks of Baseball, Soccer Painful but Necessary," *Baltimore Sun*, March 15, 2013.

163 Alejandro Zuniga Sacks, "Towson Baseball Staves Off Different Kind of Elimination," *USA Today*, May 30, 2013.

164 "FY 2016 Internal Operating Budget and Plan," Towson University, October 2015, p. 33, www.towson.edu/budgetoffice/documents/fy16operatingplan_final.pdf.

165 Kevin Armstrong, "Hofstra Eliminates 72-Year-Old Program," *New York Times*, December 3, 2009.

166 Sander, "At What Price Football?" *Chronicle of Higher Education*.

167 Armstrong, "Hofstra Eliminates 72-Year-Old Program," *New York Times*.

168 Laura A. Bischoff, "OSU President Expenses in the Millions," *Dayton Daily News*, September 22, 2012.

169 Gordon Gee, "A New (Old) Philosophy of Intercollegiate Athletics," *Phi Kappa Phi Forum* 85, No. 3 (2005): 11, 13.

170 Matt Stevens, "Third Former Vanderbilt Football Player Convicted of Rape," *New York Times*, June 23, 2017.

171 Jon Solomon, "Death of UAB Football: Anger Remains, but Study Banks on Healing," *cbssports.com*, December 23, 2014, www.cbssports.com/college-football/news/ death-of-uab-football-anger-remains-but-study-banks-on-healing/.

172 Jon Talty, "Ray Watts to Reinstate UAB Football," *AL.com*, June 1, 2015, www.al. com/sports/index.ssf/2015/06/uab_will_reinstate_football_so.html.

173 "Wichita State Suspends Football Program," Newburgh (NY) *Evening News*, December 3, 1986.

174 Lederman, "Do Winning Teams Spur Contributions? Scholars and Fund Raisers Are Skeptical," *Chronicle of Higher Education*.

175 Kevin McGuire, "AAC May Add Wichita State, But Revival of Football Program Would Be Shocking," *collegefootballtalk.nbcsports.com*, April 5, 2017.

176 Devon Fasbinder, "Study: Bringing Football Back to Wichita State Could Cost Tens of Millions," www.kwch.com, June 27, 2016.

177 Gaul, *Billion-Dollar Ball: A Journey Through the Big-Money Culture of College Football*, p. 213.

178 Liz Clarke, "Maryland Athletic Department May Have to Cut Sports to Address Budget Shortfall," *Washington Post*, August 19, 2011.

179 Allie Grasgreen, "Maryland Will Cut Eight Teams to Mitigate Athletic Budget Deficit," *Inside Higher Ed*, November 22, 2011.

180 "Club Directory," University of Maryland Recreation & Wellness, https://recwell.umd.edu/activities/club-sports/club-directory, accessed August 20, 2017.

181 C. Thomas McMillen, "Big Ten. Big Mistake," *Washington Post*, November 25, 2012.

182 Allie Grasgreen, "Another Round at Rutgers," *Inside Higher Ed*, August 24, 2011.

183 Robert Lipsyte, "Backtalk; An Eminent Voice Pleads for the Soul of Rutgers," *New York Times*, April 12, 1998.

184 William C. Dowling, "To Cleanse Colleges of Sports Corruption, End Recruiting Based on Physical Skills," *Chronicle of Higher Education*, July 9, 1999.

185 "Rutgers Prof under Fire for Comments about Student Athletes," Associated Press, September 28, 2007, www.espn.com/college-sports/news/story?id=3040343.

186 Hobson and Rich, "In NCAA, Big Revenue Means Bigger Spending," *Washington Post*.

187 Steve Berkowitz and Jodi Upton, "Rutgers Athletic Department Needs Fees, Funds to Stay Afloat," *USA Today*, June 28, 2011.

188 Jared Meyer and Neil Deininger, "The Real March Madness: Costly Subsidies for College Hoops," *Economics 21*, March 26, 2014, www.economics21.org.

189 Dan Alexander, "How Much Will Rutgers Tuition Increase in 2017–18?" *New Jersey 101.5*, July 19, 2017, http://nj1015.com/how-much-will-rutgers-tuition-increase-in-2017-18/.

190 Berkowitz and Upton, "Rutgers Athletic Department Needs Fees, Funds to Stay Afloat," *USA Today*.

191 Curtis Eichelberger and Elise Young, "Rutgers Football Fails Profit Test as Students Pay $1,000," *Bloomberg*, May 3, 2012.

192 Allie Grasgreen, "Redemption for Rutgers?" *Inside Higher Ed*, November 21, 2012.

193 Hobson and Rich, "In NCAA, Big Revenue Means Bigger Spending," *Washington Post*.

194 Ryan Dunleavy, "Paying for Rutgers Athletics: Student Fee or Student Free?" *my CentralJersey.com*, April 26, 2016.

195 Mark Gaughan, "UB Will Drop Four Sports Teams in Athletics Budget Cutback," *Buffalo News*, April 3, 2017.

196 Jay Tokasz, "Small Crowds, Big Subsidy for UB Sports," *Buffalo News*, November 28, 2015.

197 Jerry Sullivan, "UB Football, the Elephant in the Room," *Buffalo News*, April 4, 2017.

198 Bucky Gleason, "Curveball: How UB's Decision to Cut Baseball Affected the Final Season and Everyone Involved," *Buffalo News*, June 8, 2017.

199 Schalin, "College Sports: Foul Ball or Fair Play?" John William Pope Center for Higher Education Policy.

200 Sperber, *Beer and Circus: How Big-Time College Sports Is Crippling Undergraduate Education*, p. 65.

201 Ibid., p. 68.

202 George Leef, "Winston-Salem Tries the Hail Mary Pass," John William Pope Center for Higher Education Policy, July 26, 2004.

203 John Dell, "Division I Gambit a Distant Memory for Rams," *Winston-Salem Journal*, December 13, 2012.

204   Clotfelter, *Big-Time Sports in American Universities*, p. 49.
205   Ibid., p. 50.
206   "Denver University Drops Football," Spokane *Spokesman-Review*, January 10, 1961.
207   Steve Fisher, "Thanksgiving Day Marks 50 Years Since Last Pioneers Football Game," *University of Denver Magazine*, www.magazine.du.edu, November 23, 2010.
208   Mitchell, "Big-Time Sports Should Be Banished from Campus," *The Center Magazine*: 22–4.

7

"A GAME FOR EVERY GIRL AND A GIRL FOR EVERY GAME"?

A brief look at how women's sports lost their virtue and became carbon copies of the male game

Welch Suggs, a historian of women's sports, paints this evocative picture:

> There was a golden age of American sports. An age when coaches were respected teachers in their field, when athletes ran out into sunlight to play for the love of the game, to match strength and skill in defending their school's honor and to stride across campus in their letter sweaters, where baseball and basketball were harmless pastimes played out in Norman Rockwell paintings.[1]

This golden age was a feminine one, organized by female phys-ed teachers and played on campuses across America. If it is somewhat idealized—the men, after all, organized their own sports, and thus have a better claim, in the earliest years, to being a bottom-up DIY enterprise—it nonetheless contains a good deal of truth.

In the beginning, it was going to be different with women's sports. Away from the glare of publicity, unbothered by an indifferent public, largely an afterthought in coed schools, women's sports had about them a purity, an integrity, that had largely disappeared from big-time football and men's basketball by the dawn of the twentieth century.[2] "We are setting forth under our own sail, with women at the helm and women manning the whole craft," said Agnes R. Wayman, chairman of the Barnard College Department of Physical Education, in 1924.[3] Female physical education instructors were determined that women not ape male athletes, elevating competition over sport for the sake of sport.

Strenuous physical activity was thought to be inconsistent with femininity, but there was also "a general suspicion of competition." Women had seen how an "excessive focus on winning games caused male participants to lost sight of fair play and sporstmanship."[4] Healthiness and invigorating physical activity were to be the goal and the means of women's athletics. Despite concerns about the effect that vigorous athletic activity might have on women, most states required physical education for all high school students, regardless of sex, and more than one in five (22 percent) universities offered women at least one intercollegiate sport in 1920.[5]

Senda Berenson, a physical education instructor at Smith College and a pioneer of late nineteenth-century women's basketball, decried the competitiveness of male sports. Athletics "should never overemphasize winning," Berenson said.[6] She modified the rules of James Naismith's new sport of basketball by limiting the number of dribbles one player can make and dividing the court into regions from which they could not stray. This was neither better nor worse than the men's game; it was merely different. Women's teams would also eschew excessive travel, gate receipts, championship tournaments, and the other paraphernalia of men's sports. The emphasis was on the game and the players, and the most widespread possible participation.

The Women's Division of the National Amateur Athletic Federation, one of multiple competing organizations overseeing women's amateur sports, was formed in 1922 to promote physical fitness and deal with scholastic, ethical, and social issues related to sport. It "stressed participation, good sportsmanship, and character development rather than competition, breaking records, and winning champion-ships." Lou Hoover, wife of the future president, was at its head.[7] Hyper-compe-titiveness, argued Hoover and her sisters, was antithetical to the ideal of mass participation. It also encouraged a cut-throat attitude that might carry into one's personal and professional life. For this reason the Women's Division opposed the addition of women's sports to Olympic competition, a position for which it was ridiculed then and now. The Women's Division emphatically did not believe, as modern Olympic founder Pierre de Coubertin said, that "Women have but one task, that of crowning the winner with garlands, as was their role in ancient Greece," but it was very easy for more conventional feminists to caricature them in this way.[8]

The Women's Division of the National Amateur Athletic Federation issued a 16-point platform in 1923 that championed "the spirit of play for its own sake and . . . the promotion of physical activity for the largest possible proportion of persons in any given group." In an obvious allusion to men's intercollegiate sports, the Women's Division urged "programs of physical activities for all members of given social groups rather than for a limited number chosen for their physical prowess." It abjured commercialism, publicity, and gate receipts and stressed "enjoyment of the sport and the development of sportsmanship." It also emphasized that "well-trained and properly qualified women" should be in charge of "all physical education activities for girls and women" as well as athletic competition among women.[9] This was a distinctly pre-equal rights feminism; it viewed women's athletics and physical training not as identical to that of men but separate, segregated, and loftier than mere grubbing for dollars and victories. These women would not have been pleased by the way that women's Division I basketball has developed into a big-time and glitzy sport played by a relative handful of superior women athletes who are often coached by men.

Individual awards and travel were discouraged. The emphasis was on informality and widespread participation and it would remain so for several decades, even though in the professional world outstanding women athletes achieved fame and sometimes fortune in such individualized sports as golf, tennis, and swimming.

The likes of Fielding Yost would have scoffed at such Women's Division planks as:

> Promote competition that stresses enjoyment of sport and development of good sportsmanship and character rather than those types that emphasize the making and breaking of records and the winning of championships for the enjoyment of spectators or for the athletic reputation or commercial advantage of institutions or organizations.
>
> Promote educational publicity that places the emphasis on sport and its values rather than on the competitors.
>
> Promote the training and employment of women administrators, leaders, and officials who are qualified to assume full responsibility for the physical education and recreation of girls and women.[10]

Intramurals, or athletic contests confined to the school's population rather than held against girls from other schools, was the pride of early women's collegiate athletics. The ideal, as Pauline Hodgson of the University of Michigan told a 1927 convention of the American Physical Education Association, was "*every* girl receiving the benefits of athletic competition."[11] Hodgson and others derided mere "spectatorism," insisting that "our big objective is *extension*, universal participation."[12] Intramurals were not the poor stepchild in women's sports; they were the centerpiece, the jewel, the glorious expression of the motto "a game for every girl and a girl for every game." Men's sports were held up as a negative example, since few boys participated in intercollegiate athletics. The vast majority sat and watched as the few got the glory (and the exercise).

Intramurals sometimes branched out into *play days* in which women would engage in athletic competition with women from neighboring schools. On "Play Day," women from multiple colleges would gather, divide themselves into teams by lottery, irrespective of talent level, and spend the day engaged in sport for enjoyment. This doubtless frustrated the more skilled girls, who would wish to test their abilities against similarly skilled athletes, but it hewed to the early ideals of women's physical education theorists. It was the triumph, however transitory, of the Women's Division/physical educator philosophy. The days of Play Day were numbered, as it would fade into the dim mists of history, along with maypoles and Sadie Hawkins dances.

As an example, Stanford, the University of California, and Mills College engaged in "triangle tournaments" in tennis, basketball, and field hockey. The young women representing their schools were not necessarily the top athletes; young women of varying skill levels participated, as each school was represented by intramural athletes who ranged from talented to mediocre. The goal was *extension*, or the most widespread participation possible. Winning was nice, but the competition and sorority were better. Vince Lombardi's aphorism that *winning isn't everything, it's the only thing* would have been met with a mixture of incomprehension and horror. (UC Berkeley and Stanford and the University of Washington and Ellensburg Normal School played the first women's intercollegiate basketball games in 1896.[13] The score in that first Battle of the Bay was Stanford 2, Berkeley 1. Apparently both teams played suffocating defense.)[14]

But even in that halcyon era, observers glimpsed "signs, unfortunately, that some of the excesses which have come to characterize men's athletics are beginning to spread to athletics for women." The observer in this instance was Helen N. Smith, director of physical education for women at the University of Cincinnati. The title of her article in a 1932 number of the *Journal of Health and Physical Education*, "Evils of Sports for Women," invites mockery and ridicule, but Miss Smith was not recommending that young women eschew physical activity for the joys of watching the boys. Far from it. Her goal, rather, was to move young people from the bleachers to the playing fields. Men's sports were being corrupted by large national organizations (read: NCAA) that stressed record-breaking over participation. Women in the colleges and universities had so far been spared the misfortune of intercollegiate athletics, with their attendant commercialization, degradation of academic standards, and rampant spectatordom because, Smith said, responsible authorities in women's schools:

> believe that there should be a broad program of sports activities with opportunities for every girl in the university to indulge and reap their benefits, rather than a narrow program of varsity basketball and swimming teams with the resultant training of a few star performers and the neglect of the mediocre or average girl.[15]

The numerous industrial athletic leagues, which sponsored basketball, baseball, softball, and other sporting opportunities for employees, were of greater concern to Smith, as factory-employed women usually played for male coaches and under male rules. Although the female physical education instructors' cautions against the masculinization of women's sport may be seen as "extremely conservative," their views line up with those of some radical feminists today.[16] As Nancy Theriot documents in an article on the Women's Division of the National Amateur Athletic Federation for the *Journal of Women's Studies*, modernists in the sporting world of the 1920s wished to model women's sports along male patterns, while the so-called conservatives supported a mass participation model quite unlike what was happening in big-time football.

The defeat of the lady gym teachers

Any hope that women's intercollegiate sports would develop along a different, perhaps more humane or human-scale path than that of the men, was dispelled in the modern era. As early as 1979, George H. Hanford, a member of the American Council on Education's Commission on Collegiate Athletics, was drawing the sobering lesson that "Women in sports are not, it would appear, more moral than men."[17] Coaches' salaries, the admission of unqualified students who excel in basketball (the one big-budget women's sport), the disappearance of the "a girl for every sport and a sport for every girl" principle—the dream of something different died fast in Division I.

It died with the AIAW—and, ironically, with the vaunted Title IX. The AIAW, or Association for Intercollegiate Athletics for Women (1971–82), an organization controlled by female phys-ed teachers, sought to keep a separate space for women's sports. While certainly not as competition-averse as their predecessors had been—intercollegiate athletes of both sexes want to play hard and win, and the AIAW recognized that—the AIAW did not wish to mimic the male model or be subsumed by the male-dominated NCAA. The AIAW was the organizing body for the women's sports programs of more than 800 colleges, overseeing many of the conferences and the rules of the games and overshadowing the NCAA, which largely neglected its women's sports membership.[18]

The AIAW Policy Statement of May 1974 laid down its core principles:

> The sense of enjoyment, self-confidence, and physical well-being derived from demanding one's best performance in a sport situation is a meaningful experience for the athlete. These inner satisfactions are the fundamental motivation for participation in sports. Therefore, programs in an educational setting should have these benefits as primary goals.[19]

The AIAW agreed with the liberal feminist goal of equitable funding, but it wanted women's athletics to be more humane, less competition-driven, and less spectacle and more sport. Participation, not glory, was the goal. Not for the AIAW the scandals of men's sport: for instance, it barred flying recruits in for campus visits.

The AIAW was the redoubt of those female physical education instructors who wanted women's intercollegiate sports to develop along a different path than men's sports had: less commercial, less focused on winning, less willing to admit unqualified jocks, and more focused on broad participation by as many women as possible. Female athletic directors had actively campaigned against sex-integrated squads, fearing injury, corruption, and reduced opportunities for young women.

The organization, which had been created by the Division of Girls' and Women's Sport of the American Association for Health, Physical Education and Recreation, an offspring of the National Education Association, was no distaff carbon copy of the NCAA. It featured generous transfer rules (it did not punish transfers by requiring that they sit out a year), an emphasis on self-policing through an honor system rather than centralized control, a ban on athletic scholarships, and strict limits on recruiting. Although circumstances had changed, the AIAW carried the torch of the old women's physical education agenda.

By the early 1970s, though, the times they were a-changing. The AIAW, which had outlawed athletic scholarships, was sued in 1973 by women tennis players; after much debate, it dropped the ban, though scholarships remained tied to academic performance. This change was enormous; instead of a physical education program tailored to the women of an AIAW-member college, the college was now recruiting top athletes. The emphasis shifted to winning over participation; whereas once women's sports were for students, now the "student-athlete" recruited for her athletic skill alone was served.

In the AIAW debate over changing the athletic scholarship policy, the losing side, the traditionalists, spoke in the melancholy language of loss. Protested Donna Mae Miller and Mary Pavlich Roby of the University of Arizona in 1973:

> The earmarks of bad athletics, whether they involve men or women, have been well documented historically and have always centered around such practices as scholarships and recruitment . . . [W]e are at this moment preparing to write history which may, in fact, indicate that we have resigned ourselves to pale replicas of men's programs. If we are really talking about the "rights of women". . . the question of whether women have the same access to "talent" scholarships as men do appears to be a minuscule point when it is contrasted to the greater question of whether women have the same right that men do to determine their own rules and regulations in their own athletic contests.[20]

The surrender to the male model was proceeding apace. By 1974 both the AIAW and NCAA schools offered athletic scholarships to women.

The NCAA, which had been indifferent at best toward women's athletics, saw an opportunity for empire-building and took aim at the AIAW. It hit the group in a soft spot: the AIAW's ambivalence toward cut-throat competition. The NCAA, which had for years brushed aside requests from advocates of women's sports to sponsor national championship tournaments, reversed field and established women's national championships by convention votes in 1980 and 1981 in various sports, most notably basketball, swimming, tennis, track and field, and volleyball. By the 1981–2 season, the NCAA was sponsoring 29 championship competitions for women in 12 sports. Major financial benefactors such as NBC and Eastman Kodak bailed on the AIAW.[21] As Welch Suggs writes, by those votes to sponsor championships "the AIAW was rendered irrelevant."[22] A failed Sherman Act lawsuit sealed its fate. The felling blow, as sports economist Rodney D. Fort writes, "was the inclusion of the women's basketball championship tournament in the men's championship TV package and scheduling it at precisely the same time as the AIAW's championship."[23] (The last AIAW basketball champion was Rutgers, which defeated Texas 83–77 in 1982.) It was a quick death; in 1980, AIAW had 961 colleges within its ambit, and two years later it was gone.[24]

By 1982, the AIAW was as dead as the Play Day. Yet as Walter Byers, head of the NCAA, said, "The men and the NCAA, itself, didn't discriminate against women. Women's athletics leaders discriminated against themselves through the years by refusing to accept competitive athletics as a proper pursuit for teenage women."[25] Byers strenuously defended himself against the AIAW charge that he and the old boys network took over women's sports once they sensed that a few bucks could be made off it. He positioned himself as a proto-feminist, a critic of women's college "play days" and such rule modifications as half-court basketball, limits on dribbling, and a de-emphasis on winning or even keeping score. "Long-smoldering female resentment ignited in the AIAW. The NCAA, with its publicized wealth and male-dominated hierarchy, was an obvious target, and Walter Byers as head of the masculine empire was the prime quarry." he wrote, referring to himself in the third person.[26]

The age of Title IX

The instrument of revolution—or, revisionists would argue, reaction—was Title IX of the Education Amendments of 1972, signed into law on June 23, 1972, by President Richard M. Nixon. Its central element was this: "No person in the United States shall, on the basis of sex, be excluded from participation in, be denied the benefits of, or be subjected to discrimination under any education program or activity receiving federal financial assistance."[27] Henceforth, the gender balance of intercollegiate athletics would be subject to oversight by the federal government. Title IX was not specifically directed at sports, though this is where it has had the most significant impact. In 1973, while colleges offered an average of 7.3 sports for men, they offered an average of 2.5 for women.[28] The imbalance was lopsided, though the level of interest probably was, too.

At the congressional hearings on what became Title IX, athletics were mentioned only twice, and briefly. In the floor debate, Senator Peter Dominick (R-CO) asked sponsor Birch Bayh (D-IN) if he was "thinking in terms of dormitory facilities, is he thinking in terms of athletic facilities or equipment?" Bayh replied:

> I do not read this as requiring integration of dormitories between the sexes, nor do I feel it mandates the desegregation of the football fields. What we are trying to do here is provide equal access for women and men students to the educational process and the extracurricular activities in a school, where there is not a unique facet such as football involved. We are not requiring that intercollegiate football be desegregated, nor that the men's locker room be desegregated.

Dominick jokingly replied that "I would have had much more fun playing college football if it had been integrated."[29]

Welch Suggs notes that this lighthearted Bayh-Dominick exchange "was the only discussion of college sports during the entire debate over the sex discrimination bill."[30] Had members of Congress known that Title IX would—in the opinion of some—encourage colleges to drop men's sports such as wrestling in order to comply with federal regulations, the legislation likely would have hit severe roadblocks. The House-Senate conference kicked the responsibility for setting regulations pertaining to Title IX to the Department of Health, Education, and Welfare (HEW). HEW promulgated the enforcement regulations in 1975, giving schools until 1978 to comply. While HEW was drawing up regulations for Title IX, Sen. John Tower (R-TX) of the football-crazed Lone Star State offered a successful amendment on the Senate floor during debate in 1974 over the Elementary and Secondary Education Act. Senator Tower wished to clarify that "revenue-producing sports"—read football and basketball—were exempt from Title IX. The Tower amendment was dropped in conference committee and replaced by language offered by Senator Jacob Javits (R-NY) directing the Secretary of HEW to make "reasonable provisions considering the nature of particular sports" with respect to Title IX implementation.[31]

Some feminist groups, for instance the National Organization for Women (NOW), scorned "separate but equal" arrangements and supported open tryouts—that is, men and women trying out for a single team for intercollegiate sports. (Except in isolated cases such as football, where not even the most ideological feminist believed women could compete on a level playing field with men.) The AIAW, by contrast, supported "proportionate funding" for sex-segregated sports.[32] HEW actually considered permitting open tryouts to satisfy the requirements of Title IX, but the approach was rejected in favor of equal opportunities for sex-segregated teams.

HEW's three-part test stated that to fall within Title IX guidelines, a school must demonstrate compliance in one of the following three areas:

1. Whether intercollegiate level participation opportunities for male and female students are provided in numbers substantially proportionate to their respective enrollments;
2. Where the members of one sex have been and are underrepresented among intercollegiate athletes, whether the institution can show a history and continuing practice of program expansion which is demonstrably responsive to the developing interest and abilities of the members of that sex; or
3. Where the members of one sex are underrepresented among intercollegiate athletes, and the institution cannot show a continuing practice of program expansion, such as that cited above, whether it can be demonstrated that the interest and abilities of the members of that sex have been fully and effectively accommodated by the present program.[33]

There were, to be sure, gross inequities in intercollegiate sports. One of the first Title IX complaints filed revealed that in 1977, the University of Oregon (pre-Phil Knight) spent $413,768 on the men's basketball team and $24,171 on the women's squad.[34]

Though Title IX is only part of the reason, and probably a much less significant reason than other societal changes, the number of women playing intercollegiate sports has risen from fewer than 32,000 in 1971 to more than 120,000 in 1986–7 to over 200,000 in 2017. Between 1971 and 1978, "the number of colleges offering athletics to women rose from 280 to 825 and the number of teams rose from 1,831 to 4,797."[35] This might fairly be called an explosion—and it happened before the Title IX regulations had been promulgated. So clearly women's sports were trending upward in a big way, Title IX or no Title IX.

Today Title IX is interpreted by the Office of Civil Rights within the U.S. Department of Education. (More recently, Title IX has been used to expand the federal government's role in the matter of sexual assaults or alleged assaults on campus.) The three-prong compliance test has been a consistent rope in the tug of war between liberal feminists and defenders of low-profile men's sports, though the details are beyond the scope of this book.

The goals of some Title IX advocates go well beyond merely ensuring equal expenditures or opportunities for women in sport. Typically, one feminist writer urges the federal government to take "a more active role in getting women into contact sports." True, young women have shown very little interest in playing tackle football at the intercollegiate level, but perhaps if the feds would "make a more concerted effort to break down the gender barriers" that define a sport distinguished by concussions and broken limbs as "masculine," then the mass of unenlightened young women would be encouraged to don shoulder pads.[36]

Title IX marked a significant advance in federal regulation of intercollegiate sports. Consider the case of Grove City College in Pennsylvania, which proudly and famously refuses to accept federal monies. The fact that some Grove City students received federal Pell Grants gave HEW its entering wedge. The receipt of federal financial aid by these students brought Grove City within the boundaries of Title IX, asserted federal officials. Grove City College officials bucked, district and appeals courts ruled crosswise, the former agreeing with the college, the latter with the government, and the U.S. Supreme Court, in the case of *Grove City College v. Bell* (1984), sided with Grove City. As Justice Byron White's majority opinion had it, "we have found no persuasive evidence suggesting that Congress intended that the Department's regulatory authority follow federally aided students from classroom to classroom, building to building, or activity to activity."[37] Since the athletic department is not a direct recipient of federal aid, it is not subject to Title IX. Or so said the Supreme Court. Congress effectively restored the federal government's broad pre-*Grove City* powers with the Civil Rights Restoration Act of 1987, passed over President Reagan's veto.

Grove City responded in best principled dissident fashion by removing itself from the federal financial aid network and setting up its own such programs. Ignoring what it regarded as nanny-state hectoring in the matter of athletics, Grove City pursued gender equity in its own way. It currently fields 20 NCAA Division III athletic teams: ten male, and ten female.[38]

Title IX and its enforcement may be seen as marking the triumph of liberal feminists not only over male and female conservatives but also over radical feminists.[39] In the words of Suzanne E. Estler and Laurie Nelson, authors of the 2005 monograph "Who Calls the Shots? Sports and University Leadership, Culture, and Decision Making," Title IX "resulted in the subordination of women's sports to the dominant male model."[40] Title IX set women's athletics down a path parallel to men's; gone were the female physical education instructors who had long controlled women's sports. Mass participation would soon be as anachronistic among female college students as it is among males: only the top athletes played and were feted. The duty of the mass of students was simply to watch, to cheer, and in many cases to subsidize the athletic department with their student fees.

Moreover, one perhaps unintended consequence of Title IX was the squeezing out of women athletic administrators. The dream of those early female physical education teachers that women's sports would be guided by women died. As the AIAW gave way to the NCAA, separate men's and women's athletic departments were merged. Typically, the erstwhile women's AD was made subordinate to the male, who oversaw both programs. The ideal of sport organized by and for women vanished. As Deborah L. Brake writes, "Once women's programs were integrated into a unified athletic structure, women lost control over women's sports."[41] (Title IX is gender-neutral on the matter of head coaches and administrators.)

According to the most recent figures, only 37 of 352, or 11 percent, of Division I's women athletic directors are female.[42] Yet before Title IX, more than 90 percent of athletic directors for women's sports were women.[43] In 2015–16, the most recent year for which data were available, 152 of the 348, or 44 percent, of the Division I women's basketball coaches were men.[44] Basketball was the only D-I sport with at least 300 teams in which even a majority of women's teams were coached by women: figures for other major sports include Cross Country (M: 285, W: 67); Soccer (M: 241, W: 91), Tennis (M: 212, W: 114), Indoor Track (M: 268, W: 60), Outdoor Track (M: 272, W: 65), and Volleyball (M: 186, W: 149).[45]

The highest-paid coach of a women's team, 11-time national championship basketball coach Geno Auriemma of the dynastic University of Connecticut, signed a five-year, $13 million-plus contract in late 2016. The fact that women are a bare majority of women's basketball coaches at the Division I level has been ascribed to "sexism" by Stanford coach Tara VanDerveer; with greater nuance, Notre Dame coach Muffet McGraw suggests that women themselves may be more reluctant to put in the 70-hour workweeks of a D-I coach, for "the work-life balance, I think, is a bigger issue for women than it is for men."[46] (Women's basketball is a financial black hole even at traditional powerhouses like UConn and the University of Tennessee due to "inexpensive tickets, high salaries for coaches, and less interest" from the public and media.)[47]

There is another underside to Title IX. As Welch Suggs wrote in his history of the act, "Title IX undoubtedly played a pivotal role in many athletics directors' decisions to cut teams."[48] To say that Title IX has not led to the abolition of some men's teams is to subordinate truth to ideology. A study by Professor Jerome Kravitz of Howard University found that from 1982 to 2001, "women gained 2,046 to 2,384 teams and 51,967 athletic opportunities, while men lost between 1,290 to 1,434 teams and 57,100 to 57,700 participation opportunities."[49] The complaint, as Jessica Gavora wrote in the *Washington Post*, is that "Title IX, a law intended to expand opportunity for women in the classroom and on the playing field, is now being used to restrict opportunity for both men and women." Wrestlers, swimmers, divers . . . if you are a young man playing a non-money sport, especially in a big football school, the thought that you may be team-less next near is never far from your mind. Just between 1992 and 1997, according to the NCAA, "more than 200 men's teams and 20,000 males athletes disappeared from the ranks of America's colleges."[50] Between the passage of Title IX and 2002, "170 wrestling teams, 80 men's tennis teams, 70 men's gymnastics teams, and 45 men's track teams" had bitten the dust, according to a General Accounting Office report.[51] A 2017 report by the NCAA admitted that since 1988, 330 Division I men's teams had been cut while 803 women's teams have been added.[52]

Many sportswomen bewail this trend. Nancy Hogshead, attorney, gold medal swimmer, and former president of the Women's Sports Foundation, has said, "It's never in women's interests to be cutting men's sports because that's where our power comes from—having strong men's sports programs."[53] One casualty was the Boston University football team, which broke its last huddle in November 1997, ending 91 years of Terriers football. Citing annual football-related losses of $2.91 million and "pressures to achieve compliance" with Title IX, the BU Board of Trustees disbanded the Division 1-A team, which lost 26 of its last 28 games. In protest, the Terriers covered up the BU logo on their jerseys in their last game (a 45–7 loss to Connecticut), playing instead as "University X." BU became the 22nd school to drop football in the 1990s, but the administration's ascription of this action to Title IX was unusual.[54] It's common sense that a disproportionately expensive sport that has no female analogue will throw gender-measured spending way out of balance, and that one obvious way to achieve balance is by eliminating that sport, but this is one of those unsayable truths in the current atmosphere on many campuses.

When sadsack Rutgers had a football year for the ages in 2006, finishing 11–2 with a #12 ranking in the final Associated Press poll, the New Jersey school dropped six varsity teams: men's tennis, men's swimming and diving, men's lightweight and heavyweight crew, and men's and women's fencing. The football budget in the following year increased by $1 million, which exceeded the cost of the six canceled sports—five of which were men's. Obviously Title IX played a role here, though administrators are usually careful not to cast aspersions on that federal law.

As Jon Vegosen of the U.S. Tennis Association pointed out at the time, the per-athlete expenditure for football and basketball at Rutgers was $128,500, while the per-athlete expenditure for the dumped sports was $5,600.[55] Even a modest reduction in football scholarships could have helped fund the Olympic sports. FBS schools can and usually do have up to 85 players on scholarship; reducing that to 60, plenty to field a team, a second string, and a third string, would save the average school enough to field two full wrestling teams, as Andrew Zimbalist has written.[56] But that, like criticism of Title IX, is a nonstarter. (If colleges professionalized football, it would no longer fall under an education rubric, and thus its numbers would not count against Title IX. Problem solved.) Since reducing spending on football and weakening Title IX are off the table, the response by the powers-that-be to the protests of heavyweight rowers and lithe male swimmers is little more than a sheepish shrug of the shoulders. But they do have their ways of fudging or finessing the situation.

Crew, or rowing, is the only women's sport in which squad numbers can even hope to approach those of football. So whether demand exists or not, schools seeking Title IX compliance are eager to put oars in the hands of physically fit young women. After all, rowing is an inexpensive sport; all you need is "some water, a boathouse, and a few boats," as well as a head coach and an assistant.[57] So between 1995 and 2017, Division I women's rowing expanded from 44 teams and 1,804 athletes to 88 teams and about 5,000 athletes. (By contrast, men's D-I rowing had 35 teams and 1,896 athletes in 2017.)[58] Women's rowing teams routinely outnumber football squads. Gilbert Gaul found that Wisconsin had an incredible 205 women rowers and 120 football players. Other big football schools had similar numbers. Washington: 154 rowers to 111 footballers; Michigan: 147–114; Ohio State: 103–103.[59] Those numbers may be taken with a gulp of salt water, however; Gaul noted that while 205 women tried out for the Badgers' rowing team, the number who actually made the team and stayed was probably half that. Yet the NCAA accepts tryout numbers. The budget for that putatively 205-member team, by the way, was $2.3 million, compared to the Badger football budget of $24 million.[60]

The rowing sham "aggravates a common complaint among Title IX opponents," writes Welch Suggs.

> Wrestlers, swimmers, and other male athletes train for their sports starting in elementary school and even earlier, yet are excluded from college teams. Women with little sports experience are allowed and even wooed with scholarship funds to go out for varsity crews—or equestrian teams or even bowling squads, both of which have become popular among colleges desperate to attract more female athletes.[61]

College football, as Quinnipiac College School of Law Professor Robert C. Farrell wrote, "devours financial resources, and college football teams seem as big as invading armies."[62] But does that army protect or ravage women's sports, or is it all a wash?

The handful of profit-generating football programs may actually help finance women's sports. Leeds, Suris, and Durkin, in a study of 201 schools representing all college football divisions, found that in 1997, a "$1,000 increase in spending on football actually reduces expenditure on women's sports by $112," though in those schools with *profitable* football programs, a "$1,000 increase in a football program's net revenue increases expenditures on women's sports by $34." Only nine schools in their sample subsidized women's sports from their football profits, and in only six cases—Auburn, the University of Florida, Penn State, the University of Washington, the University of Georgia, and Texas A&M—did this subsidy exceed $100,000.[63]

Patrick James Rishe, using data from Division I universities in 1995–6, found that the more prominent a school's football team, the more it spent in absolute—but not relative—terms on female athletes. So in an absolute sense, female athletes benefit from the presence of big-time football, but in a relative sense—the gender equity equation—they do not.[64] Contrariwise, Donald W. Agthe and R. Bruce Billings, writing in 2000 in the *Journal of Sport Management*, found a positive link between football profitability and gender equity at the Division I-A level.[65] So let's call it a draw, bearing in mind that the easiest way to iron out imbalances in sheer numbers of participants would be to drop football.

You can't make an omelette without breaking a few eggs. Or abolishing a few wrestling teams. Or erasing the legacy of female physical-education teachers, the game for every girl and a girl for every game philosophy, and adopting instead the male sports model. The federal government played a role in this, however inadvert.

Notes

1 Welch Suggs, *A Place on the Team: The Triumph and Tragedy of Title IX* (Princeton, NJ: Princeton University Press, 2005), p. 13.
2 Women constituted 40 percent of the national college population by 1900. Sack and Staurowsky, *College Athletes for Hire: The Evolution and Legacy of the NCAA's Amateur Myth*, p. 55.
3 Sojka, "Evolution of the Student-Athlete in America," *Journal of Popular Culture*: 61.
4 Suggs, *A Place on the Team: The Triumph and Tragedy of Title IX*, p. 23.
5 Nancy Theriot, "Towards a New Sporting Ideal: The Women's Division of the National Amateur Athletic Federation," *Journal of Women's Studies* 3, No. 1 (Spring 1978): 2.
6 Sack and Staurowsky, *College Athletes for Hire: The Evolution and Legacy of the NCAA's Amateur Myth*, p. 58.
7 "The National Amateur Athletic Federation: Innovative Approach to Women's Athletics," Herbert Hoover Presidential Library Museum, https://hoover.archives.gov/education/nhd/historydayWomensAthletics.html, accessed May 9, 2017.
8 Theriot, "Towards a New Sporting Ideal: The Women's Division of the National Amateur Athletic Federation," *Journal of Women's Studies*: 5.
9 R. Vivian Acosta and Linda Jean Carpenter, "Women in Sport," in *Sport and Higher Education,* edited by Donald Chu, Jeffrey O. Segrave, and Beverly J. Becker (Champaign, IL: Human Kinetics Publishers, 1985), pp. 321–2.
10 Alice Allene Sefton, *Sixteen Years of Progress in Athletics for Girls and Women, 1923–1939* (Stanford, CA: Stanford University Press, 1941), pp. 10–11.
11 Pauline Hodgson, "The Development of Intramural Athletics for College Women," *American Physical Education Review* XXXII, No. 7 (September 1927): 491.
12 Theriot, "Towards a New Sporting Ideal: The Women's Division of the National Amateur Athletic Federation," *Journal of Women's Studies*: 3.
13 Sojka, "The Evolution of the Student-Athlete in America: From the Divinity to the Divine," p. 26.
14 Suggs, *A Place on the Team: The Triumph and Tragedy of Title IX*, p. 21.

15 Helen N. Smith, "Evils of Sports for Women," *Journal of Health and Physical Education* 2, No. 1 (1931): 8.

16 Theriot, "Towards a New Sporting Ideal: The Women's Division of the National Amateur Athletic Federation," *Journal of Women's Studies*: 1.

17 George H. Hanford, "Controversies in College Sports," *Annals of the American Academy of Political and Social Science* 445, Issue 1 (September 1979): 77.

18 Suzanne E. Estler and Laurie Nelson, "Who Calls the Shots? Sports and University Leadership, Culture, and Decision Making," *ASHE Higher Education Report* 30, No. 5 (2005): 50.

19 Suggs, *A Place on the Team: The Triumph and Tragedy of Title IX*, p. 50.

20 Sack and Staurowsky, *College Athletes for Hire: The Evolution and Legacy of the NCAA's Amateur Myth*, p. 118.

21 Loretta M. Lamar, "To Be an Equitist or Not: A View of Title IX," *Sports Lawyers Journal* 1, No. 1 (1994): 245.

22 Suggs, *A Place on the Team: The Triumph and Tragedy of Title IX*, p. 64.

23 Fort, *Sports Economics*, p. 457.

24 Robert C. Farrell, "Title IX or College Football?" *Houston Law Review* 32 (1995–6): 1004.

25 Byers with Hammer, *Unsportsmanlike Conduct: Exploiting College Athletes,* p. 243.

26 Ibid., p. 242.

27 20 U.S. Code 1681 (a).

28 Acosta and Carpenter, "Women in Sport," in *Sport and Higher Education*: 317.

29 Suggs, *A Place on the Team: The Triumph and Tragedy of Title IX*, p. 41. See also Deborah L. Brake, *Getting in the Game: Title IX and the Women's Sports Revolution* (New York: New York University Press, 2010).

30 Suggs, *A Place on the Team: The Triumph and Tragedy of Title IX*, p. 41.

31 Ibid., pp. 67, 69.

32 Ibid., p. 70.

33 "Compliance Resolution," U.S. Department of Education, www2.ed.gov/about/offices/list/ocr/docs/investigations/06116001-a.html, accessed April 5, 2017.

34 Lamar, "To Be an Equitist or Not: A View of Title IX," *Sports Lawyers Journal*: 250.

35 Hanford, "Controversies in College Sports," *Annals of the American Academy of Political and Social Science*: 76. See also Michael A. Leeds, Yelena Suris, and Jennifer Durkin, "College Football and Title IX," in *Economics of College Sports*, edited by John Fizel and Rodney Fort (Westport, CT: Praeger, 2004), pp. 138–9.

36 Brake, *Getting in the Game: Title IX and the Women's Sports Revolution*, p. 106.

37 *Grove City College v. Bell* (1984), No. 82–792.

38 "Grove City College Athletics," http://athletics.gcc.edu/, accessed October 25, 2017.

39 See Dorothy J. Lovett and Carla D. Lowry, "Is Liberal Feminism Working in the NCAA?" *Journal of Sport Management* 9 (1995): 263–72.

40 Estler and Nelson, "Who Calls the Shots? Sports and University Leadership, Culture, and Decision Making," *ASHE Higher Education Report*: 61.

41 Brake, *Getting in the Game: Title IX and the Women's Sports Revolution*, p. 203.

42 "Athletics Administrative Staff, NCAA," http://web1.ncaa.org/rgdSearch/exec/instSearch, accessed April 5, 2017.

43 Brake, *Getting in the Game: Title IX and the Women's Sports Revolution*, p. 202.

44 "Head Coaches—Basketball," NCAA Sport Sponsorship, Participation and Demographics Search, http://web1.ncaa.org/rgdSearch/exec/instSearch, accessed March 11, 2017.

45 "Head Coaches," NCAA Sport Sponsorship, Participation and Demographics, http://web1.ncaa.org/rgdSearch/exec/instSearch, accessed March 11, 2017.

46 Jere Longman, "Number of Women Coaching in College Has Plummeted in Title IX Era," *New York Times*, March 30, 2017.

47 Nixon, *The Athletic Trap: How College Sports Corrupted the Academy*, p. 75.

48 Suggs, *A Place on the Team: The Triumph and Tragedy of Title IX*, p. 139.

49 "Open to All: Title IX at Thirty," The Secretary of Education's Commission on Opportunity in Athletics, U.S. Department of Education, February 28, 2003, p. 24.

50 Jessica Gavora, "A No-Win Numbers Game," *Washington Post*, January 14, 2001.

51 Jon Sanders, "Of Title IX and 30 Years of Bureaucratic Miasma," John William Pope Center for Higher Education Policy, May 31, 2002.

52 Luke Meredith, "NCAA Title IX Report: Spending Up, Gender Gaps Remain," Associated Press, June 21, 2017, www.usnews.com/news/sports/articles/2017-06-21/ncaa-title-ix-report-spending-up-gender-gaps-remain.

53 Clarke, "Maryland Athletic Department May Have to Cut Sports to Address Budget Shortfall," *Washington Post*.

54 Malcolm Moran, "Banned in Boston: One Football Team," *New York Times*, November 2, 1997.

55 Jon Vegosen, "Starve Football, Feed Athletics," *New York Times*, January 28, 2007.

56 Andrew Zimbalist, "What to Do About Title IX," *Gender Issues* 21, Issue 2 (March 2003): 57.

57 Gaul, *Billion-Dollar Ball: A Journey Through the Big-Money Culture of College Football*, p. 170.

58 Ibid., p. 171; "College Rowing & Scholarship Opportunities," www.scholarshipstats.com/rowing.html, accessed December 13, 2017.

59 Gaul, *Billion-Dollar Ball: A Journey Through the Big-Money Culture of College Football*, p. 180.

60 Ibid., p. 184.

61 Suggs, *A Place on the Team: The Triumph and Tragedy of Title IX*, p. 140.

62 Farrell, "Title IX or College Football?" *Houston Law Review*. 994.

63 Leeds, Suris, and Durkin, "College Football and Title IX," pp. 148–9.

64 James Patrick Rishe, "Gender Gaps and the Presence and Profitability of College Football," *Social Science Quarterly* 80, No. 4 (December 1999): 702–17.

65 Donald E. Agthe and R. Bruce Billings, "The Role of Football Profits in Meeting Title IX Gender Equity Regulations and Policy," *Journal of Sport Management* 14 (2000): 37.

8

REFORM—OR RENEWAL?

For better or worse, Americans—at least those who achieve positions of power—are congenital reformers. Presidents Eliot and Hutchins, Howard Savage and his Carnegie Report, John Hannah and the ACE commission—each sought, in his own way, to alter or even retard the development of intercollegiate athletics. Yet the one thing all these reforms have in common is that they failed to derail the juggernaut of big-time college sports, or subordinate them to the academic mission of the university. As Bradley David Ridpath of Ohio University writes in his assessment of reform efforts since 1929, the "same exact issues"—academic fraud, special treatment for athletes, unethical behavior by boosters and recruiters—recur in each generation.[1] Players bulk up, game strategies change, stadia are modernized, but the fundamental problems are never addressed. The song remains the same. Reforms are futile, inutile; the combined might of television, coaches, boosters, alumni, and fans overwhelm the Mugwumps every time.

Yet the reformers keep on coming. Matthew Denhart, Richard Vedder, and Robert Villwock of the Center for College Affordability and Productivity imagine a serious reform effort originating among the leaders of 25 to 30 top-tier FBS universities who might agree to a number of significant changes in the way big-time sports is conducted, including:

—Reducing the number of games, the length of the season, the size of the coaching staffs, and the size of the team.

—Playing at least 80 percent of their games against other schools that accept the reform principles.

—Creating two new conferences, thus gutting the Power Five conferences.

—Outlawing redshirting and prohibiting the playing of games during exam periods.

—Strictly limiting institutional subsidies.[2]

These salutary steps would help to rein in out-of-control football programs and perhaps lessen the injustice of forcing students to pay an athletic tax at public universities. As the authors point out:

> Long before sports became as commercialized as they are now, huge crowds gathered to watch Harvard play Yale, Michigan play Ohio State, Army take on Navy, etc. School spirit can exist, entertainment can be provided, and athletic programs can be at most a minor financial drain on institutions.[3]

This would require, among other things, strong leadership from school presidents, and that is the obstacle over which many a previous reform effort has tripped and fallen.

In his history of collegiate athletic reform, the distinguished scholar of sport Ronald A. Smith concluded that "it is not likely that presidents of institutions of higher learning will be successful in reforming college athletics." They are given to lofty rhetoric, and they may even mean it, but they are also "cheerleaders for their institution," and is it almost inconceivable that a president of, say, the University of Alabama will ever do anything to bring the football team in line with the school's academic mission.[4] (If he or she tried, said president would find himself out the door before you could say "Nick Saban.") Thus the Knight Foundation's Commission on Intercollegiate Athletics was a "failure," judged Smith in 2011, pursuing as it did the shopworn solution of presidential leadership.[5]

The Drake Group, with its emphasis on the faculty as prime movers of reform, had a better idea, but college faculties are by and large powerless in the institutional framework. Even the well-intentioned do not have the ability to effect significant change. The Drake Group's central demands—integrate athletes into the general student body, abolish athletes-only academic support services and even the term *student-athlete,* give academics priority over athletics in scheduling, end freshman eligibility, require athletes to maintain a 2.0 GPA in order to play—are in the reform mainstream. Its goal of a world in which "college students play college sports" is admirable, though probably not achievable without a far more radical set of reforms.[6]

The Coalition on Intercollegiate Athletics (COIA), an association of 62 faculty senates of FBS schools, was founded in 2002 at the University of Oregon, where football and basketball were calling the shots in the Nike-fied world of the twenty-first century. The first of COIA's core values is that "Student Athletes are Students First," which is perhaps a bit of wishful thinking. Its proposals on subjects such as academic integrity and the shortening of athletic calendars are solidly in the reform mainstream, though as a veteran of faculty senate meetings the author doubts the efficacy of any coalition of five dozen faculty senates.[7]

James Duderstadt, the former University of Michigan president, has said:

> All hope is not lost. There is one important ally left . . . the university faculty. . . It is now time to challenge the faculties of our universities,

through their elected bodies such as faculty senates, to step up to their responsibility to defend the academic integrity of their institutions, by demanding substantive reform of intercollegiate athletics.[8]

This hope is belied by history: faculty have not been effective overseers of athletics, nor are they equipped to be so at large football and basketball factories. Romantics imagine the faculty to be the "conscience of the university," jealously guarding its integrity and reputation, but this has never really been the case, nor is it likely to evolve as such.[9]

The manifest failure of college presidents, faculty, and athletic directors to clean up big-time intercollegiate sports has led, inevitably, to calls for federal intervention. Not that the feds have looked the other way all these years: witness Theodore Roosevelt's labors to change the rules of football. The first instinct of a politician is to *do* something, not by private means but by employing the powers of the government. Thus in recent years Rep. Charles Dent (R-PA) and a bipartisan group of cosponsors have proposed the creation of a Presidential Commission on Intercollegiate Athletics, which would almost certainly regurgitate the findings of previous commissions, though perhaps in less striking or academic prose. About nine in ten of Dent's cosponsors represent districts with schools in the Big Ten, so this is hardly President Eliot or Robert Maynard Hutchins territory.[10]

What is different about the Dent proposal, denominated the National Collegiate Athletics Accountability Act, or NCAA—ha! ha!—is that it advances forcefully the notion that intercollegiate athletics are a concern of the U.S. government rather than the institutions themselves. Its first preambulary finding is that the federal government spends as much as $200 billion on higher education under Title IV of the Higher Education Act of 1965 and $30 billion annually on federal Pell Grants. The nose, in other words, is under the tent in a big way. When you accept the king's shilling, you become the king's man.

The Dent bill would forbid a school from joining any nonprofit athletic association—read: NCAA—unless it annually tests each student-athlete participating in a contact or limited-contact sport for concussion. A wise policy, perhaps, but a subject that traditionally has been thought to be the province of the NCAA. It also requires guaranteed four-year scholarships, though its main thrust is the creation of a commission of wise, or at least very well-connected, men and women. Dent's national commission would consist of 17 members appointed by the President (5), the Speaker of the House of Representatives (3), the House Minority Leader (3), the Senate Majority Leader (3), and the Senate Minority Leader (3). It would be charged with reviewing, and recommending action on, a host of issues related to the intersection of athletics and academics on campus, among them graduation rates, academic integrity, eligibility standards, financing (including student fees), transparency, and compensation for student-athletes.[11]

In other words, the same subjects—with the exception of student fees—that every previous panel and committee has grappled with, and failed to make any appreciable dent in the collegiate-athletic complex. "Many will ask the question why Congress is getting engaged in this," said cosponsor Rep. Joyce Beatty (D-OH). "The reason is, talk is not enough."[12] Well, it's been enough in the past, Congresswoman Beatty, and there is no reason to suspect that talk and more talk will not suffice in the future, solons to the contrary.

The Dent bill did draw the enthusiastic support of the Drake Group, which noted that "the threat of losing federal Higher Education funding appears likely to move the needle toward meaningful change."[13] Once again, the warnings of those 1950s conservatives and radicals who said that accepting federal assistance would permit national politicians to jerk the strings of institutions of higher education look prescient.

A less-publicized but more far-reaching legislative proposal coeval with the NCAA Act is the College Athlete Protection, or CAP Act, formulated by the Drake Group and still in search of a congressional sponsor at this writing. Like Rep. Dent's bill, CAP envisions a more active, or intrusive, role for the federal government in the realm of intercollegiate sports. Its central provisions would mandate that athletic scholarships extend to graduation, with a maximum of five years; place academic counseling for athletes within the academic affairs division rather than the athletic department; restrict practice and participation by (and ban from freshman eligibility) athletes with low GPAs and test scores; and, in its two most provocative provisions, bar the use of student fees to support athletics unless otherwise directed by a vote of the student government every four years, and cap salaries of coaches and administrators "at the average salary of a full professor in the 95th percentile at doctoral granting institutions."[14]

Those not enamored of federal solutions to educational problems must look to the schools themselves—a prospect not exactly brimming with possibilities. Conceivably, schools, whether acting as members of conferences or within the broader NCAA, could enact many of these long-bandied-about reforms on their own. If every school were bound by the same rules on recruitment, eligibility, expenses, and suchlike, "competitive balance would be maintained," says Robert Frank, the Cornell economist. This would not drain the sport of spectators, he says, because:

> [I]t is much less the absolute performance of teams that matter than the fact of there being spirited contests. If absolute performance were of primary concern to spectators, they would have long since deserted college athletic contests in favor of their professional counterparts.[15]

What would have happened if the early reformers had triumphed, and intercollegiate football, while not abolished, had been de-emphasized, subordinated to intramurals, and confined to limited geographic areas, so that teams played a smaller number of games, mostly against natural rivals, using students as athletes? Surely, as W. Burlette Carter speculates, private enterprise would have filled the void, in the form of the National Football League. While the Oklahomas and Penn States would not have garnered the headlines or the huge TV and bowl game purses, schools also would have lost out on "crippling athletic expenses and troubling ethical dilemmas." Salaries, stadia, equipment, scholarship costs: these would be, by comparison to the present state of affairs, minuscule. Academic standards may have eroded for other reasons, but not because of pressure from gargantuan athletic departments.[16] But that was only one of the roads not traveled.

Should we pay the help?

If football and basketball players at the Division I level are not real students, as virtually everyone this side of the nation's sports information directors believe, then should we strike a blow for honesty and just pay them as employees of the college? Or maybe we could make an end-run around the hypocrisy by permitting them to major in football or basketball? Lewis Grizzard, the late *Atlanta Constitution* columnist and humorist, proposed the latter option. Grizzard wrote:

> We give Lorenzo Linebacker a scholarship and allow him to major in football. He learns to play football, goes to daily classes to learn how to fill them with air, how to make one, how to coach others in the game, and even how to sell a football . . . Lorenzo gets his degree in football. Maybe he can go and play in the pros and make millions of dollars. Or maybe he can become a coach. Or maybe he can get a job in a sporting-goods store. Either way, it's better than what he could have had otherwise. It's silly to offer a degree in football? I had a friend from high school who majored in music in college, learned to play guitar, and was last seen doing five nights a week in a Holiday Inn lounge. Life could turn out that way for Lorenzo, too, if we just give him a chance.[17]

More seriously, Johnny Majors, the swashbuckling football coach of the University of Tennessee and Pitt, said in 1978:

> Look, a person who's a woodworker and is in school to learn to carve isn't interested in the guy working on computers in the engineering department. And the saxophone player who wants to become a music teacher couldn't care less about the law classes. If a kid wants to play football, with the idea of turning professional, then he ought to be allowed to earn a degree in college football.[18]

Instituting a football major would send President Eliot or President Hutchins for the smelling salts, and it would belie any pretense that the usual football factories have about the paramountcy of intellectual pursuits, but it would have the virtue of honesty. Lewis Grizzard had his tongue only partially in cheek, and Johnny Majors was dead serious if a little on the ethically shady side, but David Pargman, a professor emeritus of educational psychology at Florida State, was entirely sober-sided when he proposed in the *Chronicle of Higher Education* that the pursuit of a professional career in football, basketball, and baseball be recognized as a legitimate academic specialty, in the manner of music or ballet or dance. He even laid out a course of study: two years of basic studies, similar to those of regular students, and then a junior year filled with anatomy and physiology, sports psychology and sports strategy, contract law and scrimmages; and a senior year with courses in nutrition, public speaking (to pare "y'knows" from the vocabulary), coaching, business law, and kinesiology. All this would lead to a B.A. in Sports Performance. And as Pargman concludes, it "would be infinitely more honest than the charade that now prevails." Or as a partial concession to reality, Mitch Albom, the Detroit sports-writer and author of the best seller *Tuesdays with Morrie*, suggests permitting college athletes to get paid for non-college competition. If the actress Jodie Foster could make movies during the summertime during her college years at Yale, says Albom, why shouldn't football or basketball players be able to ply their trade for money during the off-season?[19]

Rick Telander, a former All-Big Ten cornerback at Northwestern and a senior writer for *Sports Illustrated*, concluded in his 1989 indictment *The Hundred Yard Lie: The Corruption of College Football and What We Can Do to Stop It* that "big-time college football is out of control, rotten from the foundation up."[20] At major colleges, writes Telander, football players "aren't part of the college populace; they're unpaid workers imported for the entertainment delight of, by and large, TV viewers and alumni."[21] And that, really, is a function more compatible with professional sports, which exist for the amusement, if not edification, of the spectator, and the financial gain, or at least the opportunity therefor, of the team owner, the media that broadcast and cover the games, and the players and employees of the franchise. Amateur sport, by contrast, is first and foremost for the participants, and spectators are, or should be, an afterthought. Amateur athletes measure themselves against objective standards as well as competitors, and learn or enhance all those character-building qualities that fusty nineteenth-centurians spoke of with due reverence.[22]

Given the extinction of this amateur ideal in big-time college football, would it be better to end the charade and pay these players a market-sensitive wage? Is it fair that Nick Saban makes $7 million a year coaching the Alabama Crimson Tide but his star quarterback or linebacker is compensated in academic credits (in which he may have no interest) and the perks of the high-profile athlete? This is not a new question. When Red Grange, the "Galloping Ghost" of the University of Illinois, quit school in 1925 to sign a contract with the professional Chicago Bears of the fledging National Football League, the extollers of the amateur ideal denounced him. His college coach, Bob "The Little Dutchman" Zuppke, expressed disappointment in his star player, but Grange pointedly noted that Zuppke made his living coaching football, "so what's the difference if I make a living playing football?"[23] (Zuppke, no musclehead himself, was also a Western landscape artist.)[24]

Most of today's unpaid athletes are African American: 57 percent of football players and 64 percent of men's basketball players in the six largest conferences are such, though African American men account for less than 3 percent of the student bodies at those schools. Donald H. Yee, a prominent agent for pro athletes, notes that to the (limited) extent that the money sports of football and basketball help subsidize non-revenue sports, it is a case of African American athletes subsidizing white athletes—of University of Texas football players generating the revenue that supports University of Texas men's rowing.[25]

Roger G. Noll argues that "intercollegiate athletics is primarily a mechanism whereby poor, primarily black students are used to finance the educational and athletic activities of wealthy white students." He bases this claim on the fact that the only two "money" sports, FBS football and Division I basketball, have dis-proportionately African American rosters, while the Olympic sports that these money sports *sometimes* subsidize have overwhelmingly white rosters. Of course the budgets for fencing and wrestling are considerably smaller than the football budget, and as we have seen, a small percentage of money-sport teams actually make money. One could argue that for schools in, say, the Sun Belt Conference, it is the largely white student bodies that are subsidizing the decidedly unprofitable and largely African American football teams.[26]

In retirement, Walter Byers, executive director the NCAA from 1951–87, accused the association of harboring a "neoplantation belief that the enormous proceeds from college games belong to the overseers (the administrators) and the supervisors (coaches). The plantation workers performing in the arena may receive only those benefits authorized by the overseers."[27] For most of his tenure, Byers said in his memoir *Unsportsmanlike Conduct*, he "passionately believed" in the NCAA's purported ideal of amateurism, but this had become a hopeless ana-chronism by late in his career. As Byers points out, in 1975, his final year of coaching basketball, the legendary John Wooden, who had guided UCLA to ten national championships, had a salary of $32,500 and, by his choice, no shoe deals. A decade later, Jimmy Valvano, who led North Carolina State to one NCAA title, was pulling in $850,000 from his salary, shoe deals, and other business arrange-ments.[28] But Valvano's players, while likely receiving under-the-table gifts and the social perquisites of the famous athlete, were officially limited in compensation to tuition, room, and board.

If college football and basketball players do join the ranks of the officially salar-ied, we will have the strange spectacle of ordinary students paying increased fees in order to subsidize not just the education but the livelihoods, the salaries, of their far more feted and famous and celebrated sports-playing fellow "students." And if you pay those who play revenue sports, the big-time sports factories may need to shutter non-revenue sports, which would run afoul of Title IX. A star halfback at Alabama may be worth hundreds of thousands of dollars to his school; the best women's lacrosse player at Alabama is, from a strictly utilitarian view, a debit who is costing her school the price of her scholarship as well as a proportional share of the women's lacrosse budget. But you can bet your *Roll, Tide, Roll* party bus that that lacrosse player will sue if the halfback starts cashing astronomical checks from the university while she is salary-less.

Charles Clotfelter notes that the idea of paying players—"serfs of the turf"—is "in sync with both the libertarian sensibilities of free-market economics and leftist sympathies for the oppressed."[29] But this would perhaps shine too bright a light on the hypocrisy of the spurious "student-athlete" model. An alternative—schools corrupted by big-time athletics could drop down to Division III, where sport is played at relatively small expense for the love of the game—appeals to the romantics among us, but the chance that Ohio State and the University of Alabama will do so absent some cataclysmic and utterly unforeseeable event is on a par with the chance that the D-III University of Chicago Maroons will knock off Ohio State in next year's Rose Bowl—or that Ohio State will reject a Rose Bowl invite ever again.

Sports economist Andrew Zimbalist notes, "No other industry in the United States manages not to pay its principal producers a wage or salary."[30] Paying college athletes would, in effect, make them employees, or subcontractors. They would be more like NFL or NBA athletes than unlike them, only somewhat less lucratively paid and less talented. The emotional or sentimental bonds linking the college fan to his team would be weakened, as the fiction that these young men are putting themselves on the line for the glory of good old State U. would be finally and fully exploded.

When the aptly surnamed Allen L. Sack, professor of sociology and management at the University of New Haven, was a defensive end on Notre Dame's 1966 national championship team, he was treated like a king, he recalls, though academics had to come a distinct second to football. The mid-60s were also a period of freshman ineligibility (a rule that was reversed in 1972), and Notre Dame was still refusing to play in bowl games. In his career as an academic and advocate for college athletes, Sack has taken the position that these athletes are, in essence, employees of the school, and therefore deserve workers' compensation, the right to form labor unions, and the right to bargain collectively. The term "student-athlete," argue Sack and Ellen J. Staurowsky, was invented in part to make clear that scholarship athletes were not parties to a "contract for hire," and thus were not to be considered employees eligible for the panoply of protections and benefits provided by federal and state labor laws.[31] But should they be?

Periodically, talk of unionization invades college athletics, but the advance is quickly repulsed. For the transient nature of college athletes militates against unionization; four or (for redshirts) five years is the most they will spend on campus, and in basketball, the best sometimes opt for "one and done." Athletes also lack an independent basis for action. Coaches exercise enormous sway at the college level, far more so than in the professional ranks, and it is the rare (or supremely talented) athlete who will brave his coach's disfavor and agitate for a union. Moreover, as Richard Vedder and Matthew Denhart note in the *Wall Street Journal*, "most players don't have a lot of contact with the members of other teams."[32] Nationwide organization would be a logistical nightmare, even in the age of Facebook and texting.

The frank professionalization of college sports, whereby schools sponsor teams of paid athletes—not necessarily student-athletes—in football and basketball would end the rampant hypocrisy surrounding these sports but it would also snap, or at least weaken, the emotional link between fans and the teams. These would be akin to minor league baseball clubs, whose fan bases are often passionate but also modest in size. The University of Alabama might call its professional team the Crimson Tide, but the glory would be a fading memory, and in reality the team would be more like a minor-league version of the Jacksonville Jaguars.

Rick Telander proposed the creation of a clumsily acronymed AGPFL, or Age Group Professional Football League, analogous to baseball's minor leagues, hockey's junior leagues, and the lesser professional basketball leagues. It would consist of those big-time college football schools that would accept a "reasonable pay scale" for its 18- to 22-year-old players. They would not need to be college students, though they would play for and wear the traditional colors of Nebraska, Texas, Penn State, and the other football factories who chose to join the league. Those schools refusing to pay their players would revert to a Division III-type model, with shortened schedules. The nonprofessional college teams would forswear spring practices, freshmen players, athletic dorms, athletic scholarships, games outside a Labor Day-Christmas window, and other aspects of what Telander views as a corrupt system. Hypocrisy would be the first casualty: "The AGPFL coaches won't have to think about education at all, and the college coaches will no longer be celebrities, but rather career college teachers who can afford to be concerned about their players' education." No longer would the fiction of the "student-athlete" be maintained; the lie would be unnecessary, and colleges "can become ethical and honorable places once again."[33]

Or, suggest Randy R. Grant, John Leadley, and Zenon Zygmont in *The Economics of Intercollegiate Sports* (2008), the NFL could be assigned responsibility for Division I football programs by lottery to its 32 member teams, who would "run the football program at each school. Not only would this solve the financial difficulties that plague so many D-I schools, it would also allow the athletes to receive a salary just like minor leaguers in baseball and ice hockey."[34] But the NFL (and NBA) are unlikely to take over the support of 120-plus FBS teams and 300-plus Division I basketball teams; perhaps they would subsidize the Michigan Wolverines or the Buckeyes of Ohio State, but the Cal-Irvine Anteaters and Idaho State Bengals would be on their own.

For now, the NFL and NBA have no real incentive to create an extensive minor league system as has developed in baseball, since the NCAA functions perfectly well in that role. Yet the absurdity of the current system is jarring, as well as tremendously unfair to talented young athletes who have a real shot at a lucrative professional career. A gifted 18-year-old wide receiver may not pursue his desired career path without first taking a detour through the nation's higher education system. He must take up residence on a college campus, and enroll in and—putatively—attend classes in an at least nominally academic subject that interests him not in the slightest. He is a participant in a charade but the charade is not of his own making; he has been forced to play his role therein due to the accumulated hypocrisies of many generations. Isn't it time we tried honesty?[35]

Striking at the root

Paying players is only one of the more radical suggestions for reform. And while it gets points for frankness, it is no more consistent with the educational mission of a university than is the current system. One option is to eliminate varsity sports altogether from the formal offerings of colleges and universities. After all, as the education writer George Leef has argued, the nation's largest school of higher education, the online University of Phoenix, has no athletic program, and its over 140,000 students (and almost one million alumni) get along just fine without one.[36]

Somewhat less quixotic, though still a long-shot, is the abolition of athletic scholarships. This proposal has a fusty quality about it, redolent of debates in the 1920s and 1930s, yet the principles undergirding it remain just as valid today as then. John R. Gerdy, a star basketball player at Davidson College in the 1970s who was drafted by the NBA New Jersey Nets and is now a professor of sports administration at Ohio University—the epicenter of intercollegiate sports reform and provocative thought—has proposed, in the pages of the *Chronicle of Higher Education* and elsewhere, the replacement of athletic scholarships by institutional need-based aid. Pointing to the often pathetic graduation rates of African American football and basketball players, he denies that this would reduce the presence of African Americans on campus; rather, they would, on the whole, be "less talented" athletes and "better students." The great rivalries—Alabama-Auburn, Michigan-Ohio State, Oklahoma-Texas—would still be played, with as much fire and enthusiasm and spirit as ever, if at a somewhat lower talent level. But the schools would be represented by actual students—fellows you might see in Bio 201 lab, or in the dorm (since athletic dorms would be thing of the past). When Texas beat Oklahoma, it really would be a case of Texas students defeating Oklahoma students on the gridiron. Wouldn't that be something new?[37]

Murray Sperber offers a clear-eyed and unadorned proposal based in the not always abundant virtue of *honesty*: "*Stop pretending that athletes can get decent college educations.*" Steer those whose ambition is professional sport to minor leagues, which, if Sperber's vision were to take hold, would spring up in football and basketball. Athletes desiring a college education would be held to the same standards as other students: no special admits, no "jock privileges." Subsidies should be transparent; athletic department deficits should be abolished by scaling down operations.[38] In recommending that schools abolish athletic scholarships and grant aid only on the basis of need, Sperber quotes Bill Stern, pioneering sports radio broadcaster of the 1930s and 1940s:

> Getting a higher education should be the primary reason for any youngster going to college. Athletic achievements, however sensational, should be secondary and should serve as a means to an end, namely a legitimate college diploma. Let's keep the record straight, when a college athlete plays for pay, receiving money through athletic scholarships, he's a professional no matter what uniform he wears.[39]

At the very least, colleges could sharply reduce the number of football scholarships they award. And there is a tradition-shrouded way to do this.

Responding to those who believe that college football reform must be namby-pamby, Douglas S. Looney of *Sports Illustrated* proposed a return to "a time when men were men and football players played real football"—that is, the era of one-platoon football, wherein footballers play both offense *and* defense. (The first coach Looney quoted in support of the idea was Penn State's Joe Paterno, who gushed, "If it were up to me, I'd love to go back to one-platoon football right now. It would get us back to a lot of basic values. Wouldn't that be great?") The single-platoon system held sway in college football until 1941, when unlimited substitution was introduced. The year is no coincidence; as is so often the case, war had domestic consequences—in this case, a perceived shortage of "versatile young men," since so many were in fatigues rather than shoulder pads. In 1953—the year the Korean War ended—the single platoon system was restored, only to be scrapped—for good?—in 1964.

The cost implications of unlimited substitution football were real. As the Associated Press noted in 1953, the two-platoon system "bankrupted the football programs of many small colleges." Football rosters consist of many more members than there are positions on the field at any one time. The current FBS scholarship limit of 85 would be reduced considerably if one-platoon football were restored. Dave Nelson of the NCAA Rules Committee told Looney that scholarships could be cut to at least 60, which would mean, under current rules, a reduction of approximately 30 percent in scholarship costs.[40] Taking the average FBS scholarship amount of $36,070 and multiplying by 25 equals an average savings per FBS school of $901,750.[41] And of course that doesn't include additional savings in uniforms, travel, and such. Jon Wefald, then president of Kansas State, estimated that this reform would cut football expenses by at least 40 percent. There would be other benefits too, argues Looney, among them better-conditioned players and, as a result, fewer injuries; an emphasis on all-around athletes instead of specialized speed burners, which would lessen the severity of collisions and resultant injuries; and a dispersed balance of power, as the Alabamas and Clemsons could no longer stockpile players.

Even without reverting to single-platoon football, schools could reduce football scholarships to save money, ensure Title IX compliance, and perhaps achieve greater parity. Of course, fewer star high school players would get the chance to play FBS football (or at least serve as an FBS practice tackling dummy and sit at the end of an FBS bench). NFL teams carry 53 players; surely college teams can make do with a similar number, supplemented by walk-ons.

When smaller schools sought scholarship number limits in the 1960s and 1970s, Darrel Royal, head coach of the Texas Longhorns, sniffed, "I don't want Hofstra telling Texas how to play football."[42] Hofstra has since dropped the game; Texas still plays football the way it wants to. The NCAA set a scholarship ceiling of 95 in 1977 and cut that to 85 in 1992. The assumption was that this would keep the A-list programs from "stockpiling" players and thereby spread the wealth a bit, since a marginal recruit no longer signed by the University of Texas might blossom as a fine player for the University of Texas at El Paso. This was a victory, however modest, for the have–nots, right?

Yet the story may be more complicated than that. Daniel Sutter and Stephen Winkler, writing in the *Journal of Sports Economics*, examined the interplay between scholarship limits and parity. The evidence was mixed. But then perhaps that's what we should have expected. Scholarship limits apply to the outsider schools, too, and may be a deceptive means by which the Ins "protect the existing powers by restricting the efforts of outsiders to break into the football elite." For their limits apply to the Hofstras as well as the UTs, and thus prevent Hofstra-level programs from offering, say, 120 scholarships in order to increase their chances of finding diamonds in the rough.[43] This, note the authors, is what University of Pittsburgh coach Johnny Majors did when he handed out an eye-popping 83 scholarships to his first recruiting class—which went on to win the national championship in 1976.[44]

So perhaps, suggest Sutter and Winkler, scholarship limits were actually intended to fortify and entrench the existing power programs. Universities that had enjoyed recent success on the football field were more likely than others to vote to reduce the scholarship limit from 95 to 85, suggesting that there may have been various factors at play in this issue.[45]

The way out: go clubbing!

Robert Maynard Hutchins, the man who abolished football at the University of Chicago, was no more an advocate of sedentary eggheadism than was Amos Alonzo Stagg. But he was, despite his elitist reputation, a democratizer. "A football squad usually numbers 45," he said in 1954. (The number on scholarship has almost doubled in the years since.)

> It is absurd to talk as though an institution that spends hundreds of thousands of dollars on this select group, ordinarily the group that needs physical training least, and pays little attention to opportunities for intramural sport, is doing so in the name of health, exercise and recreation. The only exercise for the majority is climbing up and down stadium stairs.[46]

Intramural sports, which were first formally organized at Ohio State and the University of Michigan in 1914, offer opportunities for students of any and all skill levels to run, throw, hit, hurl, stumble, fall, and triumph in dozens of sports and games.[47] Teams are sometimes single-sex, sometimes coed, and the incidence of raucous laughter is far higher on the fields and courts of intramural sports than in Division I contests.

John D. Colombo, professor at the University of Illinois College of Law, says:

> The idea that college football evokes a Greek ideal of well-rounded athletes—
> that's just nuts. That's just crazy. The Greek ideal, if there is one, is intramural

sports. Big-time college football is nothing more than the minor leagues for the pros, and everyone knows it.[48]

Maurice Mitchell, the former chancellor of the football-dropping University of Denver and foe of all intercollegiate athletics, grew almost misty-eyed in recalling his success in converting an unused football field and complex to a center of intramural athletics. "It is an exciting thing on a nice day to see eight thousand kids out there playing baseball, playing soccer, running around in the fresh air and sunlight, and getting the blood circulating through their veins," said Mitchell in 1982.

> You certainly do not achieve that when you set them all down in a cold sta-
> dium with a bottle of booze and a joint in their hands, so they can watch
> twenty-two benighted kids lurch up and down the field in search of a pro-
> fessional career that only two of them will ever enjoy.[49]

But intramurals, though fiercely contested at some schools, have a reputation for frivolity. They don't quite measure up for many students who'd like to exercise body as well as mind. And this leads us to an alternative to the present madness: an alternative that does not require inactivity, passivity, a rejection of athletes and athleticism, or the jettisoning of football and basketball and the whole panoply of sports played today at the college level. That alternative is club sports. Early inter-collegiate sports resembled club sports, as they were student-run, and not under college sponsorship or the auspices of an organization like the NCAA or NAIA.

NIRSA, the National Intramural-Recreational Sports Association, defines clubs as "Student-run organizations with a shared interest in a particular competitive sport. Club sports are not regulated by the NCAA and do not include inter-collegiate or varsity sports. Examples include club hockey and club volleyball."[50] The most extensive recent survey found that as many as two million college students play club sports. They are, in a way, a throwback to the nineteenth-century model of student-run athletic competition. The academic institution has a very limited role; the onus, or opportunity, rests on the players. They run the practices, they draw up the schedules, they take care of all the administrative duties for which massive athletic departments have otherwise been constructed.

The student activities association may throw a few hundred or even thousand dollars at the club team, but membership dues are usually required. Team selection varies by school; some have tryouts, others are open to all comers. The talent level can be impressive; most of these young people played high school sports, and their drive to succeed can be as strong as that found at the varsity level. "Intramural sports can be too loose and not competitive enough," explained Tiffany Villalba of the Villanova women's club soccer team to the *New York Times*. "But the varsity teams, even if you make one, can be intense and require a lot of your free time. The club team fills that gap between the two. It's not too demanding, but it's not trivial."[51]

Sports range from meat and potatoes (football and basketball) to the exotic (bass fishing and *Harry Potter*-derived quidditch) to the granddaddy of all club sports, the ever-popular rugby. In their survey of the college sports scene, James Shulman and William G. Bowen wrote that "Those who play on student-run clubs today certainly enjoy themselves. Moreover, the club sports model has the advantage of encouraging student initiative."[52] David Gerstle, player-coach of the club water polo team at Yale, told the *New York Times*'s Bill Pennington, "It's a ton of work, but we do it because we take ownership of our team. I think it's a more collegial experience than the varsity team model."[53]

Although club sports may sound like an archaism in our age of Urban Meyer and March Madness, their popularity grows—perhaps in reaction to the 12-month madness that is intercollegiate sport. For instance, in 2017, the National Collegiate Club Volleyball Championships in Kansas City attracted over 440 men's and women's teams competing in ten divisions. Winning teams came from various schools from all parts of the United States, from San Diego State to the University of Wisconsin at LaCrosse to Messiah College.[54] Three decades earlier, the club volleyball tournament had drawn just 20 teams.[55]

From a purely practical, or perhaps mercenary, point of view, research has demonstrated that "alumni who participated in extracurricular activities were much more likely to donate to the school later in life than varsity athletes." That diminutive but game fullback on the women's club rugby team is much more likely to be writing checks to the alumni fund-raising drive 20 years hence than is the husky, male varsity linebacker.

As Leon Lifschutz of the Department of Student Life at the University of Vermont points out in *Recreational Sports Journal*, travel and medical coverage are the primary challenges faced by club teams. The curling club team doesn't travel by private jet or gaily decorated megabus; the unprepossessing van is the usual mode of transportation. "[P]oor vehicle maintenance and driver error" are concerns. And medical insurance practices vary greatly among schools: most require proof of private medical coverage, though 43 percent of schools in one survey offered blanket insurance coverage to all club teams.[56] But somehow the students navigate these obstacles. The teams are put together, the contests scheduled, the games go on. And the managers and schedulers and coaches learn or hone valuable skills.

Games are sparsely attended, if attended at all, but this is as many early partisans of sport intended. The game is for the players, not the watchers. And besides, it's not like the NCAA varsity women's cycling team draws anything more than flies. "It's a return to pure amateurism and a lot closer to the original model for college athletics," Jim Guinta, executive director of the National Collegiate Wrestling Association, told Bill Pennington of the *New York Times*.

> Nobody competes for the money or the fame because there are no scholarships and not a lot of attention. The kids have to do all the work to make their club function. They do it because they love their sport, and I'll tell you

what, we don't have the prima donnas you see at the higher levels of college athletics.

David Gerstle, the Yale water polo player-coach, compared the club and varsity models:

> If you look at in economic terms, varsity sports are like a high-regulated industry with restrictions, caps, and incentives. But club sports eliminates the barriers and lets anyone in, much like libertarian economics. It raises the level of competition because it inspires people's competitive nature. It frees them to want to do it and do their best.[57]

With club sports, universities would be, in some sense, going forward to the past. They evoke an age of student-run athletics in which participants knew—or at least accepted—that sports were distinctly a sideline, an enjoyable if marginal activity, and clearly, wholly subordinate to education. ESPN wouldn't like it, but Robert Maynard Hutchins—perhaps even President Eliot—would approve. And what are colleges for, anyway?

Notes

1 Bradley David Ridpath, "Can the Faculty Reform Intercollegiate Athletics?" *Journal of Issues in Intercollegiate Athletics* 1 (2008): 16.
2 Denhart, Villwock, and Vedder, "The Academics-Athletics Trade-Off," pp. 41–2.
3 Ibid., p. 43.
4 Smith, *Pay for Play: A History of Big-Time College Athletic Reform*, p. x–xi.
5 Ibid., p. 5.
6 Ridpath, "Can the Faculty Reform Intercollegiate Athletics?" *Journal of Issues in Inter-collegiate Athletics*: 19–22.
7 See "Academic Integrity in Intercollegiate Athletics: Principles, Rules, and Best Prac-tices," Coalition on Intercollegiate Athletics, adopted April 1, 2005, www.thecoia.org.
8 "Why Should Faculty become Involved?" 2003 AAUP Meeting, www.math.umd.edu/~jcohen/COIA/AAUPconference.htm, accessed October 15, 2017.
9 John C. Weistart, "College Sports Reform: Where Are the Faculty?" *Academe* 73, No. 4 (July–August 1987): 12.
10 Kadence A. Otto, "A Value Oriented Analysis of Proposed Collegiate Athletic Reform Legislation," *Journal for the Study of Sports and Athletes in Education* 8, No. 3 (November 2014): 199.
11 H.R. 2731, U.S. House of Representatives, introduced June 11, 2015.
12 Travis Waldron, "Lawmakers Take Aim at 'Abysmal Cesspool' of College Sports," *Huffington Post*, June 12, 2015.
13 "Position Statement: Establishment of a Presidential Commission on Intercollegiate Athletics Reform," The Drake Group, p. 11.
14 Otto, "A Value Oriented Analysis of Proposed Collegiate Athletic Reform Legislation," *Journal for the Study of Sports and Athletes in Education*: 192–3.
15 Myers, "Winning College Sports Teams Rarely Attract More Alumni Gifts or Better Student Applicants, Cornell Report Shows," *Cornell Chronicle*.
16 Carter, "The Age of Innocence: The First 25 Years of The National Collegiate Athletic Association, 1906 to 1931," *Vanderbilt Journal of Entertainment and Technology Law*: 289.

17 Telander, *The Hundred Yard Lie: The Corruption of College Football and What We Can Do to Stop It*, pp. 25–6.

18 Thelin, *Games Colleges Play: Scandal and Reform in Intercollegiate Athletics*, p. 166.

19 David Pargman, "End the Charade: Let Athletes Major in Sports," *Chronicle of Higher Education*, November 26, 2012.

20 Telander, *The Hundred Yard Lie: The Corruption of College Football and What We Can Do to Stop It*, p. 17.

21 Ibid., p. 55.

22 See Peter Gent, "Some Hard Thoughts on Games People Play. . ." *Los Angeles Times*, November 26, 1978.

23 Ingrassia, *The Rise of Gridiron University: Higher Education's Uneasy Alliance with Big-Time Football*, p. 135.

24 "Sport: Football Artist," *Time*, October 18, 1937.

25 Donald H. Yee, "The Color of Money in the NCAA," *Washington Post*, January 10, 2016.

26 Noll, "The Economics of Intercollegiate Sports," in *Rethinking College Athletics*, pp. 198, 204.

27 Byers with Hammer, *Unsportsmanlike Conduct: Exploiting College Athletes*, pp. 2–3.

28 Ibid., pp. 5, 9.

29 Clotfelter, *Big-Time Sports in American Universities*, p. 215.

30 Zimbalist, *Unpaid Professionals: Commercialism and Conflict in Big-Time College Sports*, p. 6.

31 Sack and Staurowsky, *College Athletes for Hire: The Evolution and Legacy of the NCAA's Amateur Myth*, p. 48.

32 Richard Vedder and Matthew Denhart, "The Real March Madness," *Wall Street Journal*, March 20, 2009.

33 Telander, *The Hundred Yard Lie: The Corruption of College Football and What We Can Do to Stop It*, pp. 214, 218.

34 Grant, Leadley, and Zygmont, *The Economics of Intercollegiate Sports*, p. 455.

35 On a parallel track, James Duderstadt, reformist ex-president of the University of Michigan, offers recommendations, some practicable, others quixotic, including barring freshmen from playing varsity football, basketball, and hockey (he is not unaware of the irony that Michigan won the NCAA men's basketball tournament during his tenure with the "Fab Five," a starting quintet of freshmen); the shortening of seasons and elimination of spring football practice; and the "decoupling" of pro from college sports, specifically by requiring professional teams to finance the continuing education of undergraduates whom they poach from the colleges. If these cannot be achieved, he suggests spinning off football and basketball from colleges and universities to minor pro leagues: a recommendation similar to that of Rick Telander. Duderstadt, *Intercollegiate Athletics and the American University: A University President's Perspective*, p. 302.

And to prove once again that there is nothing new under the sun, in 1905 David Starr Jordan, president of Stanford, urged, "Let the football team become frankly professional. Cast off all the deception. Get the best professional coach. Pay him well and let him have the best men the town and alumni will pay for . . . Let the teams struggle in perfectly honest warfare, known for what it is and with no masquerade of amateurism or academic ideas . . . The evil in current football rests not in the hired men, but in academic lying and in the falsification of our own standards as associations of scholars and men of honor." Boyer, "College Athletics: The Control of the Campus," in *Sport and Higher Education*, p. 408.

36 George Leef, "Do Sports Programs and Community Colleges Mix?" John William Pope Center for Higher Education Policy, July 11, 2007; statistics from University of Phoenix, www.phoenix.edu/, accessed August 8, 2017.

37 John R. Gerdy, "For True Reform, Athletics Scholarships Must Go," *Chronicle of Higher Education*, May 12, 2006.

38 Sperber, "College Sports, Inc.: The Athletic Department vs. the University," *The Phi Delta Kappan*: K10.

39 Sperber, *Beer and Circus: How Big-Time College Sports Is Crippling Undergraduate Education*, p. 271.

40 Douglas S. Looney, "One Is More Like It," *Sports Illustrated*, September 3, 1990, www.si.com/vault/1990/09/03, accessed December 7, 2016.

41 "College Football & Scholarship Opportunities," www.scholarshipstats.com/football.html, accessed June 21, 2017.

42 Branch, "The Shame of College Sports," *The Atlantic*.

43 Daniel Sutter and Stephen Winkler, "NCAA Scholarship Limits and Competitive Balance in College Football," *Journal of Sports Economics* 4, No. 1 (February 2003): 4.

44 Ibid.: 16.

45 More predictably, there is a significant relationship between recruiting and team performance. See George Langelett, "The Relationship Between Recruiting and Team Performance in Division IA College Football," *Journal of Sports Economics* 4, No. 3 (August 2003): 240–5.

46 Hutchins, "College Football is an Infernal Nuisance," *Sports Illustrated*.

47 Sarah K. Fields, "Intramural and Club Sports: The Impact of Title IX," *Journal of College and University Law* 33, No. 3 (2006–7): 530.

48 Gaul, *Billion-Dollar Ball: A Journey Through the Big-Money Culture of College Football*, p. 59.

49 Mitchell, "Big-Time Sports Should Be Banished from Campus," *The Center Magazine*: 24.

50 John P. Dugan, Mark A. Torrez, and Natasha T. Turman, *Leadership in Intramural Sports and Club Sports: Examining Influences to Enhance Educational Impact* (Corvallis, OR: NIRSA, 2014), p. 8.

51 Bill Pennington, "Open Membership: Rapid Rise of College Club Teams Creates a Whole New Level of Success," *New York Times*, December 2, 2008.

52 Quoted in Leon Lifschutz, "Club Sports: Maximizing Positive Outcomes and Minimizing Risks," *Recreational Sports Journal* 36 (2002): 106–7. See also James L. Shulman and William G. Bowen, *The Game of Life: College Sports and Educational Values* (Princeton, NJ: Princeton University Press, 2001).

53 Pennington, "Open Membership: Rapid Rise of College Club Teams Creates a Whole New Level of Success," *New York Times*.

54 "NCVF National Tournament," www.ncvfvolleyball.org/pages/nationals.aspx, accessed August 9, 2017.

55 Pennington, "Open Membership: Rapid Rise of College Club Teams Creates a Whole New Level of Success," *New York Times*.

56 Lifschutz, "Club Sports: Maximizing Positive Outcomes and Minimizing Risks," *Recreational Sports Journal*: 107–9.

57 Pennington, "Open Membership: Rapid Rise of College Club Teams Creates a Whole New Level of Success," *New York Times*.

INDEX

Page numbers followed by "n" refer to notes.

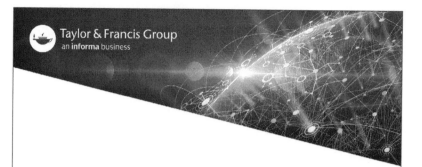